D1375024

## About the author

Garry Leech is a journalist and editor of
*Colombia Journal* <www.colombiajournal.
org>. He is also a lecturer in the Depart-
ment of Political Science at Cape Breton
University and author of *Killing Peace:
Colombia's Conflict and the Failure of US
Intervention* (Inota, 2002).

GARRY LEECH

# Crude interventions

The US, oil and the new world (dis)order

**SIRD**
KUALA LUMPUR

University of KwaZulu-Natal Press
PIETERMARITZBURG

Zed Books
LONDON | NEW YORK

*Crude Interventions: the US, oil and the new world (dis)order* was first published in 2006.

Published in Malaysia by Strategic Information Research Development (SIRD), No. 11/4E, Petaling Jaya, 46200 Selangor

Published in South Africa, Lesotho, Swaziland, Botswana, Namibia and Zimbabwe by the University of KwaZulu-Natal Press, Private Bag X01, Scottsville 3209, South Africa

www.ukznpress.co.za

Published in the rest of the world by Zed Books Ltd, 7 Cynthia Street, London N1 9JF, UK, and Room 400, 175 Fifth Avenue, New York, NY 10010, USA

www.zedbooks.co.uk

Cover designed by Andrew Corbett
Set in Arnhem and Futura Bold by Ewan Smith, London
index: <ed.emery@britishlibrary.net>
Printed and bound in Malta by Gutenberg Press Ltd

Distributed in the USA exclusively by Palgrave Macmillan, a division of St Martin's Press, LLC, 175 Fifth Avenue, New York, NY 10010.

A catalogue record for this book is available from the British Library
US CIP data are available from the Library of Congress

ISBN  1 84277 628 2 | 978 1 84277 628 5  hb
ISBN  1 84277 629 0 | 978 1 84277 629 2  pb
SIRD ISBN  983 2535 840  pb
UKZN ISBN  1 86914 092 3  pb

# Contents

# Acknowledgements

I would like to thank Sean Howard, Thomas Wright, Eric Fichtl and Emeka Duruigbo for their close readings of the text and invaluable suggestions. I would especially like to thank Terry Gibbs for her uncompromising commitment, endless patience and insightful analysis during our many long debates about the issues addressed in this book. Without her unfailing support, this book would not have been possible.

# Introduction

At the beginning of the twenty-first century, a new world disorder is emerging in which battles over resources are playing an increasingly prominent role. The importance of oil to this picture is underscored by the unilateral and militaristic foreign policy of the world's largest power in its attempt to secure access to this critical resource. In this global context, oil-rich communities of the South are being drawn into struggles to defend their sovereignty, cultural integrity, human rights and threatened ecosystems.

With only 4 per cent of the world's population, the United States consumes 25 per cent of global energy production. In 2004, the United States consumed over 16 million barrels of oil a day with imports accounting for more than 10 million barrels a day, or 65 per cent of consumption.[1] This thirst for energy has played a significant role in determining US foreign policy in recent decades. The desire to secure access to reliable supplies of oil has played an even more prominent role in determining the foreign policy of the government of George W. Bush than of previous administrations.

*Crude interventions* examines the military and economic policies of the Bush administration in oil-rich regions of the world. More precisely, it examines the socio-economic and human rights consequences of these policies, as well as those of recent US administrations and multinational energy companies, for the peoples of oil-producing nations in the global South.

By the time President George W. Bush assumed office on 20 January 2001, the new world order pronounced by his father following the end of the cold war a decade earlier was already showing signs of strain. The growing trans-national resistance to economic globalization, however, did not deter the new Bush White House, stocked with neo-conservatives from the administrations of George H. W. Bush and Ronald Reagan, from attempting to defend and expand the US-led global capitalist system. Two themes that dominated the new Bush administration's foreign policy initiatives – both before and after the 9/11 terrorist attacks – were the continued promotion of neo-liberal, or 'free market', economic reforms and securing access to new sources of oil to serve ever growing US energy needs.

One of the distinguishing factors of the Bush administration has been its preponderance of high-ranking officials who were formerly executives in the oil industry: President Bush served on Harken Energy's board of directors from 1986 to 1993; Vice-President Dick Cheney amassed a fortune of more than $50 million as CEO of Halliburton during the 1990s; National Security Advisor, and later Secretary of State, Condoleezza Rice served on Chevron's board of directors; Commerce Secretary Donald Evans was the CEO of Tom Brown Inc., an oil and gas exploration firm. Energy companies were also major contributors to George W. Bush's presidential campaigns, providing the former governor of Texas with more than $1.8 million in contributions for his successful campaign in 2000 and more than $2.5 million four years later.[2]

The Bush administration's oil policies have not been dictated solely by its close ties to US energy companies; they have also been influenced by pressing geo-political realities. First, there is a finite supply of oil in the world. And second, the growing energy consumption of industrializing nations of the South such as China and India has dramatically increased the global demand for oil and resulted in a race to control the world's reserves. In 2003, China passed Japan to become the world's second-largest energy consumer. Its rapidly growing thirst for oil has led Beijing to seek new supplies throughout the world, including in such

2

faraway places as South America. China's economic growth suggests that it may soon become the next superpower to seriously challenge US hegemony, potentially ushering in a new cold war motivated not by ideology – despite China's official communism – but rather a desire to control the world's resources, particularly oil and other fossil fuels.

In order to ensure access to the world's largest oil reserves, Washington has maintained close ties with several members of the Organization of Petroleum Exporting Countries (OPEC). OPEC's member nations – Iran, Iraq, Saudi Arabia, Kuwait, Venezuela, Qatar, Libya, Indonesia, the United Arab Emirates, Algeria and Nigeria – control about 40 per cent of the world's oil production. Consequently, OPEC can manipulate the global price of oil whenever its members agree to increase or decrease production in unison. In the United States, OPEC has often been portrayed as a dangerous cartel with an undue influence over the US economy. In reality, OPEC production policies are rarely determined by a specific desire to aid or harm US interests, with the obvious exception of the 1973 Arab oil boycott due to US support for Israel in the Arab–Israeli war that year. The production policies of OPEC countries are primarily driven by the needs of their own oil export-dependent economies, which often result in disagreements among member states over the establishment of production quotas.

OPEC also represents an important component of the contradiction that exists between the two principal US energy concerns: meeting national energy needs and the interests of US energy companies. The US public prefers low global oil prices that translate into cheap gasoline and heating-oil. The oil industry's interests are often in conflict with the US national interest because energy companies earn greater profits when oil prices are high. Consequently, the Bush administration's approach to developing its energy-driven foreign policy has not been monolithic.

3

On the one hand, some members of the administration seek to undermine OPEC and achieve greater US control over global reserves in order to ensure access to cheap oil to serve growing US energy needs. Others in the administration have focused on ensuring that US energy companies can access global reserves on profitable terms, which may mean defending OPEC and high oil prices. In either case, a primary objective of US foreign policy is to secure access to the world's oil reserves.

Sometimes, US foreign policy benefits US companies; at other times it helps European-based multinationals that supply oil to the US market. US oil policy does not exist in a vacuum; it has been intricately intertwined with the implementation of the US-pushed global neo-liberal project and, since 9/11, the war on terror. *Crude interventions* looks at how US energy policy has led to interventions in various oil-rich regions of the world. In particular, it focuses on three types of intervention: military, economic and corporate. US military interventions have played an important role in securing access to global oil reserves for multinational companies and to serve US energy needs. They have helped provide security for oil operations – albeit imperfectly at times – in countries such as Iraq and Colombia, and in the oil-rich regions of Central Asia and West Africa. At the same time, US military interventions, particularly under the umbrella of the war on terror, have worked to establish favourable conditions for implementing the US-directed neo-liberal project in Iraq and Colombia.

The United States, either directly or through Washington-based international financial institutions such as the International Monetary Fund (IMF) and the World Bank, has intervened economically in the South through the implementation of neo-liberal reforms that open up economies, and their resources, to multinational corporations. US economic intervention has been particularly evident in the oil-rich nations of

Kazakhstan, Azerbaijan, Iraq and Colombia, and in Venezuela until the late 1990s. Despite the growing resistance to a globalization process that has mostly benefited multinational companies and the economies of the North, while citizens of the South have endured increasing poverty and greater inequalities, the Bush administration has continued to promote its 'free trade' doctrine around the globe.

For their part, multinational oil companies have not relied solely on US military interventions and neo-liberalism to create favourable conditions in oil-rich nations; they have developed their own close ties to corrupt and repressive regimes in Central Asia and West Africa. They have also worked closely with the military apparatuses in Nigeria and Colombia, which have been responsible for gross violations of human rights while protecting the operations of foreign oil companies.

While all three intervention strategies – military, economic and corporate – are often present in most instances, the degree to which each form of intervention is relevant varies from case to case. *Crude interventions* begins by looking at the history of US policy in Iraq and how it has been influenced by oil. It examines how the Bush administration's March 2003 invasion and subsequent occupation has been used to lay the groundwork for the implementation of neo-liberal policies intended to open up Iraq's oil reserves for exploitation by multinational companies. Chapter 2 looks at the oil-rich regions of Central Asia and the South Caucasus following the collapse of the Soviet Union. It examines how post-cold-war neo-liberal economic intervention made the natural resources of Kazakhstan and Azerbaijan, the two countries with the largest oil reserves in the region, accessible for exploitation by multinational, particularly US, oil companies. The Bush administration has also used the war on terror to establish a military presence in what has traditionally been Russia and China's 'own back yard'. The cost to the local populations has been a dramatic increase in poverty and increased repression at the hands of US-backed authoritarian regimes.

Chapter 3 explores the role played by multinational corporations in oil-rich West African nations. The close ties that foreign oil companies have developed with Nigeria's authoritarian government and brutal military have contributed to increased poverty and human rights abuses. The lives of people in the Niger river delta region have been further afflicted by the environmental destruction resulting from oil operations. In Angola, meanwhile, the lack of transparency in relations between foreign oil companies and the Angolan government has contributed to exorbitant levels of official corruption and widespread poverty.

Chapter 4 examines how all three forms of intervention have occurred simultaneously in Colombia. Neo-liberal policies have provided some of the most favourable contract terms in the world for foreign oil companies. The wars on drugs and terror, meanwhile, have been used to justify US military intervention in Colombia's long-running civil conflict, in part to provide security for foreign oil companies. At the same time, foreign oil companies work closely with US-backed Colombian military units responsible for gross violations of human rights. In the eyes of many Colombians, US intervention and oil exploitation have increased poverty and fuelled a dirty war against the civilian population.

The final case study examines how Venezuela has challenged the neo-liberal doctrine and the traditional manner in which oil-rich nations of the South manage their natural resources. President Hugo Chávez has used the country's oil wealth to fund his 'revolution for the poor'. In sharp contrast to neighbouring Colombia, Venezuela has restructured the terms of oil contracts to better benefit the state – and the Venezuelan people. Chávez has implemented social and economic policies that directly contradict the prevailing neo-liberal wisdom in order to undertake redistributive programmes intended to benefit the country's impoverished majority. As a result, Chávez has incurred the wrath of the Bush administration, which has intervened in Venezuela's domestic affairs in a variety of attempts to achieve regime change.

The Bush administration's efforts to ensure US hegemony in the twenty-first century have contributed to political, social, economic, ethnic and religious disorder in many regions of the world. As this book went to press, the Bush White House was continuing its interventions in oil-rich regions, albeit in the face of increasing resistance. Consequently, many of the issues addressed herein remain unresolved. It is my hope, however, that *Crude interventions* will prove to be a useful tool in helping all those interested in US foreign policy to better understand the connections between US energy needs, the war on terror, globalization, human rights abuses and other social injustices endured by those peoples of the South who are cursed with an abundance of the world's most sought-after resource.

# 1 | Iraq: seeking the riches of Babylon

On 16 March 2003, four days before the United States invaded Iraq, US Vice-President Dick Cheney declared that the conflict would be over in 'weeks rather than months' and that 'from the standpoint of the Iraqi people, my belief is we will, in fact, be greeted as liberators'.[1] Six weeks later, President George W. Bush landed on the aircraft carrier USS *Abraham Lincoln* and, standing under a sign that read 'Mission Accomplished', declared that major combat operations in Iraq had ended. At that time, 109 US soldiers had been killed in the campaign to overthrow Iraqi leader Saddam Hussein. But one year later, a *USA Today*/CNN/Gallup poll, the most extensive nationwide survey conducted up until that point, showed that 71 per cent of Iraqis saw the US-led coalition forces as 'occupiers' rather than 'liberators'.[2] In September 2004, the number of US troops killed in Iraq surpassed the 1,000 mark as resistance to the US military occupation continued to intensify.[3] Of greater concern for the Iraqi people, and a contributing factor to the escalating insurgency, was the fact that the country's 'liberators' were primarily responsible for the deaths of 100,000 Iraqis during the first eighteen months of the occupation.[4]

While it became evident that the Bush administration had underestimated the degree to which Iraqis would resist the occupation, it did not prevent the US president from attempting to implement his plan for 'democracy promotion' and the imposition of neo-liberal, or 'free market', economic reforms in Iraq. Such policies were intended to facilitate the access of US energy companies to Iraqi oil, a commodity that had remained beyond the grasp of foreign corporations since Baghdad nationalized the oil industry in 1972. With 112 billion barrels of proven reserves, Iraq contains the second-largest supply of oil in the world after Saudi Arabia. Iraq and its vast oil reserves figured prominently in US foreign policy during the latter decades of the twentieth century. Washington's stance towards Baghdad shifted dramatically during this period from undermining the Iraqi regime in the 1970s to supporting it during the 1980s and then seeking its overthrow in the 1990s.

## The rise of Saddam Hussein

Until 1967, a consortium of foreign oil companies ironically named the Iraq Petroleum Company (IPC) held a virtual monopoly over Iraq's oil-producing capabilities. The IPC consortium consisted primarily of British companies including Shell Oil, although US energy giants Standard and Mobil equally shared a 23.75 per cent stake (Tripp 2000: 60). As a result, Iraq was dependent on Western oil companies, and by extension Western markets, for decades. The 1967 Arab–Israeli war, however, helped set the stage for Iraq to finally nationalize the IPC.

Baghdad responded to US and British support for Israel during the war by severing diplomatic relations with the two Western powers and establishing closer ties with the Soviet Union. A military coup on 17 July 1968 that brought the Ba'ath Party to power did not affect the country's blossoming relationship with the Soviet Union. In fact, if anything, the new Ba'athist government, led by Hasan al-Bakr and Saddam Hussein, developed even closer ties to the communist superpower.

The new regime backed up its socialist rhetoric by introducing subsidies for basic commodities, providing social services and establishing agricultural cooperatives. These government initiatives, along with the development of a patronage network in the primarily Sunni Muslim regions of the country, helped the Sunni-dominated Ba'th Party to consolidate its control over

9

Iraq's political and economic affairs. Still, President al-Bakr was concerned with the Iraqi economy's ongoing vulnerability to IPC decisions regarding oil production. In 1969, al-Bakr decided to address this issue by negotiating a deal with the Soviet Union to help the recently established Iraq National Oil Company (INOC) exploit new oilfields. When these fields began production in 1972, following the signing of the Soviet–Iraq Treaty of Friendship and Cooperation, the IPC decided to punish Iraq by immediately halving oil production in its Kirkuk fields in the north of the country. Unhappy with the latest in a long history of IPC attempts to hold Iraq's economy hostage whenever the consortium's business interests were threatened, al-Bakr finally nationalized the oil consortium in June 1972.

Iraq had prepared itself for any possible economic retaliation by the IPC and Western governments by having Saddam Hussein negotiate a trade agreement with the Soviet Union, guaranteeing that the communist superpower would purchase Iraqi oil. The nationalization was hugely popular among the Iraqi people and the timing of it proved fortuitous as it occurred just over a year prior to the dramatic increases in global oil prices that resulted from the 1973 Arab–Israeli war. The signing of the oil agreement with the Soviets, however, also situated Iraq in the middle of the cold war.

In 1972, Washington responded to Iraq's burgeoning relationship with the Soviets by providing covert aid to Mustafa Barzani and his Kurdistan Democratic Party (KDP). KDP rebels were seeking to establish an independent Kurdistan in northern Iraq that included the oil-rich city of Kirkuk. The US-backed Shah of Iran, himself suspicious of the Ba'athist regime's growing ties with Moscow and its nationalist and socialist rhetoric, also provided aid to the Iraqi Kurds. US and Iranian support for the KDP contributed to an escalation of the conflict between the Iraqi military and Kurdish rebels. Both Iraq and Iran became

*1 Iraq*

increasingly concerned that the Kurdish issue might lead to a war
between the two countries. In order to address these concerns,
Saddam Hussein and Iranian officials met in Algiers in 1975 and
agreed that Iraq would recognize Iran's territorial claims in the
border region of Shatt al-Arab in return for Tehran ending its
support for the Kurds. Not willing to undermine the Shah's position, the United States also stopped aiding the Kurds. When US
Secretary of State Henry Kissinger was asked about the morality
of abandoning a people that the United States had encouraged
to rebel just because it was no longer politically expedient, he

11

simply declared 'that covert military activity is not to be confused with missionary work'.[5]

Many Kurdish leaders accused the United States, and Kissinger in particular, of betraying them. The KDP's Dr Sami Abdul-Rahman declared: 'It was the most cruel betrayal in our history – which is full of betrayals. Kissinger was instrumental in this betrayal. And it was totally unfair to promise the Kurdish people help and support and to give the impression that if the Iraqi government attacks we will help you – which they did at the beginning. Then in the middle of the road, to drop you.'[6] With the cessation of US and Iranian aid, many Kurds accepted a government amnesty offer while others fled across the border into Iran in the face of an Iraqi military offensive. The KDP split into two factions with Jalal Talabani leading the newly formed Popular Union of Kurdistan (PUK). After fleeing Iraq, the KDP's Barzani went into exile in the United States, where he died in 1979.

In an attempt to ensure that the Kurdish conflict did not flare up again, the Iraqi government relocated close to half a million Kurds from their villages and towns in the north to Shiite communities in the south. At the same time, the Ba'athist regime encouraged Arabs to move northward in order to boost the Arab population in the oil-rich city of Kirkuk.

There was not only conflict between the Iraqi government and the Kurds; there also existed a history of confrontation between the minority Sunnis and the majority Shiites – the two Muslim groups constitute approximately 25 per cent and 65 per cent of Iraq's population respectively. Many Arab tribes in southern Iraq, particularly around the cities of Najaf and Karbala, were converted to Shiism in the mid-nineteenth century. Over the next half-century, they sought to establish an independent Shiite state in southern Iraq, a quest that ended when Britain determined the borders of the new Iraqi state in 1921. The country's Sunnis continued to maintain political dominance over the Shiites under

British rule and following independence. Unlike in neighbour-ing Iran, where the majority of the population were Shiites of Persian origin, Iraq's various Arab Shiite sects failed to establish a central religious hierarchy. Consequently, according to Middle East historian Yitzhak Nakash (2003: 87), 'Successive Iraqi govern-ments achieved a clearer separation between religion and state in Iraq than that achieved in Iran, thus preventing the *mujtahids* [Islamic legal scholars] from emerging as a major player in Iraqi national politics.'

In February 1977, large numbers of Shiites protested against their continued marginalization from the patronage networks that were benefiting from the government's vast oil revenues, which had reached $8 billion annually. The government res-ponded to the protests by arresting thousands of Shiites and executing eight Islamic scholars. At the same time, Saddam Hus-sein, who had become a master of the carrot-and-stick strategy, incorporated certain Islamic values into the government's mostly secular policies and expanded his patronage network to include more Shiite communities. During this period, Hussein also con-solidated his control over the state's security forces and in Sep-tember 1977 assumed authority over the country's oil policies.

When the Ayatollah Khomeini's revolutionary movement in Iran overthrew the Shah in February 1979, Baghdad became concerned that Iraq's Shiite population might be influenced by the Islamic revolution that had occurred next door. In a pre-emptive strike, Hussein's security forces ruthlessly cracked down on underground Shiite groups such as al-Da'wa, and arrested clerics, including the Ayatollah Sayyid Mohammad Baqir al-Sadr, who had been speaking out against the Sunni dominance of the governing elite. Hussein's security forces then violently suppressed the Shiite protests that followed al-Sadr's arrest, executing several Shiite clerics, arresting thousands of Shiites and sending many more into exile. The Shiites in the south rose up and, with the country in a national crisis, al-Bakr resigned as president. Hussein was sworn in as the country's new leader and immediately turned his security forces against anyone in the Ba'ath Party he thought might challenge his ascension to the presidency. Hundreds of immediate and potential future enemies within the party were executed. According to Middle East expert Charles Tripp, the forty-two-year-old Hussein 'had triumphed by using the disconcerting combination of charm, generosity and ruthless terror that was to serve him so well in maintaining his position as ruler of Iraq for longer than any predecessor' (Tripp 2000: 223).

After consolidating his position within the party, Hussein targeted those Shiites who, spurred on by the new regime in Tehran, continued to revolt against the government. The new president ordered his security forces to round up thousands of Shiites, many of whom were executed. The extent of Hussein's ruthlessness became apparent following an assassination attempt against Deputy Prime Minister Tariq Aziz, when the new president ordered the execution of Ayatollah al-Sadr, his sister and hundreds of Shiites. Never before had an Iraqi government killed such a prominent cleric. Hussein then expelled as many as 100,000 Shiites from the country.[7]

Not surprisingly, relations between Iraq and Iran began to deteriorate. Despite his ongoing confrontations with certain sectors of Iraq's Shiite population, Hussein tried to create a sense of national identity among both the Sunni and Shiite population by emphasizing the country's distinctly Iraqi and Arab traits. He attempted to instil in the population a consciousness of Iraq embracing leadership in the Arab world. In an effort to rally the Iraqi people around a nationalist cause, and believing that the new Iranian regime was vulnerable because it had not yet consolidated its hold on power, Hussein decided to reassert Iraq's sovereignty over the Shatt al-Arab region ceded to Iran five years earlier. Hussein was also taking advantage of the post-revolution rupture in US–Iranian relations and the resulting cut-off in US military aid to Tehran. In late September 1980, believing that an overwhelming display of force would lead the Ayatollah Khomeini to quickly call for negotiations, Hussein ordered Iraq's military to invade Iran.

Iran did not respond to the attack in the manner that Hussein had anticipated. In fact, the new Iranian regime successfully rallied the Iranian people to defend the nation. By 1982, the Iranian military was effectively counter-attacking, eventually regaining control of the territory initially seized by Iraqi forces. The conflict turned into a war of attrition, with each country targeting the oil facilities of the other in an attempt to cripple its economy. In 1982, the conflict took a turn for the worse when Iraq began using chemical weapons on the battlefield in a desperate attempt to stave off an Iranian offensive. By the time the two nations agreed to a ceasefire in 1988, the Soviet Union and much of the West, particularly the United States, Great Britain and France, were aiding Iraq. The US Navy had become directly engaged in the Persian Gulf in order to ensure the safe passage of oil tankers. In the process, US forces virtually destroyed Iran's naval capabilities and even shot down an Iranian airliner, killing 290 people.

Meanwhile, in 1985, the rival KDP and PUK parties in Kurdistan formed an alliance and with support from Iran became increasingly effective at attacking Iraqi forces based in Kurdish regions. Hussein responded by dispatching his cousin 'Ali Hasan al-Majid to the Kurdistan region to orchestrate a brutal response to the Kurdish rebels. In 1987, captured rebels were summarily executed, while villages were destroyed and their inhabitants sent to government-run camps. By the following year, the Iraqis were no longer transferring the local population to camps; instead they had launched a scorched-earth campaign called *al-Anfal* (the spoils of war) that involved the destruction of villages and

15

the massacre of all inhabitants. The Iraqi military also expanded its use of chemical weapons beyond the targeting of armed opposition on the battlefield to the general Kurdish population, including women and children. During a March 1988 attack on the Kurdish town of Halabja, Iraqi forces killed at least three thousand residents with chemical weapons.[8]

By August 1988, KDP and PUK resistance was almost non-existent. As many as 80 per cent of Kurdish villages had been destroyed and 60,000 Kurds killed. As Tripp points out: 'The devastation of *al-Anfal* had demonstrated not only to the Kurds, but to all Iraqis, in the circles of power and elsewhere, the fate of those who stepped out of the "national ranks", as defined by Saddam Hussein himself' (Tripp 2000: 245–6). The cost of the Iranian and Kurdish conflicts proved staggering, with some quarter of a million Iraqis and Kurds killed and the incurrence of a national debt of $80 billion (ibid.: 248).

## US–Iraqi relations in the 1980s

Following the overthrow of the Shah in 1979 and the seizure of fifty-two US hostages, Washington severed diplomatic ties with Iran and cut off aid to the new revolutionary regime. The United States viewed Iran's Islamic fundamentalist government and its anti-Western views as a new destabilizing force in the oil-rich Middle East. Washington's break with Iran meant that the United States had lost a major oil supplier. Securing an alternative source of oil became even more critical when the Reagan administration announced an embargo of Libyan oil in 1982. Consequently, the United States turned to Iraq. Despite its officially 'neutral' stance with regard to the Iran–Iraq war, the Reagan administration began aiding Iraq in order to ensure a steady flow of oil from the region – although diplomatic relations were not officially renewed until 1984. Throughout the 1980s, US oil imports from Iraq rose dramatically from fewer than five hundred barrels a day in 1982 to over half a million barrels a day by the time Hussein invaded Kuwait in 1990.[9]

James Akins, an attaché at the US embassy in Baghdad from 1963 to 1965 and later the US ambassador to Saudi Arabia, claimed that following the overthrow of the Shah in Iran, 'The power structure of the Middle East changed dramatically with the most important country in the Gulf becoming, not one of the pillars of American policy in the area, but one of the strongest opponents of America, and the entire world, because of our close association with the Shah.'[10] From the beginning of the war, the United States provided Iraq with military intelligence about Iranian troop movements. In March 1982, the same month that the Reagan administration imposed an oil embargo on Libya for its links to international terrorism, the United States removed Iraq from its list of state supporters of international terrorism, thereby allowing US companies to export 'dual-use' chemical and biological technology to Hussein's government. The 'dual-use' categorization included equipment and technology that could be used for both civilian and military purposes. Over the next few years, dual-use equipment sold to Iraq included not only chemical and biological technology, but also aircraft and helicopters.

Howard Teicher, a former staff member of the National Security Council during the Reagan administration, testified in a 1995 affidavit that, in June 1982, 'President Reagan decided that the United States could not allow Iraq to lose the war to Iran'. Consequently, says Teicher:

CIA Director [William] Casey personally spearheaded the effort to ensure that Iraq had sufficient military weapons, ammunition and vehicles to avoid losing the Iran–Iraq war. Pursuant to the secret NSDD [National Security Decision Directive issued by President Reagan in June 1982], the United States actively supported the Iraqi war effort by supplying the Iraqis with billions of dollars of credits, by providing military intelligence and advice to the Iraqis, and by closely monitoring third country arms sales to Iraq to make sure Iraq had the military weaponry required. The United States also provided strategic operational advice. ... For example, in 1986, President Reagan sent a secret message to Saddam Hussein telling him that Iraq should step up its air war and bombing of Iran. This message was delivered by Vice President Bush who communicated it to Egyptian President Mubarek, who in turn passed the message to Saddam Hussein.[11]

Reagan administration officials were aware of Iraq's use of chemical weapons as early as 1983. A partially declassified internal US State Department memo dated 21 November 1983 states: 'In October 1982, unspecified foreign officers fired lethal chemical weapons at the orders of Saddam during battles in the Mandali area. ... In July and August 1983, the Iraqis reportedly used a chemical agent with lethal effects against and [sic] Iranian forces invading Iraq at Haj Umran, and more recently against Kurdish insurgents.'[12]

Another internal State Department memo issued three weeks earlier had stated: 'We also know that Iraq has received a CW [chemical weapons] production capability, primarily from western firms, including possibly a US foreign subsidiary.'[13] The memo notes Iraq's 'almost daily use of CW' and suggests to Secretary of State George Schultz that if the National Security Council 'decides measures are to be undertaken to assist Iraq, our best present chance of influencing cessation of CW use may be in the context of informing Iraq of these measures'.[14] This memo appears to suggest that if the Reagan administration was to decide to directly provide military aid to Iraq then it should use that as leverage to get Hussein to stop using chemical weapons. In other words, rather than condemning and punishing Iraq for its use of chemical weapons, the memo proposed rewarding it with US military assistance.

By early December 1983, the United States was becoming concerned that the war would interrupt Iraqi oil exports, which were becoming increasingly important to the United States. The State Department approached the Bechtel Corporation to discuss the possibility of building an oil pipeline from Iraq to the Gulf of Aqaba in Jordan as a means of bypassing Iraq's Persian Gulf export terminals, which had been damaged by Iranian attacks. Later that month, President Reagan dispatched special envoy Donald Rumsfeld to the Middle East, where he met with Saddam Hussein in Baghdad. The State Department's partially declassified report on the meeting stated: 'Rumsfeld told Saddam US and Iraq had shared interests in preventing Iranian and Syrian expansion. He said US was urging other states to curtail arms sales to Iran and believed it had successfully closed off US-controlled exports by third countries to Iran.' The report went on to note: 'Our initial assessment is that meeting marked positive milestone in development of US–Iraqi realtions [*sic*] and will prove to be of wider benefit to US posture in the region.'[15] Rumsfeld then raised the possibility of building the Aqaba pipeline, which Hussein said he would consider. Several years later, however, the Iraqi leader would reject the pipeline proposal. According to the declassified sections of the report covering Rumsfeld's ninety-minute meeting with Hussein, Iraq's use of chemical weapons was not discussed.

On 5 March 1984, in response to Iran's raising of the chemical weapons issue in the United Nations, the US government issued a public condemnation of Iraq's use of such weapons. Several weeks later Rumsfeld returned to Baghdad to address the deteriorating relations that had resulted from Washington's condemnation. While discussing Rumsfeld's Iraq visit, a State Department official said that Iraq's use of chemical weapons would not affect US efforts to expand trade between the two countries and restore diplomatic relations. The official added: 'We are interested in being involved in a closer dialogue with Iraq.'[16] Two months after its condemnation of Iraq for using one type of weapon of mass destruction, the Reagan administration reviewed its policy for the sale of dual-use technology to Iraq's nuclear programme. A State Department memo recommended that 'US nuclear-related trade with Iraq should now allow the sale of insignificant dual-use items' and that the 'Iraqi government is not disposed to give meaningful assurances' that such items would not be used to develop nuclear weapons.[17] On 26 November 1984, Iraq's Deputy Prime Minister Tariq Aziz and US Secretary of State George Schultz met in Washington to officially restore diplomatic relations between the two countries.

In early 1986, the United Nations dispatched a team of specialists to investigate new Iranian claims of chemical weapons use by Iraqi forces. The team examined survivors as well as soil and shrapnel in targeted areas and unanimously concluded that Iraq had indeed used chemical weapons against Iranian troops. In March, the Security Council issued a statement declaring that Council members were:

> Profoundly concerned by the unanimous conclusion of the specialists that chemical weapons on many occasions have been used by Iraqi forces against Iranian forces, most recently in the course of the Iranian offensive into Iraqi territory, the members of the Council strongly condemn this use of chemical weapons in clear violation of the Geneva Protocol of 1925 which prohibits the use in war of chemical weapons. (UNSC 1987: 11–12)

The United States was the only Security Council member to vote against the issuance of the statement.

The Reagan administration also opposed congressional efforts to rein in Hussein's use of weapons of mass destruction. Following Iraq's chemical weapons attack on Halabja, which killed at least three thousand Kurds, the US Senate passed a bill entitled 'Prevention of Genocide Act of 1988'. The bill called for ending US military and non-military aid to Iraq and the application of sanctions, including a boycott of Iraqi oil. The Reagan administration announced its opposition to the bill and worked with its allies in the House of Representatives to ensure that it did not pass.

The Reagan administration did not limit itself to undermining legislation and condemnations of Iraq's use of weapons of mass destruction; it actually helped Baghdad develop chemical and biological weapons programmes. According to a 1994 report issued by Senator Donald Reigle, chairman of the Senate Committee on Banking, Housing and Urban Affairs with Respect to Export Administration, between 1985 and 1989 the US Commerce Department licensed dozens of sales of anthrax, botulism and other biological research materials. The Reigle Report noted: 'The United States provided the Government of Iraq with "dual use" licensed materials which assisted in the development of Iraqi chemical, biological, and missile-system programs.' Furthermore, the senator's report revealed that 'Microorganisms exported by the United States were identical to those the United Nations inspectors found and recovered from the Iraqi biological warfare program.'[18]

Following Iraq's 1988 chemical attacks against Kurdish civilians, the United States continued to issue export licences to companies selling dual-use equipment to weapons factories controlled by Iraq's Ministry of Industry and Military Industrialization (MIMI). The administration of President George H. W. Bush issued dozens of these export licences despite CIA intelligence 'showing that these MIMI controlled entities were involved in Iraq's clandestine nuclear, chemical, and biological weapons programs and missile programs'.[19] Throughout the 1980s, it wasn't only US corporations which were contributing to Iraq's non-conventional weapons programmes; British, French, West German, Italian, Austrian and Swiss companies also played a role. By the time Iraq invaded Kuwait in 1990, according to the US Department of Defense, 'It's [sic] advanced and aggressive biological warfare program was the most advanced in the Arab world.'[20] Also, by 1990 the close ties that the Reagan and Bush administrations had forged with Saddam Hussein had led to the United States importing record amounts of Iraqi oil – more than half a million barrels a day – to serve US energy needs.

## The Gulf War and UN sanctions

Despite having successfully increased its oil exports throughout the 1980s, Iraq was still burdened with a huge debt load owing to the costs of its war with Iran. With the country's economy in shambles, Hussein asked Saudi Arabia, Kuwait and other states in the region to write off the $40 billion in loans that they had provided to aid Iraq's war effort. According to Tripp, their refusals led Hussein to decide to invade Kuwait and threaten the Saudi regime in order to 'extract resources and concessions from the Gulf states generally and particularly from Saudi Arabia' (Tripp 2000: 252). Hussein publicly justified the invasion by claiming that Kuwait was part of Iraq because it was historically a district of Basra province, which along with two other former Ottoman provinces – Baghdad and Mosul – constituted Iraq when the country was formed in the early 1920s. At the time of Iraq's formation, however, Britain separated Kuwait from Basra province and retained control over the tiny kingdom until granting it independence in 1961.

On 2 August 1990, Iraqi forces invaded Kuwait and successfully seized control of the country in less than twenty-four hours. Hussein believed that such a show of force would pressure Saudi Arabia into renegotiating the debt. He also believed that the

United States would support his new military endeavour in much the same way it had his invasion of Iran ten years earlier. Such thinking on Hussein's part may not have been as absurd as it now seems. As US diplomat Akins points out:

> We were very tolerant of Saddam. There was no great outcry when the Kurdish villages were destroyed and the Kurds were all murdered. There was not really much outcry after Saddam allegedly used gas against the Kurds. Saddam could quite reasonably conclude that, with all of these signals, the testimony in the congress, people talking about the economic importance of Iraq, he would be able to get away with what he intended to do in Kuwait.[21]

As it turns out, it was a gross miscalculation on the part of the Iraqi leader. Saudi Arabia immediately requested US military assistance, the Arab League condemned the invasion and the United Nations imposed a trade embargo on Iraq. In actuality, the United States did respond in much the same way it had when Iraq invaded Iran: it defended its oil interests. In 1990, Saudi Arabia was exporting 1.3 billion barrels of oil a day to the United States, almost three times as much as Iraq. As it had done a decade earlier, the United States sided with its most important oil supplier.

In November 1990, the UN Security Council passed Resolution 678, which demanded that Iraq withdraw from Kuwait by 15 January 1991 or face eviction by military force. Hussein stood his ground and on 16 January a US-led coalition launched Operation Desert Storm with a six-week bombing campaign against Iraq that targeted both military and civil infrastructure. Following the aerial campaign, coalition forces recaptured Kuwait, although retreating Iraqi troops set the country's oil wells ablaze. Coalition troops did not invade Iraq itself because Resolution 678 authorized only the removal of Iraqi forces from Kuwait. On 28 February

1991, a ceasefire agreement was signed and the Kuwaiti royal family was returned to power. While the war and corresponding UN-imposed sanctions severed the flow of Iraqi oil to the United States, the US-led Desert Storm had defused the threat against Saudi Arabia, the most important supplier of Middle Eastern oil to the United States.

Civilian casualties on both sides were extensive. Iraqi soldiers massacred Kuwaiti civilians before fleeing the arrival of coalition troops. The coalition's aerial bombardment of Iraq, meanwhile, killed hundreds, if not thousands, of civilians, with the worst case being the Amirya bombing on 13 February. In that incident, a US stealth bomber dropped two 900-pound, laser-guided bombs on a shelter, killing 314 civilians, including 130 children.[22]

The atrocities continued after the war. Almost immediately following the signing of the ceasefire agreement, Shiite uprisings occurred throughout southern Iraq in an attempt to take advantage of the government's seemingly vulnerable position. But Hussein had kept most of his elite Republican Guard troops in reserve during the brief war to protect his regime against just such a revolt. The Iraqi leader dispatched these troops to the troubled cities, where they ruthlessly put down the uprising. The Shiites had responded to a call by President Bush for the Iraqi people to rise up against Hussein, but the US support they had anticipated never materialized. Apparently, the Bush administration had second thoughts about the chaos and possible disintegration of Iraq that might result from Hussein's overthrow. Instead, US officials believed that, for the time being, a contained Hussein was better than the possible establishment of a Shiite regime similar to the one in neighbouring Iran.

At the same time, the Kurds also believed that the United States would come to their aid if they heeded Bush's call to revolt. Rebels fought Iraqi forces and seized control of several towns in the north, including Kirkuk. But after putting down the Shiite uprising, Hussein dispatched his Republican Guard troops to the north to deal with the Kurds. The rebellion soon collapsed and 2 million Kurds fled to Iran and Turkey, fearful that Hussein would again use chemical weapons against them. When Hussein realized that US military forces amassed on Iraq's borders were not going to intervene to protect the Kurds, the Iraqi military brutally repressed the Kurdish population. Ultimately, according to Frank Anderson, chief of the Central Intelligence Agency's Near East Division in 1991, 'Neither the Shias in the south, nor the Kurds in the north, nor any combination of them without really significant outside military assistance had the means to defeat even what was left of Saddam's army.'[23]

The United Nations decided to continue the sanctions regime imposed on Iraq even though its original objective, to end the occupation of Kuwait, had been achieved. The new post-war objectives for the sanctions under Resolution 687 included the elimination of Iraq's weapons of mass destruction and long-range missiles, Baghdad's recognition of Kuwaiti sovereignty, the payment of reparations, and an end to Hussein's repression of the Iraqi people. Unofficially, the United States and Britain were also hoping that the sanctions would eventually lead to Hussein's downfall.

Over the next few years it became apparent that the harsh sanctions were not weakening Hussein's grip on power. They were, however, causing massive depredations of food, water and medicines for the Iraqi people. The sanctions restricted the importation of many items that were needed to produce food and medicines as well as to repair electricity power stations, hospital machinery and water and sewage treatment plants, many of which had been damaged by US bombing during Operation Desert Storm. The sanctions were proving to be especially harsh on children. A 1995 report published by the British medical journal, *The Lancet*, stated that 567,000 children under the age of five had died between 1990 and 1995 as a result of the sanctions.[24] Despite the report's shocking statistics, the Clinton administration appeared to be unmoved by the escalating humanitarian crisis in Iraq. During a 12 May 1996 interview on the US television news show *60 Minutes*, US ambassador to the United Nations Madeleine Albright was asked about the morality of maintaining sanctions that were responsible for the deaths of more than half a million children, to which she responded: 'We think the price is worth it.'[25]

In 1995, the UN Security Council attempted to address the humanitarian crisis with the passage of Resolution 986, which proposed the Oil-for-Food Programme. It permitted Iraq to sell $4 billion of oil annually with all the proceeds to be deposited in a UN-controlled bank account. The funds would be used to cover the administrative costs of the programme and to purchase food and medicines for the Iraqi people.

The Oil-for-Food Programme, however, fell short of providing the assistance needed to effectively alleviate the suffering of Iraq's children. Three years after the programme had been launched, a UNICEF study concluded that Iraqi children were still dying as a result of the sanctions. According to the report, the country's infant mortality rate – children who die before reaching their first birthday – was double what it had been a decade earlier. UNICEF's executive director, Carol Bellamy, stated that 'whenever sanctions are imposed they should be designed and implemented in such a way as to avoid a negative impact on children'.[26] US diplomat James Akins went farther when he declared: 'Most Arabs in the area think that the sanctions should be lifted, that the sanctions have in no way weakened Saddam. The sanctions have certainly hurt the Iraqi people, and there is no rational reason to continue the sanctions.'[27] A 2000 study conducted by the UN World Food Programme confirmed that 'rations provided by the Oil-for-Food Programme are not sufficient to cover all the nutritional needs of the population' and that the 'poorest families barely get by on the ration, facing some days without food each month'.[28] In December 2000, the distribution of proceeds from the Oil-for-Food Programme was restructured so that a greater percentage of the funds would be used for humanitarian needs.[29] After the programme was terminated in March 2003, it was alleged that Hussein had pocketed billions of dollars in kickbacks paid by individuals and foreign companies seeking to participate in the Oil-for-Food Programme.

The Oil-for-Food Programme facilitated the re-entry of Iraqi oil into the global market. As a result, US imports of Iraqi oil rose quickly from none in 1995 to 795 million barrels a day in 2001, making Iraq the seventh-largest supplier of oil to the United States. Owing to the Oil-for-Food Programme, Iraqi oil exports to the United States in 2001 were more than 50 per cent higher than before Hussein's invasion of Kuwait.[30]

In addition to its imposition of economic sanctions on Iraq, the UN Security Council also demanded that Hussein allow UN inspection teams into the country to ensure that Iraq's nuclear, chemical and biological weapons programmes, as well as its long-range ballistic missiles, were fully dismantled. The United Nations Special Commission on Disarmament (UNSCOM) was established on 3 April 1991 under Resolution 687 and was responsible, along with representatives from the International Atomic Energy Agency (IAEA), for conducting weapons inspections in Iraq.

In the ensuing years, Iraq repeatedly impeded the activities of UNSCOM weapons inspectors, although Hussein would back down on most occasions when threatened by the Security Council. In all likelihood, Hussein's obstructionist actions were motivated as much by a desire to convince the Iraqi people that he remained firmly in control as by a desire to hide WMDs. It is also possible that Hussein wanted to create the impression that he still possessed WMDs, believing that the United States would be less likely to invade Iraq if faced with the possibility that he might use such weapons.

The cat-and-mouse game played by Hussein and the weapons inspectors continued throughout the decade. In 1998, however, it intensified when the Iraqi leader accused US members of the UNSCOM weapons inspection team of being spies and refused any further cooperation. On 6 January 1999, the *Washington Post* ran a front-page story confirming Hussein's oft-repeated claims. In the article, an adviser to UN Secretary-General Kofi Annan stated: 'The secretary general has become aware of the fact that UNSCOM directly facilitated the creation of an intelligence collection system for the United States in violation of its mandate. The United Nations cannot be party to an operation to overthrow one of its member states.'[31] Former weapons inspector Scott Ritter also acknowledged that the United States was running an intelligence-gathering operation through UNSCOM. Ritter admitted that his UNSCOM inspection team included 'nine covert operatives from the CIA's covert activities branch'.[32]

The United States and Britain, without any authorization from the UN Security Council, responded to Hussein's refusal to co-operate with UNSCOM by launching Operation Desert Fox, which consisted of missile strikes against multiple military and strategic targets. Faced with the imminent bombings, UN Secretary-General Annan ordered the withdrawal of UNSCOM inspectors. Security Council members France and Russia were opposed to both Operation Desert Fox and the existence of US and British patrolled 'No-Fly Zones' in the north and south of the country, from which Iraqi aircraft were forbidden to operate. Both France and Russia insisted that these zones were not authorized under any Security Council resolution and were, therefore, illegal.

The revelations about the Clinton administration's use of weapons inspectors to conduct espionage ensured that the

UNSCOM mission was no longer viable. The situation deteriorated further in November 1999 when the United Nations renewed the Oil-for-Food Programme for only two weeks instead of the six months called for by Iraq. Hussein responded by cutting off oil exports, which drove the global price of oil up to a nine-year high of $27 a barrel.

In 1999, the Security Council officially dissolved UNSCOM and replaced it with the United Nations Monitoring Verification and Inspection Commission (UNMOVIC). In an attempt to avoid a repetition of the espionage activities that brought down UNSCOM, the UNMOVIC inspection teams were staffed with UN employees instead of representatives from member nations. The following year, the UN Security Council renewed the Oil-for-Food Programme for six months and Iraqi oil once again began to flow. But it wasn't until 16 September 2002 that Hussein finally agreed to allow the UNMOVIC weapons inspectors to enter the country. Less than one month after weapons inspectors returned to Iraq, the US Congress authorized President Bush to use military force against Iraq as he deemed necessary in order to '(1) defend the national security of the United States against the continuing threat posed by Iraq; and (2) enforce all relevant United Nations Security Council resolutions regarding Iraq'.[33]

### The US invasion and occupation

On 8 November 2002, the UN Security Council passed the US- and UK-sponsored Resolution 1441, which deplored 'the fact that Iraq has not provided an accurate, full, final, and complete disclosure, as required by resolution 687 (1991), of all aspects of its programmes to develop weapons of mass destruction and ballistic missiles'. It also condemned 'the absence, since December 1998, in Iraq of international monitoring, inspection, and verification, as required by relevant resolutions'. The resolution concluded by stating that 'the Council has repeatedly warned Iraq that it will face serious consequences as a result of its continued violations of its obligations'.[34]

Critics of Resolution 1441, concerned with the Bush administration's increasingly militaristic rhetoric towards Iraq, believed that the intent of the resolution was to provide a justification for future military action. Following the adoption of the resolution, US ambassador to the United Nations John Negroponte deflected criticism by declaring: 'As we have said on numerous occasions to Council members, this resolution contains no "hidden triggers" and no "automaticity" with respect to the use of force. If there is a further Iraqi breach, reported to the Council by UNMOVIC, the IAEA or a Member State, the matter will return to the Council for discussions as required in paragraph 12.'[35] Negroponte also suggested, however, that the United States could respond unilaterally if it did not agree with a future UN decision: 'If the Security Council fails to act decisively in the event of a further Iraqi violation, this resolution does not constrain any member state from acting to defend itself against the threat posed by Iraq, or to enforce relevant UN resolutions and protect world peace and security.'[36]

It was evident that the Bush administration was seeking to justify military intervention in Iraq with the goal of achieving regime change. The White House was becoming increasingly critical of the weapons inspection programme and resistant to any proposals that allowed Hussein to remain in power. Bush administration officials intensified their rhetoric against Iraq in order to convince the US public that Hussein posed an imminent threat to the United States. One month before the adoption of Resolution 1441, Bush had publicly stated: 'Evidence indicates that Iraq is reconstituting its nuclear weapons program' and that it 'could have a nuclear weapon in less than a year'.[37] Bush's comments echoed those made by US National Security Advisor Condoleezza Rice one month earlier when she had declared: 'We do know that [Hussein] is actively pursuing a nuclear weapon. ... We don't want the smoking gun to be a mushroom cloud.'[38]

Throughout the second half of 2002, Bush administration officials voiced a stream of claims about Iraq's chemical and biological weapons capabilities in order to instil fear in the US public and justify military intervention. In August 2002, US Vice-President Dick Cheney announced: 'Simply stated, there is no doubt that Saddam Hussein now has weapons of mass destruction. There is no doubt that he is amassing them to use against our friends, against our allies, and against us.'[39] The following month, US Secretary of Defense Donald Rumsfeld told the US Senate Armed Forces Committee that Hussein had 'amassed large, clandestine stockpiles of biological weapons, including Anthrax, botulism, toxins and possibly smallpox'.[40] One week later, in his national radio address, Bush told the US public: 'The Iraqi regime possesses biological and chemical weapons ... and, according to the British government, could launch a biological or chemical attack in as little as 45 minutes after the order is given.'[41]

The US president also focused attention on Hussein's past atrocities in an attempt to vilify the Iraqi leader: 'Iraq's weapons of mass destruction are controlled by a murderous tyrant. ... He has ordered chemical attacks on Iran, and on more than forty villages in his own country. These actions killed or injured at least 20,000 people, more than six times the number of people who died in the attacks of September the 11th.'[42] Naturally, Bush was careful not to remind the US public that the United States was not only supporting Hussein when he committed these crimes against humanity, but was also helping him to develop weapons of mass destruction.

The propaganda campaign continued into 2003 when, in January, Rumsfeld stated: '[Hussein's] regime has large, unaccounted-for stockpiles of chemical and biological weapons – including

VX, sarin, cyclosarin and mustard gas; anthrax, botulism, and possibly smallpox'.[43] Just over a week later, Bush announced to the nation during his annual State of the Union speech: 'Our intelligence officials estimate that Saddam Hussein had the materials to produce as much as 500 tons of sarin, mustard and VX nerve agent.'[44] And in February, only six weeks before the United States invaded Iraq, US Secretary of State Colin Powell told the UN Security Council: 'There can be no doubt that Saddam Hussein has biological weapons and the capability to rapidly produce more, many more. ... Our conservative estimate is that Iraq today has a stockpile of between 100 and 500 tons of chemical weapons agent. That is enough agent to fill 16,000 battlefield rockets.'[45]

The Bush administration's rhetoric was not restricted to convincing the US public and the international community that Iraq had weapons of mass destruction. Officials also desperately tried to link Saddam Hussein to al-Qaeda and the 9/11 attacks in order to justify making Iraq a target in the war on terror. On 25 September 2002, Bush told reporters that 'you can't distinguish between al-Qaeda and Saddam when you talk about the war on terror'.[46] In January 2003, Vice-President Cheney stated on National Public Radio: 'There's overwhelming evidence there was a connection between al-Qaeda and the Iraqi government. I am very confident that there was an established relationship there.'[47] Despite the Bush administration's failure to produce a single piece of the alleged evidence linking Saddam Hussein to al-Qaeda or the 9/11 attacks, a significant percentage of the US public believed the government's assertions. A public opinion poll conducted in February 2003 showed that one in five Americans believed that Iraq was directly involved in 9/11, with 13 per cent of Americans believing that they had been given conclusive evidence. A further 36 per cent of Americans believed that Iraq provided substantial support to al-Qaeda.[48] The Bush administration's case was bolstered by the US mainstream media's unwillingness to seriously challenge the government's baseless assertions. On 18 March, with 56 per cent of Americans believing that Iraq was directly or indirectly involved in the 9/11 attacks, Bush sent a letter to Congress explaining that an invasion of Iraq was permitted under legislation authorizing force against 'those nations, organizations, or persons who planned, authorized, committed, or aided the terrorist attacks that occurred on September 11, 2001'.[49]

In early March 2003, the United States, Britain and Spain had drafted a Security Council resolution authorizing the use of force against Iraq. The resolution was never voted on because the sponsors knew that it would not be approved. A tripartite declaration by Russia, Germany and France two days earlier had stated that they believed the full and effective disarmament of Iraq could be 'achieved by the peaceful means of the inspections. We moreover observe that these inspections are producing increasingly encouraging results. ... In these circumstances, we will not let a proposed resolution pass that would authorise the use of force.'[50] A report submitted to the Security Council on 7 March by Hans Blix, the executive chairman of UNMOVIC, supported the claims of progress made in the tripartite declaration: 'There is a significant Iraqi effort underway to clarify a major source of uncertainty as to the quantities of biological and chemical weapons, which were unilaterally destroyed in 1991. ... Inspection work is moving on and may yield results.'[51] Still, the Security Council failed to achieve a consensus, leading UN Secretary-General Annan to warn: 'The members of the Security Council now face a great choice. If they fail to agree on a common position, and action is taken without the authority of the Security Council, the legitimacy and support for any such action will be seriously impaired.'[52]

Bush chose to ignore Blix's progress report and Annan's

warning that the use of force without the authorization of the Security Council would be illegitimate. On 19 March, the United States, supported by Britain and several dozen other countries in a 'coalition of the willing', attacked Iraq. The invasion of Iraq also appeared to contradict US ambassador to the United Nations John Negroponte's assurances that Resolution 1441 contained 'no "hidden triggers" and no "automaticity" with respect to the use of force' and that 'the matter will return to the Council for discussions'. The Bush administration's actions, however, were in line with Negroponte's other comments declaring that 'this resolution does not constrain any member state from acting to defend itself against the threat posed by Iraq, or to enforce relevant UN resolutions'. Indeed, the Bush White House claimed it was launching a 'pre-emptive strike' because Iraq's weapons of mass destruction posed an imminent threat to the United States. Bush administration officials also attempted to present the war as a legitimate action by claiming that Resolution 1441 authorized the use of force by warning Iraq that it 'will face serious consequences as a result of its continued violations of its obligations'. While the Bush administration publicly portrayed Iraq as a military threat to the United States and a violator of UN resolutions, the White House downplayed its ulterior motives for wanting Saddam Hussein removed from power: to secure long-term access to Iraq's oil and implement neo-liberal economic reforms that would integrate the country into the global capitalist economy.

The initial military objective of the war, the removal of Saddam Hussein from power, was quickly achieved when the Iraqi military offered little resistance and Hussein fled into hiding. Six weeks after the invasion, President Bush landed on the aircraft carrier USS *Abraham Lincoln* and declared that major combat operations were over. Bush's announcement proved to be premature, however, when, despite the eventual capture of Hussein in

December 2003, a divergent Iraqi resistance to the occupation became entrenched. One year after the war began, 71 per cent of Iraqis viewed the US troops as 'occupiers' rather than 'liberators', while only 13 per cent believed that the invasion was morally justifiable.[53] Photojournalist Jason Howe witnessed the animosity that many Iraqis felt towards the US occupation. Following most bombings, says Howe, rumours would immediately circulate 'that it was the Americans who had done it so they could justify staying here longer. ... Every single car bombing we go to someone comes and tells us they saw a US helicopter fire rockets at the police station or hotel or whatever.'[54]

Sadly, the sense of anger and distrust was not all one-sided, according to US Army infantryman Darrell Anderson, who served eight months in Iraq before seeking political asylum in Canada rather than return to combat duty at the end of his leave. Anderson claims that the behaviour and attitude of many US soldiers in Iraq made it evident that they 'hated these people [Iraqis]. There is a hatred for the Iraqi people.'[55] Anderson's assertions were supported by an April 2004 opinion poll in which 58 per cent of Iraqis said that US soldiers 'conducted themselves badly or very badly' and 46 per cent claimed US troops displayed a lack of respect towards Iraqi women.[56]

That many Iraqis held such a cynical view of the United States is not surprising when the number of Iraqis killed by US forces is taken into account. In September 2004, the number of US soldiers killed passed 1,000, but this figure paled in comparison with the more than 100,000 Iraqis who had died during the previous eighteen months. According to a field study published in the British medical journal *The Lancet*, the risk of death by violence for Iraqis was fifty-eight times higher after the invasion than before. According to the journal, 'Violent deaths were widespread ... and were mainly attributed to coalition forces. Most individuals reportedly killed by coalition forces were women and children.'[57]

Kelly Dougherty, a former US soldier who served in Iraq from April 2003 until February 2004, echoed *The Lancet*'s assertions: 'You don't hear every day how the Iraqi people are suffering at the hands of the US military, and how so many people are arrested or detained, shot and killed, or whatever – that are completely innocent, or that are trying to go about their daily business.'[58]

Intent on countering the increasing number of domestic and international critics who claimed that invading Iraq had little to do with waging a war on terror, Bush declared: 'There's no question that Saddam Hussein had al-Qaeda ties.'[59] Less than a week later, on 23 September, the US president told the United Nations General Assembly that the insurgents 'have made Iraq the central front in the war on terror'.[60] Given that the insurgents did not exist prior to the US invasion and occupation, Bush's declaration that an insurgency launched after the invasion 'made Iraq the central front in the war on terror' suggests that Iraq was not a central front in the war on terror before the US invasion, thus contradicting one of his justifications for going to war.

On 22 July 2004, the National Commission on Terrorist Attacks upon the United States, also known as the 9-11 Commission, released its final report analysing the events leading up to the 9/11 attacks and the Bush administration's response to them. The report made clear that, following 9/11, certain members of the Bush administration were intent on using the terrorist attacks to justify invading Iraq. Secretary of State Powell told the commission that Deputy Secretary of Defense Paul Wolfowitz 'was always of the view that Iraq was a problem that had to be dealt with. And he saw this as one way of using [9/11] as a way to deal with the Iraq problem.'[61] The report mentioned a 17 September 2001 meeting of the National Security Council in which 'President Bush ordered the Defense Department to be ready to deal with Iraq if Baghdad acted against US interests, with plans to include possibly occupying Iraqi oil fields'.[62] The evidence presented in the 9-11 Commission's report and the Bush administration's pre-war rhetoric suggest that it was of little consequence to the White House whether or not UN weapons inspections were proving to be effective in neutralizing any potential Iraqi military threat.

Shortly after the US invasion, the executive chairman of UNMOVIC, Hans Blix, briefed the UN Security Council on the weapons inspections that had been conducted up until the day before the war began. According to Blix, 'The Commission has not at any time during the inspections in Iraq found evidence of the continuation or resumption of programmes of weapons of mass destruction or significant quantities of proscribed items – whether from pre-1991 or later.' He went on to note that 'during the last month and a half of our inspections, the Iraqi side made considerable efforts to provide explanations. ... We did not have time to interview more than a handful of the large number of persons who were said by Iraq to have participated in the unilateral destruction of biological and chemical weapons in 1991.'[63]

Following the invasion, the Bush administration deployed its own weapons inspection team, the Iraq Survey Group. The US inspectors ultimately determined that Iraq's claims to have unilaterally destroyed most of its biological and chemical weapons following the Gulf War were apparently true. David Kay, head of the Iraq Survey Group, admitted in his 2 October 2003 testimony before the US Congress that 'Iraq did not have a large, ongoing, centrally controlled chemical weapons program after 1991. Information found to date suggests that Iraq's large-scale capability to develop, produce, and fill new chemical weapon munitions was reduced – if not entirely destroyed – during Operations Desert Storm and Desert Fox, 13 years of UN sanctions and UN inspections.'[64] Kay also noted that his weapons inspectors 'have not uncovered evidence that Iraq undertook significant post-1998 steps to actually build nuclear weapons or produce fissile material'.[65]

By late 2003, it had become clear that Iraq had no weapons of

Iraq

mass destruction and, therefore, had posed no imminent threat to the United States. If the Bush administration had allowed the UNMOVIC weapons inspectors to continue performing substantive inspections, it would soon have discovered that Iraq did not possess any weapons of mass destruction. Or, perhaps, the Bush White House was concerned with the possibility that further inspections would eliminate a primary justification for removing Hussein from power and lead to the lifting of sanctions.

There was also no evidence to support the Bush administration's pre-war claims that Saddam Hussein and al-Qaeda were allies and that Iraq had played a role in the 9/11 attacks. The 9-11 Commission's final report declared that what little contact existed between the secularist regime in Baghdad and the Islamic fundamentalist al-Qaeda never 'developed into a collaborative operational relationship. Nor have we seen evidence indicating that Iraq cooperated with al-Qaeda in developing or carrying out any attacks against the United States.'[66]

The Bush administration's human rights justification for removing Saddam Hussein from power also lost its lustre on 28 April 2004, when the CBS television news show *60 Minutes II* broadcast photographs of US soldiers abusing Iraqi prisoners in Baghdad's Abu Ghraib prison. A report issued following an internal army investigation described some of the abuses: 'Breaking chemical lights and pouring the phosphoric liquid on detainees ... beating detainees with a broom handle and a chair; threatening male detainees with rape ... sodomizing a detainee with a chemical light and perhaps a broom stick, and using military working dogs to frighten and intimidate detainees with threats of attack, and in one instance actually biting a detainee.'[67]

Among the many photographs of the abuses was one displaying a prisoner with electrical wires attached to his testicles. Another showed a female soldier holding one end of a dog leash while the other end was tied around the neck of a naked prisoner lying on the floor. There was also a photograph of a US soldier apparently forcing a naked prisoner whose body had been smeared with what appeared to be excrement to walk a straight line with his arms outstretched and ankles shackled together. At the same time these abuses were being committed, US Army General Janis Karpinsky was telling US media that, for Iraqi inmates, 'living conditions now are better in prison than at home. At one point we were concerned that they wouldn't want to leave.'[68]

Many in the Arab world were horrified at the images of US soldiers humiliating and abusing Iraqi prisoners in one of Saddam Hussein's former torture centres. Shortly after the Abu Ghraib revelations, Iraqi insurgents began beheading kidnapped Westerners, claiming it was revenge for the humiliation suffered by Iraqi prisoners. Many of the beheadings, which were videotaped, were carried out with the victims dressed in orange overalls similar to those worn by war-on-terror detainees held by the US military at the Guantanamo Bay naval base in Cuba.

It was also evident by early 2004 that the huge majority of the insurgents were not foreign terrorists, as the Bush administration repeatedly claimed, but Iraqis from among both the Sunni and Shiite populations who were simply opposed to the US occupation. This became blatantly obvious following a November 2004 military assault against insurgents led by Jordanian-born Abu Musab al-Zarqawi in the mostly Sunni city of Fallujah. US troops secured the city after one week of intense fighting and, according to US Marine colonel Michael Regner, at least 1,030 of the 1,052 captured insurgents were Iraqis. In other words, while their leader was foreign born and linked to al-Qaeda, fewer than twenty-two of the more than one thousand insurgents were actually foreigners.[69]

Following the assault, US forces refused to allow aid workers to enter Fallujah for several days, thereby limiting information about the number of civilian casualties caused by a week of relentless US bombing. Seven months earlier, in April 2004, US aircraft had also carried out an intensive bombing campaign against Fallujah, but ended their assault before capturing the city following reports by the Arab television network al-Jazeera that hundreds of civilians, including women and children, were being killed in the US offensive. The Bush administration denied al-Jazeera's reports, but British photojournalist Jason Howe entered Fallujah immediately following the attacks and described what he saw: 'I photographed Iraq's new mass graves, not this time the result of Saddam's handy work [sic], but the result of the US assault on the city. At one location alone more than 200 bodies had been buried in a football pitch. One fifteen year old was mourning his brother with whom he used to practise on the very same football field.'[70]

A few weeks after the failed April attempt to capture Fallujah, Secretary of State Powell visited Qatar, where al-Jazeera is based, and pressured the government to rein in the reporting by the most widely watched Arabic station in the Middle East. Powell even went so far as to suggest that a failure to do so would hurt relations between the two countries.[71] Two months later, US National Security Advisor Condoleezza Rice publicly criticized al-Jazeera, claiming that the station was presenting a biased account of events in Iraq. In August 2004, after US efforts had failed to influence al-Jazeera's coverage, Iraq's interim prime minister, Iyad Allawi, shut down the Baghdad studios of the network and banned its correspondents from working in the country. This violation of press freedom clearly contradicted the Bush administration's stated goal of bringing democracy to Iraq. The problem for the Bush White House was that the Iraqi people preferred al-Jazeera's critical news coverage to that offered by the Pentagon-funded Iraqi channel al-Iraqiya, which most Iraqis considered to be little more than a mouthpiece for the occupation.

Iraqi officials finally acknowledged that more than two thousand people had been killed in the November assault on Fallujah. Without the presence of al-Jazeera correspondents in the city, Allawi was able to declare that none of these casualties were civilians; they were all terrorists.[72] US Army infantryman Darrell Anderson questioned the wisdom of labelling the insurgents as terrorists, claiming that those fighting the occupation are simply Iraqis defending their homeland from foreign invaders. Based on his experience in Iraq, Anderson claimed: 'There really isn't an insurgency. It's just people fighting to defend their homes, defend their lives.'[73]

In September 2004, UN Secretary-General Kofi Annan finally criticized the US invasion of Iraq. The secretary-general claimed that the invasion should not have been undertaken 'without UN approval and much broader support from the international community'. Annan also said that 'there should have been a second resolution because the Security Council indicated that if Iraq did not comply there will be consequences. But then it was up to the Security Council to approve or determine what those consequences should be.' In his harshest criticism, the UN secretary-general stated that the war violated international law because it was 'not in conformity with the UN Charter, from our point of view and from the Charter point of view it was illegal'.[74]

## The neo-liberal restructuring of Iraq

In his speeches about regime change in Iraq, and in reference to political and economic reforms in the Middle East in general, Bush alluded to another justification for overthrowing Hussein: democracy promotion and neo-liberal economic reform. According to Bush's Middle East Free Trade Initiative, announced in February 2003, the United States intends to 'pursue comprehensive free trade agreements with countries that are ready and willing to undertake the in-depth commitment to promote economic reforms, liberalize trade systems and open their economies'.[75] The Bush administration intended for Iraq to become a democratic and economic example for the rest of the Middle East by incorporating the country into the global capitalist system through the implementation of neo-liberal reforms. Inevitably, these reforms would require the complete or partial privatization of state-owned entities and the opening of the country's economy, particularly the oil sector, to foreign investment.

Sociologist William Robinson described the Bush administration's strategy for the restructuring of Iraq:

> The US has three goals for the political system it will attempt to put into place in Iraq. The first is to cultivate transnationally oriented elites who share Washington's interest in integrating Iraq into the global capitalist system and who can administer the local state being constructed under the tutelage of the occupation force. The second is to isolate those counter-elites who are not amenable to the US project, such as nationally (as opposed to transnationally) oriented elites and others in a position of leadership, authority and influence, who do not share US goals. The third is establish the hegemony of this elite over the Iraqi masses, to prevent the mass of Iraqis from becoming politicized and mobilized on their own independent of, or in opposition to, the US project, by incorporating them 'consensually' into the political order the US wishes to establish.[76]

On 13 July 2003, Paul Bremer, head of the US-led Coalition Provisional Authority, appointed a twenty-five-person Iraqi Governing Council to run Iraq, although Bremer retained veto power over any decision made by the council. Bush administration officials were quick to point out that the council was representative of the Iraqi population with the majority of its members being Shiites and the remaining membership comprised of Sunnis, Kurds, Turkmen and an Assyrian Christian. Technically, the demographic make-up of the Governing Council was representative of the Iraqi population, but in reality most of the Shiites were moderates who had been living in exile in the United States for years and who maintained close ties to US officials. In this sense, they were not truly representative of Iraq's Shiite population, but they were trans-national elites supportive of the US project described by Robinson.

Ahmed Chalabi and Iyad Allawi represented two examples of the Bush administration's strategic selection of Iraqi Shiites as members of the Governing Council. Chalabi founded the Pentagon-funded Iraqi National Congress in 1992 while in the midst of forty-five years of exile. According to US diplomat James Akins, 'He probably has more supporters in the American Congress than he does in the entire country of Iraq, and he has exploited that. He gets support from us.'[77] Akins's claims were supported by a survey conducted in May 2004 in which Iraqis overwhelmingly declared that Chalabi was the national leader they trusted least, even less than Saddam Hussein. While 42 per cent of Iraqis said they did not trust Chalabi at all, only 14 per cent said the same about Hussein. In fact, when asked which national leader they would elect president, almost three times as many Iraqis said they would vote for Hussein than opted for Chalabi.[78]

At the same time that the survey was being conducted, the Bush administration's strategic selection of Chalabi for the Governing Council was beginning to backfire. Chalabi had begun distancing himself from the Bush administration by calling for full Iraqi control over the country's security forces and criticizing US military tactics. In May, the Bush White House ordered the

Pentagon to sever its ties with Chalabi, claiming he was passing US secrets to the Iranian government. The Pentagon ended its $340,000-a-month funding of Chalabi's Iraqi National Congress organization and US troops raided the former exile's residence in Baghdad with a warrant to arrest his intelligence chief, Aras Habib.[79] Chalabi claimed the spying allegations were Washington's excuse to clamp down on his recent nationalistic rhetoric: 'I am now calling for policies to liberate the Iraqi people and get back our complete sovereignty, and I am raising these issues in a way that the Americans don't like.'[80]

Several months later, Chalabi's Iraqi National Congress joined the Shiite coalition United Iraqi Alliance, which was closely linked to Iraq's leading Shiite cleric, Grand Ayatollah Ali al-Sistani. Chalabi's break with the United States and his decision to ally himself with the United Iraqi Alliance, which intended to run against Allawi's US-backed National Reconciliation Party in the upcoming elections, helped legitimize the former exile in the eyes of many Iraqi Shiites.

As for Allawi, he had also developed close ties with US officials during his thirty-three years in exile, while his Iraqi National Accord group primarily consisted of Iraqi military defectors. The US-appointed Governing Council appointed Allawi to be interim prime minister following the handover of sovereignty to Iraq on 30 June 2004. Ultimately, Allawi was appointed interim prime minister because of his close ties to the United States and his support for the US project.

At the same time the Bush administration was implementing its 'democracy promotion' project, it was also overseeing the economic and physical restructuring of Iraq. In addition to the tens of billions of US taxpayer dollars that were funding the reconstruction, Iraqi oil revenue was being used to pay for contracts issued to foreign companies. Neither the Governing Council nor its successor, Allawi's interim government, however, controlled the revenues generated by Iraq's post-invasion oil exports. All the country's oil revenues were deposited in an account called the Development Fund for Iraq, which was controlled by the Bush administration under a UN mandate requiring that the money be used to benefit the Iraqi people.

During the initial fourteen months of the occupation, Paul Bremer's Coalition Provisional Authority (CPA) claimed that most of the Iraqi money in the Development Fund had paid for contracts issued to Iraqi companies. But shortly after the CPA handed power over to the interim government, it was discovered that nineteen of the thirty-seven major contracts funded with Iraqi oil money, amounting to 85 per cent of the $2.2 billion spent, had gone to US companies.[81] According to a CPA Inspector General report on the disbursements of Iraqi funds in no-bid contracts, the largest recipient by far was Kellogg, Brown & Root, a subsidiary of Vice-President Dick Cheney's former company Halliburton, which pocketed $1.66 billion – in addition to the controversial $7 billion no-bid contract it had already received from the Pentagon immediately prior to the invasion. Other pay-outs to US companies included $48 million to the Harris Corporation, $16.8 million to Custer Battles and $15.6 million to Motorola. According to Fareed Yaseen, an Iraqi diplomat in Allawi's interim government, 'There was practically no Iraqi voice in the disbursements of these funds.'[82]

The Bush administration began its restructuring of Iraq's oil industry less than two months after the invasion. On 4 May 2003, the Bush White House appointed a US citizen, former Shell Oil CEO Philip Carroll, to oversee the rebuilding and restructuring of the Iraqi oil industry. Shortly after his appointment, Carroll suggested that the contracts that foreign oil companies had signed with Hussein's government might be voided. During the 1990s, Hussein had signed oil exploration and production contracts with French, Russian and Chinese companies in preparation for the lifting of UN sanctions. The Iraqi leader had refused, however, to deal with US companies. The US suggestion that Iraq void all contracts signed by the Hussein government stood in sharp contrast to US demands in years past that newly established governments in other countries, Cuba in 1959 and Nicaragua in 1979, for example, respect the contracts that US companies had signed with former dictators. As expected, in late May the new US-appointed Iraqi oil minister Thamer Gadhban began cancelling the contracts when he announced the suspension of three oil deals with Russian and Chinese companies and declared that future Iraqi oil contracts would be open for bidding to all foreign corporations.

While there was little doubt that one of the principal objectives of the US occupation was to secure access to Iraq's oil for US companies, there were differing views within the Bush administration about how this goal should be achieved. Neo-conservatives in the administration wanted Iraq's oil sector privatized and the country to withdraw from OPEC in order to diminish the cartel's influence over global oil prices. The State Department and the oil companies, on the other hand, were fearful that privatization might result in a political backlash reminiscent of the chaos that followed Russia's energy privatization, which left US oil companies on the sidelines. Ultimately, the strategy proposed by the State Department and oil companies prevailed and a new plan was developed that called for a state oil company and continued OPEC membership. The oil companies had little interest in undermining OPEC's efforts at maintaining high oil prices because that would negatively affect their bottom lines. The link between the interests of US oil companies and those of OPEC were made clear by Amy Jaffe of the Baker Institute, one of the architects of the new US plan for Iraq's oil sector: 'I'm not sure that if I'm the chair of an American company, and you put me on a lie detector test, I would say high oil prices are bad for me or my company.'[83]

The potential profits for foreign energy companies promised to be enormous even without privatizing the oil sector. Under neo-liberal restructuring similar to that implemented in other oil-producing nations of the South, foreign oil companies could enter into production agreements under terms so favourable that privatization would not be necessary to ensure huge profits. According to the New York-based NGO Global Policy Forum, favourable concession deals in Iraq would allow foreign oil companies to make a minimum of $600 billion in profits over the next fifty years.[84]

In December 2004, the US-appointed Iraqi Governing Council revealed Iraq's new oil strategy. According to Interim Prime Minister Allawi's economic adviser Hilal Aboud al-Bayati, the strategy called for the Iraq National Oil Company (INOC) to continue operating existing fields, while foreign companies would be allowed to develop all new fields; a substantial prize considering that it is estimated that up to 95 per cent of Iraq's oil reserves remain untapped.[85] While the government did not announce the terms for the proposed oil concessions, the new strategy marked the first time since Iraq had nationalized its oil industry in 1972 that foreign companies would be able to access the country's vast reserves. Many major oil companies signed post-invasion contracts with the Iraqi oil ministry to provide technical assistance in geological studies and for the repairing of pipelines and infrastructure.[86] Highly sought-after long-term oil production contracts, however, could not be signed until the Iraqi government set their terms, including the percentage of oil to which foreign companies would hold the rights.

In the meantime, a June 2005 meeting in London brought together officials from Iraq's oil ministry and executives from ExxonMobil, BP, Shell, Halliburton and other energy giants, with the apparent objective of laying the groundwork for the re-entry of foreign oil companies into Iraq. According to Hasan Juma'a,

Iraq

head of the Iraqi General Union of Oil Employees, 'The second phase of the war will be started by this conference carving up the industry. It is about giving shares of Iraq to the countries who invaded it – they get a piece of the action as a reward.'[87] The union leader's concerns about the Iraqi government handing over the country's oil wealth to foreign companies appeared to be validated by Shell spokesperson Simon Buerk's admission that 'we aspire to establish a long-term presence in Iraq'.[88]

Two years after invading Iraq, the Bush administration had succeeded in securing the country's oil for exploitation by US oil companies. The lack of security in Iraq, however, remained a major deterrent to most companies. In early 2005, owing to repeated attacks against oil infrastructure by insurgents, Iraq was producing only 500,000 barrels a day, far below the country's capacity of more than 1.5 million barrels a day.[89]

The opening up of Iraq's oil industry was only one of many neo-liberal economic reforms that were implemented during the two years following the invasion. In October 2004, Iraq's Finance Minister Adel Abdul Mahdi described the progress that had been made up to that point: 'A sound macroeconomic framework, robust economic activity, and a good start on a broad range of structural and legal reforms that are critical to making the transition from the centralized economy to an economy based on private ownership, open markets, transparency, and the rule of law.'[90] In September 2004, the International Monetary Fund (IMF) provided Iraq with a $436.3 million loan as a reward for implementing neo-liberal reforms similar to those that the IMF itself had imposed on many countries of the South. Upon issuing the loan, the international financial institution also called on the Iraqi government to reduce food subsidies to the Iraqi people, despite the fact that almost half the population was unemployed.[91] The IMF's demand proved particularly disturbing following the release of a March 2005 UN report stating that the percentage of Iraqi children going hungry had almost doubled since the US invasion – from 4 per cent under Saddam Hussein to near 8 per cent by the end of 2004.[92]

On 30 January 2005, Iraqis went to the polls to elect a new parliament, which would be responsible for drawing up the country's new constitution. The elections did not go exactly as the Bush administration had intended. First, the legitimacy of the process was called into question by the fact that most of the country's Sunni Arab population boycotted the election. And second, the US-backed candidate Allawi not only failed to win, but finished a distant third with only 14 per cent of the vote. The Shiite-dominated United Iraqi Alliance won handily with 48 per cent, while a coalition of Kurdish parties finished second with 26 per cent.[93] The principal post-election problem faced by the Bush administration was the fact that Iraq's new Shiite prime minister, Ibrahim Jafaari, maintained close ties with Iran, where he spent time in exile during Saddam Hussein's reign. Jafaari also believed that the new Iraqi constitution should be rooted in Islam. As historian Juan Cole pointed out shortly after the election: 'If the United States had decided three years ago to bomb Iran, it would have produced joy in Baghdad. Now it might produce strong protests from Baghdad.'[94]

More than two years after the US invasion, it remained unclear just how inclusive the new Iraqi government would be, to what degree Islam would influence Iraqi politics in the future, or even if the new 'democracy' would continue to exist once US troops were withdrawn from the country. Some observers in the Middle East viewed both the US occupation of Iraq and the election as a possible foreshadowing of future US efforts to promote democracy and neo-liberal economic reforms throughout the region. Others viewed the Iraqi election and the ongoing insurgency as setbacks for the Bush administration. According to Rami Khouri, editor of Beirut's *Daily Star*, 'The idea that the United

States would get a quick, stable, prosperous, pro-American and pro-Israel Iraq has not happened. Most of the neo-conservative assumptions about what would happen have proven false.'[95]

*Conclusion*

By early 2005, there appeared to be an abundance of both anti-American and anti-Saddam sentiment in Iraq as the country's civilian population continued to bear the brunt of the violence. In April, tens of thousands of pro-Islamic protesters marched through the streets of Baghdad demanding an end to the US occupation. The demonstrators held aloft effigies of George W. Bush and Saddam Hussein, while chanting slogans such as: 'No America! No Saddam! Yes to Islam!' Iraqis were becoming increasingly angry about the precariousness of life in the capital, where there was ample violence but a shortage of necessities. Electricity, for example, remained rationed and was available to the Iraqi people for only two hours a day.

The Bush administration had launched an expansive pre-invasion propaganda campaign to justify military intervention in Iraq. The invasion took place at a time when UN weapons inspections were on the verge of determining that Hussein had no weapons of mass destruction. Such a realization would, in all likelihood, have led to a lifting of UN sanctions and the opening of the world's second-largest oil reserves to Russian, Chinese and French oil companies with US firms sitting on the sidelines. Such a scenario was not acceptable to the Bush administration, which was actively seeking to secure new sources of oil to supply increasing US energy needs.

After two years of occupation, the Bush administration had successfully established an economic system that ensured access for US energy companies to Iraq's vast oil reserves. The US military and newly trained Iraqi troops, however, remained mired in a struggle to contain an insurgency that consisted of as many as 40,000 mostly Sunni fighters. The persistence of the insurgency was making it difficult for the United States to establish the security and stability required for both its neo-liberal and democracy-promotion projects to firmly take root. At the same time, US public support for the war in Iraq was waning and the Bush administration began lowering its expectations with regard to the establishment of a democratic government closely allied with Washington. As sociologist William Robinson pointed out: 'If the Iraq invasion and occupation is the most massive US intervention since Vietnam, it is also the most stunning – indeed, insurmountable – chasm that we have seen since Washington's Indochina quagmire between US intent, on the one hand, and the actual US ability, on the other hand, to control events and outcomes.'[96]

# 2 | Central Asia: the Silk Road strategy

The existence of oil in the Caspian Sea region has been known about for more than a thousand years. The first major oil boom, however, did not occur until the late nineteenth century, when the Rothschild and Nobel families established themselves in Azerbaijan's capital, Baku. At the beginning of the twentieth century, Azerbaijan was responsible for 50 per cent of global oil production, displacing the Standard Oil Company as the world's leading energy producer. But Caspian Sea oil did not dominate the global market for long. Following the 1917 Bolshevik revolution, the Soviet Union inherited Central Asia and the South Caucasus from Tsarist Russia and it would be seventy years before the Caspian Sea region would experience another oil boom.

With the collapse of the Soviet Union in 1991, republics in the region formerly controlled by the communist government in Moscow suddenly found themselves to be independent nations. The new republics consisted of Kazakhstan, Uzbekistan, Turkmenistan, Tajikistan and Kyrgyzstan in Central Asia, and Azerbaijan, Georgia and Armenia in the South Caucasus. In the midst of these new countries lay the landlocked Caspian Sea, which is actually the world's largest lake. The Caspian's littoral states consist of Russia, Kazakhstan, Turkmenistan, Azerbaijan and Iran, all of which lay claim to some of the estimated 200 billion barrels of oil situated beneath the sea and along its shores.[1]

Upon obtaining independence in 1991, many of the new republics experienced civil strife as they attempted to establish themselves as fully fledged states. The governments of Uzbekistan and Tajikistan in Central Asia waged war against Islamic militants, while Azerbaijan and Georgia in the South Caucasus battled secessionist movements within their borders. At the same time, many people in the region who had lived their entire lives under the atheist Soviet regime began rediscovering Islam. Muslim schools were opened throughout the region with funding from organizations in Iran, Saudi Arabia and Turkey.

The United States also played a leading role in the political and economic transition that took place in Central Asia and the South Caucasus during the 1990s. It wasn't until after 9/11, however, that the United States established a significant military presence in a region historically beyond its sphere of influence. Not only did the Bush administration deploy troops to Afghanistan in its war on terror, it also set up bases in Uzbekistan, Kyrgyzstan and Georgia. At the same time, the United States developed closer military ties to Kazakhstan and Azerbaijan, the region's two largest oil producers. Washington pushed the newly independent republics to implement neo-liberal economic policies during the 1990s and then, as part of the war on terror, dramatically increased its military presence in the region in order to protect burgeoning US economic interests, particularly those related to oil and gas.

In 1997, the Clinton administration's deputy secretary of state, Strobe Talbott, said the new republics in Central Asia and the South Caucasus 'have, for so much of their history, been subjected to foreign domination', but now they 'have the chance to put behind them forever the experience of being pawns on a chess board as big powers vie for wealth and influence at their expense'.[2] By the time Talbot made this statement more than five years after the collapse of the Soviet Union, it was already evident that the new republics had become pawns in a new political chess game being played by the United States, Russia, Iran and China. It was, in effect, a new version of the 'Great Game', the nineteenth-century struggle between Britain and Russia for control of Central Asia.

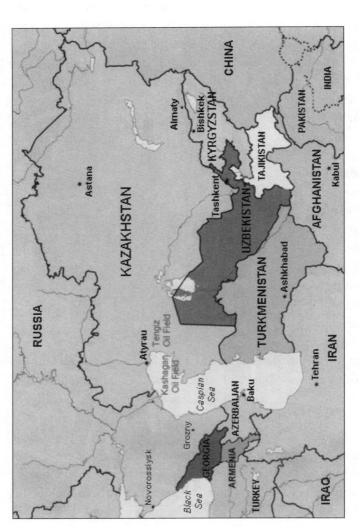

2 *Central Asia and the South Caucasus*

The original Great Game was a fight to control access to the riches of India. The new version, however, was being fought over the region's vast oil and gas reserves. Iran responded to the escalating US military presence in the region by bolstering its own military forces along its Caspian coast while simultaneously negotiating oil and gas pipeline contracts with the newly independent republics. For its part, China conducted joint military exercises with Kyrgyzstan, purchased a 60 per cent share in Kazakhstan's third-largest oilfield and agreed to build a pipeline from Kazakhstan to its western province of Xinjiang. Meanwhile, Russia's ambassador to Iran, Alexander Maryasov, claimed that the post-9/11 deployment of US troops to the region had little to do with the war on terror: 'For the Americans this is about economic interests, especially the Caspian oil.' Maryasov made it clear that Moscow had no intention of relinquishing Russia's influence in the region to the United States: 'As soon as our economy regains its strength, we will reestablish our old relations with Central Asia and the South Caucasus, and reassert our sphere of influence in that region' (Kleveman 2003: 141).

In 1998, then CEO of Halliburton Dick Cheney made clear the US attitude towards the region when he stated: 'I cannot think of a time when we have had a region emerge as suddenly to become as strategically significant as the Caspian.'[3] That same year, the US Senate Committee on Foreign Relations issued a report on a pending bill entitled the Silk Road Strategy Act. The report stated that the 'goal of the legislation is to properly focus US assistance to better achieve US interests' in Central Asia and the South Caucasus. The report warned that 'regional, hegemonic powers' – notably Russia and Iran – were striving to expand their political control in the area 'while seeking to maintain control over the flow of oil and gas resources from the region'.[4] The committee failed to note that, by strategizing to 'better achieve US interests', it was simply advocating that the region fall victim to a global hegemonic power rather than to 'regional, hegemonic powers'.

The following year, the US Congress passed the Silk Road Strategy Act, which stated: 'It shall be the policy of the United States in the countries of the South Caucasus and Central Asia ... to help promote market-oriented principles and practices ... to support United States business interests and investments in the region.' The bill also spelled out why it was so important that the United States be engaged in the new Great Game: 'The region of the South Caucasus and Central Asia could produce oil and gas in sufficient quantities to reduce the dependence of the United States on energy from the volatile Persian Gulf region.'[5] The act was named after the ancient Silk Road, which was a series of transportation routes used to move riches and goods from the Far East and Central Asia to Europe between 500 BC and AD 1500. The motivation behind the new Silk Road strategy was the transportation of oil and gas from Central Asia and the South Caucasus to Western markets.

### The Islamic revival

After 9/11, Central Asia and the South Caucasus became a principal battleground in the war on terror, while also promising to serve as a vital alternative source of oil that could diminish the US reliance on Persian Gulf producers. As in the Persian Gulf countries, a majority of the population of Central Asia are Muslims. Furthermore, Islam has been experiencing a revival in a region that had been controlled by the atheist communist regime in Moscow for more than half a century.

Islam arrived in Central Asia and the present-day South Caucasian country of Azerbaijan in the eighth century and mostly flourished until the communists seized power in Moscow in 1917. The Soviet Union inherited much of Central Asia from the tsarist empire and, in 1920, also seized Azerbaijan. In the early decades of Soviet rule, Islamic practices were suppressed and the region's Muslim population subjected to secularization campaigns.

Soviet Premier Josef Stalin divided Central Asia, then known as Turkestan, into five separate republics, creating Uzbekistan and Turkmenistan in 1924, Tajikistan in 1929 and Kazakhstan and Kyrgyzstan in 1936. According to Central Asia expert Shirin Akiner, 'These republics were entirely new state formations with no basis in historic nation-states. They were created not in response to popular demand, but at Moscow's behest' (Akiner 1995: 7). Stalin created the five republics based on the demographics of different ethnic groups with the objective of making people self-identify with their particular ethnicity rather than as Muslims.

After the Second World War, Moscow softened its stance against Islam by sanctioning an official version of the religion, which tolerated practices acceptable to the Soviet regime. There also existed, however, an 'underground Islam' that preserved ostracized traditional practices. Finally, under Soviet Premier Mikhail Gorbachev's policy of glasnost, or openness, there was a resurgence of Islamic expression in Central Asia, particularly in Uzbekistan, Kyrgyzstan and Tajikistan. Many people abandoned Russian culture and began reasserting their own cultural identity, which was rooted in Islamic teachings.

Following the collapse of the Soviet Union in 1991, the five Central Asian republics and the South Caucasus nations of Azerbaijan, Georgia and Armenia – the latter two being primarily Christian countries – became independent nation-states. Former high-ranking communist officials during the Soviet era became the leaders of the newly independent republics, which were established as secular states. With its religious demographic almost evenly split between Muslims and Russian Orthodox Christians, Kazakhstan was the only Central Asian republic in which Muslims did not constitute at least 75 per cent of the population. As had occurred during Soviet times, each of the leaders of the five newly independent Central Asian republics endorsed a state-sanctioned form of Islam and repressed those groups that refused to abide by the official version of the religion, particularly fundamentalists.

The persecution of Muslims was particularly severe in Uzbekistan, where President Islam Karimov brutally repressed all opposition Islamic groups that sought to practise any form of Islam independent of that condoned by the state. The repression intensified following al-Qaeda's attacks against the United States when Karimov used the global war on terror to justify his persecution of opposition Islamic groups. The Karimov government not only used violence against armed groups such as the Islamic Movement of Uzbekistan (IMU), it also brutally repressed the Hizb ut-Tahrir (Party of Liberation), whose members sought to establish an Islamic state through peaceful means.

For its part, the United States, particularly after 9/11, allied itself with the region's repressive regimes and ignored their persecution of Muslims. The Bush administration refused to place any of the newly independent republics on its list of nations that violated the Freedom from Religious Persecution Act of 1997, even though US State Department human rights reports clearly stated that the Uzbekistan government 'restricts freedom of religion'.[6] The Freedom from Religious Persecution Act prohibits the provision of US aid to countries on the list, something the Bush administration was unwilling to consider given its view of the newly independent republics as strategically important allies in the war on terror. According to political scientist Shahram Akbarzadeh, Bush administration policy was contributing to a 'growing radicalisation of dissidents in the face of continued state repression and disillusionment with the USA for its apparent support for authoritarian rule in Central Asia'.[7]

The 1990s saw the emergence of a struggle between the secular elites and an Islamic opposition to determine the national identity of the newly independent states. From 1992 until 1997,

Tajikistan endured a civil war waged between its secular government and Islamic opposition forces that left 50,000 dead. In Central Asia and the South Caucasus, as in various other parts of the globe, an Islamic world view replaced communist ideology as the principal alternative to the Western capitalist model that dominated the post-cold war process of economic globalization. This turn of events led Washington to portray many of those Muslims who challenged its global agenda as radical fundamentalists, often eagerly portraying them as terrorists even when their tactics involved little or no violence. Consequently, in addition to securing access to oil and implementing free trade economic reforms, US policy in Central Asia and the South Caucasus also sought to eliminate Islamic 'extremists'.

## Kazakhstan: the economic opening

When Kazakhstan became independent following the collapse of the Soviet Union in 1991, it instantly became the world's fourth-largest nuclear power owing to the thousands of former Soviet warheads located within its borders. But the government of the newly independent republic decided to unilaterally disarm all its nuclear weapons. It also shut down the world's largest nuclear test site and an anthrax production facility. A horrific Soviet nuclear legacy, in which the health of almost 1.5 million of Kazakhstan's 15 million people had been negatively affected by years of nuclear weapons testing, was one of the primary motivators behind the new government's decision to disarm. By 1995, Kazakhstan had eliminated all its weapons of mass destruction.

Kazakhstan not only found itself in possession of an abundance of nuclear missiles following independence, it was also awash in oil and gas reserves. In fact, Kazakhstan contained the largest oil reserves of all the Central Asian and South Caucasian countries. It lacked the capacity, however, to fully develop its energy reserves and to transport its prized commodities to overseas markets. In addition, its state-run economy had been under Moscow's control for decades and the sudden collapse of the Soviet Union left the newly independent republic scrambling to pay workers' salaries, feed its population, and provide healthcare and education. While Saudi Arabia, Iran and Turkey funded Islamic schools and institutions for Kazakh Muslims, who constituted almost half the country's population, the US government and the international financial institutions were also instrumental in helping Kazakhstan establish itself as a nation. In return for this desperately needed aid, however, Washington required that Kazakhstan implement neo-liberal economic reforms.

First the George H. W. Bush administration, and then the Clinton administration, demanded that the new republics of Central Asia and the South Caucasus replace their state-controlled economies with market-based systems in order to fully integrate with the global capitalist economy. According to Deputy Secretary Talbott, 'Throughout the region, we're encouraging the states there to establish ties with the World Bank, International Monetary Fund ... and other international financial and political institutions.'[8] It wasn't long before IMF-imposed structural adjustment programmes provided favourable conditions for foreign energy companies to gain access to the region's vast oil and gas reserves. As Akbarzadeh notes: 'Washington was eager to integrate Central Asian economies, especially their oil and gas extraction industries, into the global market to reduce the world's reliance on the Persian Gulf hydrocarbon.'[9]

Nursultan Nazarbayev, former First Secretary of the Central Committee of the Communist Party of Kazakhstan, became the president of the newly independent republic in December 1991. Eight months later, Kazakhstan joined the IMF and the following year received its first loan. In return for the loan, the IMF imposed a structural adjustment programme on the country which demanded that the government privatize state-run enterprises, lower tariffs and achieve macroeconomic stability by restricting public spending in order to maintain IMF-mandated debt-to-GDP ratios. On 5 July 1995, the IMF authorized a $290 million loan, noting that 'Kazakhstan made some progress in 1994 in macro-economic stabilization. ... And the attainment of the objectives of the 1995 program will, to a significant extent, hinge upon the progress made in enterprise restructuring and privatization. The privatization program is being accelerated by increasing the number of enterprises to be privatized.'[10]

By 1998, the IMF was lavishing Kazakhstan with praise for its implementation of neo-liberal policies: 'Kazakhstan has made substantial progress in transforming its economy into a market-based system. Macroeconomic stabilization has been broadly achieved, the domestic market is fairly liberalized and open to foreign competition, and the role of the state in the economy has been considerably reduced.'[11] The IMF report also praised the reduction of the state's role in the banking sector and the increased participation of foreign banks in the country. The lending institution was, however, concerned about 'the temporary suspension of the sale of enterprises in the oil and gas sector'.[12] In 1998, President Nazarbayev had consolidated the remaining publicly owned oil- and gas-producing companies into one entity known as KazMunaiGaz, supposedly in preparation for privatization. But Nazarbayev unexpectedly signed a law making KazMunaiGaz a joint stock company with the government con- trolling 100 per cent of its shares. While appearing nationalistic, in reality this move to retain state ownership of the country's remaining resources was akin to closing the barn door after the horse had escaped. Five years of IMF-imposed neo-liberal reforms had already allowed dozens of foreign energy companies to benefit from the privatization of some of Kazakhstan's oil and gas entities and from favourable concession deals. In fact, IMF-imposed reforms resulted in Kazakhstan virtually giving away its oil reserves by only requiring foreign companies to pay royalty rates of between 2 and 6 per cent a barrel.[13] Kazakhstan's royalty rates are among the lowest in the world and stand in stark contrast to those that Venezuela began demanding in 2001, which ranged between 20 and 30 per cent a barrel.[14]

The IMF was not the only international financial institution praising Kazakhstan for its implementation of neo-liberal reforms. In December 2001, Dr Peter Watson, president of the US governmental agency Overseas Private Investment Corporation (OPIC), told Kazakhstan's minister of trade and economy, Zhaksybek Kulekeev: 'OPIC is encouraged by the breadth of economic reforms undertaken by the government of Kazakhstan since its independence ten years ago, and understands that a great deal of investment opportunity remains to be tapped by American companies.'[15] Part of OPIC's mission under the congressional legislation that authorizes its existence is to 'mobilize and facilitate the participation of United States private capital and skills in ... countries in transition from non-market to market economies'.[1] To fulfil its obviously neo-liberal mission, OPIC provides loans and loan guarantees for overseas projects involving US corporations. Between 1992 and 2001, OPIC provided $98 million in loans and guarantees for projects in Kazakhstan, including $50 million for the oil and gas sector.[17]

In 2004, the IMF noted: 'Structural reforms are well advanced compared to other countries in the region, but the implementation of the reform agenda has slowed somewhat since 2000.'[18] The IMF report also praised Kazakhstan's impressive economic growth, which was primarily due to increased foreign investment in the oil industry. In 1993, for example, the Tengizchevroil consortium headed by ChevronTexaco and ExxonMobil – which owned 50 per cent and 25 per cent shares in the consortium respectively – agreed to invest $20 billion to develop the huge

Tengiz oilfield in western Kazakhstan.[19] It is estimated that there are 6 to 9 billion barrels of recoverable reserves in the Tengiz field, which was producing an average of 280,000 barrels of oil per day by the end of 2003.[20] In order to transport the oil to Western markets, the ChevronTexaco-led Caspian Pipeline Consortium (CPC) built a 935-mile pipeline from the Tengiz field to the Russian Black Sea port of Novorossiysk.

On 24 July 2000, ExxonMobil announced the discovery of the offshore Kashagan oilfield in a section of the North Caspian Sea that had not previously been explored because it was a protected nature preserve during the Soviet era. With oil reserves estimated at 13 billion barrels, Kashagan is the world's largest discovery in more than thirty years. The Offshore Kazakhstan International Operating Company (OKIOC) consortium, consisting of Exxon-Mobil, Agip, British Gas, Shell, Total, ConocoPhillips and Inpex, expects the Kashagan field to begin producing oil in 2008. Kazakhstan's former foreign affairs minister, Erlan Idrissov, claims that production should reach 400,000 barrels a day by 2013 and surpass 1 million barrels daily two years later. According to Goldman Sachs oil industry analyst Jonathan Waghorn, '[Kashagan] will provide a stable stream of cash for the next 30 or 40 years, so it is certainly a good thing for companies that are able to absorb such a project into their portfolios.'[21]

More than a decade of IMF-imposed structural adjustment had opened up Kazakhstan's resources to exploitation by multinational oil companies, but most Kazakhs had not benefited from the foreign investment in their country. Foreign corporations were investing heavily in the capital-intensive energy sector – oil and fuel account for 60 per cent of the country's total exports – but ignoring other more labour-intensive areas of the economy.[22] Even in the energy sector, it is debatable whether or not Kazakh workers were benefiting from the country's oil production. According to the local environmental group Caspian

Nature, approximately one hundred workers at the Tengiz oilfield died and many more became sick between 1996 and 2004, most of them young men who had developed blood and liver problems. The group claims that tests from 30,000 seals that died in 2002 revealed similar symptoms. US-based Halliburton, which has been involved in various oil production and pipeline projects in Kazakhstan since 1992, is one of the subcontractors responsible for operations at the Tengiz field. Caspian Nature claims that the company has been negligent in its handling of the highly toxic hydrogen sulphide gas that must be removed from Tengiz's heavy oil. According to the environmental group, this gas is responsible for the deaths and illnesses of the workers. While Halliburton admitted to illegally firing one sick employee who had filed a lawsuit against the company, the oil services giant denies it is responsible for the illnesses and deaths.[23]

ChevronTexaco, meanwhile, claims its Tengiz project has included community outreach programmes that have benefited the local population and that the company's presence in the country has led to increased 'salaries, goods and services purchased from national suppliers, tariffs and fees paid to state-owned companies and government royalties'.[24] But, according to a United Nations Development Programme (UNDP) report issued in May 2004, the two oil-rich provinces of Mangistau and Atyrau, where the Tengiz oilfield is located, are among the poorest regions in the country owing to the 'high levels of economic inequalities prompted by the monopolistic character of the oil-and-gas industry'.[25] While the communities in the Tengiz region remained mired in poverty, ChevronTexaco's global operations, of which Tengiz is the largest, earned near-record profits of $7.2 billion in 2003.[26]

Kazakhstan's transition from a state-controlled to a market-based economy proved devastating for much of the population. In 1998, the World Bank stated that a 'sharp contraction in [economic] output since independence has contributed significantly to an increase in poverty'. The bank went on to note that 'wages have fallen by over 50 percent in real terms, with serious implications for household income and consumption'.[27] Four years later, according to the UNDP, daily life for most Kazakhs had improved little with 71 per cent of the population still mired in poverty – living on less than $2 dollars per day.[28] The percentage of Kazakhs living in poverty in 2002 was substantially higher than the 15 per cent of the population that subsisted in poverty in 1989, two years prior to the collapse of the Soviet Union.[29]

A 2004 UNDP report noted the decline in many health indicators caused by reduced healthcare spending and deteriorating healthcare facilities. Ultimately, says the report, the recent economic growth brought about by neo-liberal reforms 'has failed to change the lives of the majority of the Kazakh people for the better'.[30] The UNDP's conclusions were supported by the UN's Human Development Index (HDI), which measures a country's quality of life based on life expectancy, access to education and the average citizen's purchasing power. In 1993, one year before IMF-imposed structural adjustment was initiated, the HDI ranked Kazakhstan 54th out of 173 countries (UNDP 1993: 11). But eleven years later, the country's HDI ranking had fallen to 78th out of 177 countries (UNDP 2004: 140).

In Washington's eyes, though, Kazakhstan has made great strides. On 27 March 2002, the Bush administration granted market economy status to Kazakhstan – the first former Soviet republic to achieve such a standing – allowing Kazakh goods greater access to US markets. Kazakh ambassador to the United States Kanat Saudabayev claimed his country's new status was an 'objective recognition on the part of the United States of our achievement in reforming the economy and of the democratic changes in our country'.[31]

Despite Ambassador Saudabayev's assertions to the contrary, Kazakh politics remained far from democratic in even the narrowest sense of the term – free and fair elections. Kazakhstan did not hold a multi-party election until 10 January 1999, eight years after obtaining independence. Nazarbayev won the election handily with 81 per cent of the vote. Monitors from the Organization for Security and Cooperation in Europe (OSCE) declared that 'the election process fell far short of the standards to which the Republic of Kazakhstan is committed as an OSCE participating State'.[32] Among the many problems reported by the OSCE monitors were the appointment of election officials by the president, the disqualification of opposition candidates, media coverage that disproportionately favoured the incumbent and voting-day irregularities.

As US Congressman Christopher Smith pointed out to the House of Representatives: 'The entire election was carefully orchestrated and the only real issue was whether [Nazarbayev's] official vote tally would be in the 90s – typical for post-Soviet Central Asian dictatorships – or the 80s, which would have signalled a bit of sensitivity to Western and OSCE sensibilities.'[33] Kazakhstan's parliamentary elections held in September 1999 were also fraught with irregularities according to the OSCE. Interestingly, a year later Washington imposed sanctions on Haiti owing to electoral irregularities that were minor in comparison with those that had occurred in Kazakhstan.

Like most other oil-producing nations of the South, Kazakhstan ranks as one of the world's most corrupt countries – an ignominious distinction that has played a significant role in the failure of the country's oil and gas wealth to benefit the majority of the population. In 2004, Kazakhstan ranked 122nd out of 145 countries in Transparency International's corruption index. According to Transparency International, oil-rich countries such as Kazakhstan are 'plagued by revenues vanishing into the pockets of western oil executives, middlemen and local officials'.[34]

Oil exploration and centralized political power usually go hand in hand. As a result, local communities and civil society groups are often left on the margins and there is little accountability or transparency with regard to the collection and distribution of oil wealth. A 2003 report issued by the New York-based Open Society Institute, which addressed corruption in the Caspian Sea region, noted: 'Because petroleum earnings flow to the central government and because multinational oil companies prefer to work in any country with a powerful central arbiter, petroleum production often coincides with the expansion of executive power and the evisceration of effective opposition, inside or outside of government' (Bagarov et al. 2003: 98).

In one of the biggest bribery scandals faced by a US corporation in recent decades, officials of the then Mobil Oil Company – Mobil merged with Exxon and became ExxonMobil in 1998 – were accused of paying and receiving bribes related to US companies securing oil contracts in Kazakhstan, including Mobil's share of the Tengiz field in 1993. In June 2003, Mobil's former senior vice-president, J. Bryan Williams, pleaded guilty in the US District Court to non-payment of taxes on $7 million in earnings, including $2 million he admitted certain people and governments had paid him while he was conducting business for Mobil. Another investigation led to the indictment of James Giffin, chairman of the US merchant bank Mercator, for making $78 million in illegal pay-offs to Kazakh officials to secure oil contracts. Giffin was accused of violating the Foreign Corrupt Practices Act, which prohibits the bribery of foreign officials by US citizens. Giffin acted as the middleman in negotiations between Mobil and the Nazarbayev government and was instrumental in the company securing its 25 per cent share of the Tengiz consortium.[35] A lack of transparency in oil deals contributes to corrupt practices that prevent the Kazakh people from benefiting from the country's oil wealth. A 2003 report by the British-based NGO Christian Aid noted that foreign oil companies 'sign strictly confidential product sharing agreements (PSA) with the government of Kazakhstan, forbidding them to reveal the sums they pay for being allowed to extract the oil'.[36]

It has not only been Western oil companies that have gained access to Kazakhstan's oil; China has also made its presence felt. The Chinese National Petroleum Company (CNPC) owns a 63 per cent share of the Aktobe oilfield, which contains estimated reserves of 1 billion barrels.[37] The CNPC and Kazakhstan are also constructing a 2,000-mile pipeline to transport oil from the Caspian Sea to China's western Xinjiang province. In September 2004, Kazakhstan's ambassador to Russia, Krymbek Kusherbaev, described the growing oil ties between his government and China: 'Energy cooperation between Kazakhstan and China is now on a large scale. The construction of the oil pipeline to western China, with a capacity of 20 million tonnes per year, has begun. We are not ruling out the participation of the Chinese in the exploration and development of oil deposits in the Kazakhstan sector of the Caspian Sea.'[38]

Not willing to hurt the interests of US oil companies in their race against China and Russia for access to Kazakhstan's oil reserves, the Bush administration has turned a blind eye to the country's rampant corruption, failure to democratize and human rights violations. It is economics, not democratization, that has been the priority of the governments of the United States and Kazakhstan. President Nazarbayev made this evident in a February 2004 interview when, in reference to the democratization of Kazakhstan, he declared: 'Economy first, politics second.'[39] The reason for the Bush administration's desire to maintain close ties with the corrupt and undemocratic Kazakh regime was made clear in a 2004 US Department of Energy brief: 'The country is no longer a minor world oil exporter as it was during the late 1990s, and it is poised to become an even more significant player in world oil markets over the next decade.'[40]

## Azerbaijan: the new oil boom

While the failure to democratize, high levels of poverty and corruption, and foreign control of the oil and gas sectors in Kazakhstan are clearly problematic, the situation in the much smaller country of Azerbaijan is even more troubling. Azerbaijan's first oil boom ended following the 1917 Bolshevik revolution when the new communist regime in Moscow nationalized the oil operations of the Rothschild and Nobel families in the early 1920s. During the Soviet era, Azerbaijan's importance as an oil producer declined as Moscow relied mostly on its Kazakhstan and Siberian reserves. It wasn't until it achieved independence following the collapse of the Soviet Union in 1991 that Azerbaijan experienced a significant resurgence in oil exploration and production.

Azerbaijan became embroiled in a civil conflict even before it had gained independence. In 1987, the Nagorno-Karabakh region of western Azerbaijan had tried to take advantage of Soviet Premier Mikhail Gorbachev's policy of glasnost, or openness, by requesting that the partly autonomous province populated primarily by Armenians be permitted to secede from the Soviet Union and become part of Armenia. When the Soviet government refused, Karabakh unilaterally announced its secession on 12 July 1988. Both the Azerbaijan regional government and Moscow declared the secession to be illegal and Soviet troops were dispatched to the region. The ensuing conflict between Azeris and Armenians in Karabakh escalated with the withdrawal of Soviet troops following the demise of the Soviet Union in 1991. Armenia entered the fray, fighting Azerbaijan until the signing of a ceasefire agreement in May 1994. During the conflict, Armenian forces seized control of Karabakh and almost 20 per cent of Azerbaijan. Thousands died in the conflict and 250,000 Armenians and 1.1 million Azeris became refugees.[41]

On 24 October 1992, the Armenian lobby convinced the US Congress to pass Section 907a of the Freedom Support Act, which prohibited the provision of US aid to Azerbaijan in response to an economic blockade imposed on the Karabakh region by the Azeri government. Meanwhile, US aid to Armenia continued, creating tensions with the Russians who accused the United States of meddling in their 'back yard'.

In the midst of its conflict with mostly Christian Armenia and Karabakh, the mostly Muslim Azerbaijan became an independent republic in December 1991. Following a series of regime changes during the new republic's first eighteen months of existence, a military coup led to former communist leader and Azerbaijan KGB head Heydar Aliyev assuming the presidency in June 1993. Several months later, Aliyev was 'elected' president in polls boycotted by opposition parties and condemned by international observers as fraudulent.

President Aliyev's rule was marked by rampant human rights violations. His government repressed social and political movements and, as a result, the country's jails were filled with political prisoners. The state security forces routinely harassed independent media organizations, including closing down opposition media outlets. Aliyev's regime also persecuted Muslims, particularly fundamentalists, who did not abide by the state-sanctioned form of Islam. According to the New York-based organization Human Rights Watch, 'The Interior Ministry refused identity documents to Muslim women who insisted on being photographed in headscarves.'[42]

Unlike Kazakhstan, Azerbaijan did not receive US aid during the 1990s owing to the prohibition under Section 907a of the Freedom Support Act. While Congress had tied the hands of the Bush and Clinton administrations with regard to providing monetary aid to Azerbaijan, it did not prevent White House officials from facilitating ties between the government of the newly independent republic and US oil companies.

During the political chaos of Azerbaijan's first two years of independence, US and British oil companies vied with each other to obtain the rights to the country's oil reserves – the second-largest in the region after Kazakhstan. British Petroleum (BP) gained the upper hand in 1992 when former prime minister Margaret Thatcher personally visited Azerbaijan to lobby on behalf of the company. Beginning in 1993, US oil company officials and the Clinton administration began working together and soon out-manoeuvred the British in the race to gain access to Azerbaijan's oil. On 20 September 1994, the 'contract of the century' was signed in Baku. A consortium called the Azerbaijan International Operating Company (AIOC) was to exploit three major offshore oilfields: Chirag, Azeri and Gunashli. US companies – Amoco, Unocal, Pennzoil and McDermott – dominated the consortium with a 40 per cent share, while BP held a 17 per cent share and the State Oil Company of Azerbaijan Republic (SOCAR) received 10 per cent. The following year, the US share of the consortium increased when Exxon joined.[43] Ironically, BP would eventually become the dominant member of the consortium following its merger with Amoco in December 1998.

Both Russia and Iran protested about the 'contract of the century', but to no avail. Moscow and Tehran claimed that Azerbaijan was selling the rights to oil it did not necessarily own. The Caspian littoral states had never reached an agreement demarcating ownership of oil situated beneath the landlocked lake. The question of ownership rights over Caspian Sea oil came to a head on 23 July 2001 when an Iranian warship ordered an Azeri exploration ship hired by BP-Amoco to leave South Caspian waters to which Tehran claimed it owned the oil rights.

The shortest route for BP-Amoco to transport oil from the Caspian Sea to a major ocean port was through Iran. But in order to abide by US-imposed sanctions on Iran and to avoid dependence on Russian pipelines in the north, the oil giant decided to find an alternative means of transporting Azeri oil to Western markets. A BP-led consortium of oil firms, which included US companies Unocal and ConocoPhillips, along with the governments of Azerbaijan, Georgia and Turkey, agreed in November 1999 to build the 1,087-mile Baku–Tgilisi–Ceyhan (BTC) pipeline to transport Caspian Sea oil from Azerbaijan through Georgia to the Turkish deep-water port of Ceyhan on the Mediterranean. The BTC pipeline consortium obtained financing from the World Bank's International Finance Company and the European Bank of Reconstruction and Development, despite protests by environmental groups over the use of unproven technology in the pipeline. The US engineering giant Bechtel was contracted to oversee the construction of the Azerbaijan and Georgia sections of the pipeline, which became operational in 2005.

Despite the signing of the 'contract of the century' and the building of the BTC pipeline, it would be years before the Chirag, Azeri and Gunashli oilfields would achieve full production and be capable of providing Azerbaijan with substantial revenue. In the meantime, with the economy in shambles following the war with Armenia, the Aliyev government signed two loan agreements with the IMF in 1995. In return for loans totalling $176 million, the IMF demanded that Azerbaijan begin implementing a structural adjustment programme.[44] The following year, the IMF provided Azerbaijan with another $219 million, even though the government's rate of economic reform lagged in comparison with Kazakhstan's.

The IMF stated that its medium-term programme in Azerbaijan was 'designed to prepare the country for the prospective oil boom as oil production is projected to double by the turn of the century and to quadruple shortly thereafter'.[45] Given that significant amounts of Azeri oil would soon be flowing, the IMF had only a limited time to impose neoliberal reforms on the country before oil revenues diminished the government's reliance on the international financial institution. A report issued by the Open

Society Institute alluded to this strategy: 'The key question for Azerbaijan is whether the government will commit to needed structural reforms – in the tax administration, the customs service, the treasury, privatization, and improvement of the investment climate – once the incentive to reform is diluted by the onset of petroleum revenues' (Bagarov et al. 2003: 119). In order to implement the privatization component of the reforms, the State Programme of Privatization of State Property was launched in 1995. The following year the IMF declared that 'small-scale privatization is expected to be completed by end-June 1997 and, by end-September 1999, 70 percent of state enterprises are due to be privatized. ... In addition, Azerbaijan is expected to complete its trade liberalization process during the program period.'[46]

Even the macroeconomic numbers that the IMF uses to measure progress showed that the neo-liberal reforms were not creating the promised broad-based economic growth. In 1998, GDP grew at a higher than expected rate of 10 per cent, but this was due solely to the country's oil production. Azerbaijan's non-oil manufacturing sector registered an 8 per cent decline in the same year.[47] Because of the economy's hyper-dependence on oil exports, Azerbaijan began exhibiting the early symptoms of 'Dutch Disease', in which over-dependence on the exports of a single commodity drives up the value of the national currency and makes other exported goods prohibitively expensive. Consequently, economic growth and job creation in the non-oil sectors contracted. A 2003 report released by the Open Society Institute stated: 'Most manufacturing has ground to almost a complete halt, even as the economy began a general recovery. Exports to Russia, Azerbaijan's largest trading partner, have dropped from $180.5 million in 1997 to $77 million in 2001' (Bagarov et al. 2003: 94). Clearly, Azeris in the non-oil sectors were facing the same dilemma as Kazakhs: worsening economic conditions and increasing poverty.

According to a 2000 UNDP report, despite its oil-driven economic growth in the second half of the 1990s, Azerbaijan's GDP per capita remained below that of most of the other former Soviet republics. In 2000, the average wage was a measly $1.50 a day and, as a result, 68 per cent of Azeris were living in absolute poverty – subsisting on less than $1 per day. IMF-imposed privatizations had reduced state sector employment from 71 per cent of the working population in 1990 to 36 per cent by the end of the decade. The private sector, however, had failed to create enough jobs for former state employees and by 1999 there were as many as 148 unemployed Azeris for each job vacancy, according to the UNDP.[48] The situation was most dire for the country's 789,832 internally displaced persons (IDPs) – one in ten Azeris became IDPs as a result of the war with Armenia. In April 2000, almost all IDPs lived in absolute poverty, 69 per cent of them were unemployed and more than 30 per cent of internally displaced children under the age of five suffered from chronic malnutrition.[49]

The IMF-imposed neo-liberal reforms also devastated the country's healthcare system as government cutbacks dramatically reduced healthcare spending as a percentage of GDP. According to the UNDP, even in the midst of conflict and political turmoil in 1993, the Azeri government was spending 3.3 per cent of GDP on the nation's healthcare system. By 1999, spending had declined to 1.1 per cent of GDP and healthcare was no longer free. A UNDP report stated that, owing to rising costs, 'most people tend to access healthcare only in an emergency'.[50]

By 2001, the IMF had decided it had to address the problem of poverty in Azerbaijan. On 6 July, the financial institution approved a Poverty Reduction and Growth Facility (PRGF) arrangement with the government in Baku. The PRGFs are loans issued to low-income countries with the goal of continuing structural adjustment in order to improve economic growth while simultaneously emphasizing poverty reduction. Because the IMF provides PRGF loans at a lower interest rate and with a five-and-a-half-year grace period for repaying the principal, the Azeri government's debt repayment burden would be slightly less than with conventional IMF loans. Theoretically, because the government did not have to make payments on the principal for five and a half years, it would have more money to invest in social programmes. Some of the contradictions inherent in the PRGF arrangement were made evident when the IMF approved an increase in health and education spending by the Azeri government, but called for reductions in fuel subsidies. While the country's impoverished population benefited from the increased health and education spending, these were the same Azeris who were hurt most by the reduction in fuel subsidies, which led to higher costs for heating, cooking and transportation. Not surprisingly, after two years of the PRGF arrangement an IMF review determined that 'poverty remains widespread and the economy is heavily dependent on oil-sector revenue'.[51]

In the meantime, IMF-imposed privatizations continued in 2001 when President Aliyev announced the implementation of the Second State Programme of Privatization of State Property, which included subsidiaries of the state oil company SOCAR. Only a handful of SOCAR's oil drilling and production units were privatized, but as Valekh Aleskerov, general manager of SOCAR's Foreign Investments Division, noted: 'Someday, SOCAR itself will be privatized.'[52]

In August 2003, the ailing eighty-year-old Aliyev appointed his son Ilham to the post of prime minister and then withdrew from the September presidential election. Ilham became the ruling party's candidate and won the presidency with almost 80 per cent of the vote in an election that the OSCE condemned as blatantly fraudulent. Protesters took to the streets and fought with police, but Ilham assumed office and Azerbaijan established the first dynasty among the former Soviet republics, as the reins of power passed from father to son. While the Bush administration mostly ignored the irregularities evident in Azerbaijan's September elections, it was openly critical of neighbouring Georgia's fraudulent elections a month later when the US-backed opposition was defeated. As it had done in Kazakhstan, the United States turned a blind eye to human rights violations, corruption and poverty, while facilitating access to Azerbaijan's oil reserves for US energy companies.

### Turkmenistan: going against the flow

In sharp contrast to Kazakhstan and Azerbaijan, Turkmenistan has maintained its state-controlled economy and remained relatively isolated from the outside world. While this country of 6 million people is not a major oil producer, it does sit on one of the world's largest deposits of natural gas. As occurred in most of the former Soviet republics following independence in 1991, the head of Turkmenistan's Communist Party became the country's president. Unlike other leaders in the region, though, President Saparmurat Nyazov, who calls himself *Turkmanbashi* (leader of all Turkmens), has forgone the democratic charade of repeatedly holding rigged elections by simply becoming president-for-life.

Turkmenistan has retained a Soviet-style political and economic system, centrally controlled by an eccentric president who has gone so far as to rename the months of the year after himself and family members. Turkmenistan's socialist economy stands like a lonely island in the midst of a sea of neo-liberalism. Accordingly, President Nyazov guarantees every citizen a job and heavily subsidizes goods, food and services. He also, however, represses all dissent, and strictly limits public access to the Internet, international newspapers and foreign television broadcasts.

Nyazov's policies have kept Turkmenistan relatively isolated. It is difficult for foreigners to visit Turkmenistan and few foreign companies have been permitted to conduct business in the country. The notable exception is the Russian gas company Gazprom, which purchases almost all of Turkmenistan's natural gas. Other than a small, recently opened pipeline to neighbouring Iran, Turkmenistan is dependent on Gazprom's pipelines to pump its prized commodity to Russia and from there to European markets. While the production and sale of gas have provided the Turkmen government with relatively stable revenues, they have also given Moscow leverage over Turkmenistan. For example, when Nyazov signed a preliminary contract with Shell Oil in 1999 to build an alternative pipeline under the Caspian Sea to Azerbaijan, Moscow threatened to shut down Gazprom's pipeline. Unwilling to lose its principal source of foreign revenue, Turkmenistan pulled the plug on the Azerbaijan pipeline project. The Shell deal was not the first time that Turkmenistan had attempted to enter into partnership with a multinational company. In 1995, Nyazov had signed a contract with US-based Unocal to build a gas pipeline through Afghanistan to energy-starved Pakistan. The project collapsed when Unocal pulled out following the 1998 US missile strikes against al-Qaeda training camps in Afghanistan.

For the most part, Nyazov has tried to avoid dealing with foreign companies, preferring instead to preserve state control of Turkmenistan's economy and resources. As a result, the United States and the international financial institutions have failed to integrate Turkmenistan into the global economy with the same degree of success they have achieved with the region's other two primary energy producers, Kazakhstan and Azerbaijan. Like its neighbours', Turkmenistan's economy struggled in the years following independence. But in contrast to the leaders of the other newly independent republics, Nyazov did not turn to the IMF and foreign corporations for loans and investment. Instead, he relied on increased state spending, a policy that was anathema to the IMF and other advocates of neo-liberalism.

By 1998, Turkmenistan's economy began to recover and by 2004, according to the World Bank, 'Even by the more conservative alternative rates, economic expansion over the past five years has still been robust. A contributor to this recovery has been large-scale, largely state-driven investment, averaging over 30 per cent of GDP, in oil refineries, textiles, food processing, transportation and large construction projects.' The World Bank went on to note that Turkmenistan had enjoyed an 18 per cent average annual growth rate since 1999 and 'in 2000, massive current account deficits turned into sizable surpluses, averaging 5 per cent of GDP. ... External public debt has steadily declined since 2000.'[53]

Turkmenistan had implemented economic policies that flew in the face of prevailing economic wisdom and had achieved an economic growth rate more impressive than its neighbours', which had followed the neo-liberal doctrine pushed by the IMF and the World Bank. Astoundingly, even though it had noted Turkmenistan's successes in its own report, the World Bank continued to exhibit a blind allegiance to neo-liberalism when it declared that, among the former Soviet republics, 'Turkmenistan has progressed least in terms of economic reforms since independence. ... Privatization stalled in the late 1990s with most large and medium-scale enterprises, as well as many small firms, remaining in state hands.'[54] As of 2004, Turkmenistan owed no money to the IMF and the World Bank.

By not selling off most of its oil and gas assets, Turkmenistan ensured long-term revenue generation that helped alleviate the social suffering that followed independence from the Soviet Union. According to the World Bank, only 7 per cent of Turkmen lived in absolute poverty at the end of the 1990s. This figure stood in stark contrast to the 68 per cent of the population that were subsisting in absolute poverty in Azerbaijan and the 32 per cent in Kazakhstan, which was the IMF's poster child for neo-liberal reform in the region.[55] Also, between independence and 2004 Turkmenistan climbed fourteen places to eighty-sixth in the UN's Human Development Index, ranking it above Azerbaijan and all the other Central Asian republics except Kazakhstan. As noted earlier, the least impoverished of the Central Asian republics during the Soviet era, Kazakhstan, was headed in the opposite direction, dropping twenty-four places to seventy-eighth during the same period.

While Turkmenistan's economy remained relatively healthy by regional standards, the country had serious problems regarding civil liberties and human rights. Like his fellow leaders throughout Central Asia, President Nyazov repressed opposition groups and censored independent media. The Russian Orthodox Church and Sunni Islam are the only legal religions in the country. Those caught practising another religion have been fined and, on occasion, imprisoned. Nyazov has also ordered the forced displacement of entire neighbourhoods in the capital, Ashgabad, to make way for the construction of grandiose public monuments that often honour the president himself.[56]

Owing to Turkemenistan's political isolation and dependence on Russian pipelines, Moscow has clearly held the advantage in the new Great Game in this Central Asian country. Not only have US corporations been unable to gain access to Turkmenistan's enormous reservoir of natural gas, but the Bush administration has also failed to convince Nyazov to support Washington's war on terror in the region. In fact, Turkmenistan declared itself a neutral nation before the United Nations in 1995 and successfully maintained that neutrality following 9/11. While Nyazov refused to allow US military forces the use of his country's airbases or airspace during the invasion of Afghanistan, he did allow Turkmenistan to be used as a staging ground for the delivery of international humanitarian aid to its war-ravaged neighbour.

Following the US invasion, Nyazov pledged to provide Afghan-

istan with $500 million in aid over a ten-year period. He sup-
plied electricity and fuel at special rates, while helping to build
hospitals and develop communication and transportation infrastructure throughout the devastated country. Turkmenistan is
one of the few countries that has kept its post-invasion promises
to Afghanistan. This generosity, however, is not entirely altru-
istic. A stable Afghanistan would allow Nyazov to revive plans
to construct a gas pipeline to Pakistan and finally reduce Turkmenistan's dependence on Russia. From Washington's point
of view, a stable Afghanistan could provide an opportunity for
US corporations to finally gain access to Turkmenistan's energy
reserves, particularly if Unocal again becomes involved in the
construction of a Turkmenistan-to-Pakistan pipeline.

### Militarization of the region

For multinational energy companies operating in Central Asia
and the South Caucasus, the biggest logistical hurdle in exploiting
the region's resources has been transporting the oil and gas to
Western and Asian markets. Owing to the centralization of the
Soviet system, the only existing pipelines ran northward to Russia. In order to avoid dependence on Russian-owned pipelines,
Western energy companies operating in the newly independent
republics began seeking alternative transit routes.

Unocal was one of several US energy companies operating
in the region which was interested in selling oil and gas to the
growing Asian market, but there were no pipelines running east
or south from the Central Asian nations. In an attempt to solve
this problem, Unocal signed a deal with gas-rich Turkmenistan
in 1995 before beginning negotiations with Afghanistan's Taliban
government to build a gas pipeline from Turkmenistan through
Afghanistan and Pakistan to the Indian Ocean.

In November 1997, representatives of the Taliban government
visited the United States to discuss the project with Unocal and

State Department officials. Four months later, while explaining the gas pipeline project to the US Congress, Unocal vice-president John J. Maresca announced that the company also envisioned building an oil pipeline through Afghanistan: 'The pipeline would become an integral part of a regional oil pipeline system that will utilize and gather oil from existing pipeline infrastructure in Turkmenistan, Uzbekistan, Kazakhstan and Russia.'[57]

In sharp contrast to the repression of Islamic fundamentalism that was occurring in the former Soviet republics, the Taliban imposed its brand of fundamentalism on all Muslims in Afghanistan. The Clinton administration and Unocal, however, appeared unconcerned about the Taliban's poor human rights record, particularly its treatment of Afghan women. At the same time the US officials and Unocal were in discussions with the Taliban, the State Department was reporting that Afghan women were not permitted to attend schools or go out to work. It also noted that the 'Taliban decreed what women could wear in public. Women were forced to don a head-to-toe garment known as the chador, which has only a mesh screen for vision. ... In Kabul and elsewhere women found in public who were not wearing the chador were beaten by Taliban militiamen.'[58]

US social justice groups, particularly women's organizations, launched a campaign in support of Afghan women and began lobbying for the US government to sever ties with the Taliban regime. Feeling political pressure on the domestic front, US government officials became increasingly hesitant to support Unocal's pipeline project for fear of appearing supportive of the Taliban. The shift in Washington's stance towards the Taliban was completed after al-Qaeda bombed the US embassies in Kenya and Tanzania in August 1998. The Clinton administration responded to the bombings by launching missile strikes against al-Qaeda training camps in Afghanistan, leading Unocal to abandon its pipeline project.

The US invasion of Afghanistan following 9/11 led many critics to speculate that the Bush administration was using the war on terror to secure access to the region's resources and potential pipeline routes. After all, the US Department of Energy had stated only months prior to the US invasion that 'Afghanistan's significance from an energy standpoint stems from its geographical position as a potential transit route for oil and natural gas exports from Central Asia to the Arabian Sea'.[59] In actuality, the United States had already secured access to much of the region's oil and gas reserves over the previous decade through the imposition of neo-liberal reforms on local governments which opened the door for multinational energy companies. Clearly, though, it was in Washington's interest to stabilize Afghanistan in the hope of providing alternative and more cost-effective routes for transporting oil and gas from the region to world markets. While the war on terror in Afghanistan was intended to target al-Qaeda, which, after all, had just attacked the United States, it also provided the Bush administration with an opportunity to escalate its military influence in the region in order to better protect burgeoning US political and economic interests.

The war on terror provided the United States with a long-sought justification for escalating its military involvement in a region that had historically been under Russia's sphere of influence. Washington had begun laying the groundwork for establishing a military presence in the newly independent republics immediately following the collapse of the Soviet Union. The United States was the first country to open embassies in each of the new republics of Central Asia and the South Caucasus. And despite the fact that the newly independent republics still maintained close military ties to Russia, according to Deputy Secretary Strobe Talbott, 'It was at Paul Wolfowitz's insistence, when he was at the Pentagon [under President George H. W. Bush], that the US established Defense Attaché offices at these embassies. And it was at his behest that the first military-to-military contacts took place.'[60]

Building on the groundwork laid by Wolfowitz a decade earlier, the administration of George W. Bush deployed US military forces not only to Afghanistan under the umbrella of the war on terror, but also to Uzbekistan, Kyrgyzstan and Georgia. In addition to establishing bases in these countries, Washington increased military aid to the authoritarian and repressive regimes that held power. The Bush administration deployed US Army special forces troops to Georgia in April 2002 to train that country's military to combat Islamic insurgents. The US soldiers were stationed only a few miles from a Russian military base and close to the BTC oil pipeline that ran from Azerbaijan through Georgia to the Turkish port of Ceyhan. While officially the US troops were in the South Caucasus as part of the war on terror, US ambassador to Georgia Richard Miles admitted that the deployment 'does have a back up role I would say with regards to pipeline security. The pipeline is a strategic asset for Georgia and all of the countries that are involved'.[61]

In Central Asia, Uzbekistan's relatively small oil reserves are not economically vital to the United States, but the country has been militarily important to the Bush administration. In October 2001, Uzbekistan's President Islam Karimov gave the US military permission to station aircraft and more than one thousand troops at the Soviet-era airbase in Khanabad for use in its war against Afghanistan. Karimov, who has ruled Uzbekistan's 25 million people in a dictatorial fashion since the country gained independence in 1991, used the war on terror to justify his ongoing repression of Islamic opposition groups. By allying itself with Uzbekistan, the Bush administration became partnered with one of the world's most repressive regimes. Following the arrival of the US military, according to Human Rights Watch, 'Human rights abuses on a massive scale continued in Uzbekistan. ...

**Central Asia**

83

The government systematically violated the rights to freedom of religion, expression, association, and assembly. There was no independent judiciary, and torture was widespread in both pre-trial and post-conviction facilities.'[62]

Karimov's treatment of Muslims who refused to practise their religion according to the strict guidelines established by the state was particularly harsh. It was not only Islamic militants belonging to the Islamic Movement of Uzbekistan (IMU) who were targeted by the regime, but also members of the non-violent Hizb ut-Tahrir (Party of Liberation). In 1999, the Uzbekistan government sentenced nineteen alleged members of IMU to death in what Human Rights Watch called 'patently unfair show trials', while hundreds of members of Hizb ut-Tahrir were given harsh prison sentences solely for their religious beliefs.[63] In 2001 and 2002, as many as seven thousand Uzbeks were imprisoned on religious or political charges for non-violent acts, while more than four thousand villagers forcibly displaced by the government remained in resettlement camps hundreds of miles from their homes.[64] In 2002, rather than criticizing Uzbekistan for its human rights violations, the Bush administration instead showed its appreciation for Karimov's support in the war on terror by providing an astounding $508 million in assistance to the country, making it the fourth-largest recipient of US aid in the world that year after Israel, Egypt and Colombia.[65]

As far as Karimov was concerned, the US aid was vital in light of the IMF's 1996 decision to suspend its loan programme with Uzbekistan because of the government's failure to implement neo-liberal economic reforms. After Uzbekistan became a strong ally in the war on terror, however, Washington convinced the international financial institution to renew its ties with the Karimov regime. Uzbekistan soon frustrated the IMF again by failing to implement the structural reforms called for by the lending institution. With the IMF unable to make any headway, US State

Department spokesman Richard Boucher announced on 13 July 2004 that the Bush administration was suspending $18 million in military aid to the Karimov regime, not because of Uzbekistan's atrocious human rights record, but because Washington was 'disappointed by lack of progress on democratic reform and restrictions put on US assistance partners on the ground'. In other words, Karimov was getting his wrist slapped for not implementing the reforms called for by the IMF. While Uzbekistan is of little economic importance to the United States, its implementation of neo-liberal reforms would put into place another small piece of the free trade puzzle that Washington is trying to methodically construct throughout the world. Boucher did make it clear, however, that 'Uzbekistan is an important partner of the United States in the war on terror' and that the withholding of aid 'does not mean that either our interests in the region or our desire for continued cooperation with Uzbekistan has changed'.[66]

The following month, the Bush administration performed an abrupt about-face when General Richard Meyers, chairman of the Joint Chiefs of Staff, visited Uzbekistan in August and announced that Washington would provide the Karimov government with $21 million in military aid – $3 million more than had been cut off the previous month.[67] The decision to reinstate the military aid was inspired by Karimov's refusal to allow US military planes to use the Khanabad airbase following the aid suspension.[68]

While the Bush administration withheld aid in an attempt to pressure Uzbekistan into implementing free market economic reforms, it did not use the same tactic to try to bring an end to the Karimov regime's rampant human rights abuses against Muslims. Washington's portrayal of Karimov as a close ally in the war on terror clearly contradicted the Bush administration's human rights justifications for removing Saddam Hussein from power in Iraq. Karimov, who some Uzbeks have labelled 'our Saddam', has repeatedly used torture and imprisonment against his political opposition, particularly Muslims. Former British ambassador to Uzbekistan Craig Murray was the only Western diplomat willing to speak out against Karimov's human rights abuses. Murray paid a price for his candour, however, when the Blair government removed him from his post in October 2004. One month after his dismissal, Murray claimed that there was 'political support for Karimov from all the senior figures in the US administration, from Bush down'. He went on to declare that supporting 'such a vicious dictatorship can never be right and as the Tashkent regime tortures innocent Muslims, US support for him can only increase hatred for the West in the Islamic world'.[69]

US Secretary of Defense Donald Rumsfeld downplayed human rights when he visited Tashkent in February 2004, stating that Washington's relationship with Uzbekistan is 'multifaceted' and that it also involves political, economic and security issues. Rumsfeld noted that 'Uzbekistan is a key member of the coalition's global war on terror' and that the military-to-military relationship of the two countries 'is strong and is growing stronger every month'.[70] The importance of that military-to-military relationship for the Bush administration was never so evident as following the massacre of hundreds of civilians by Uzbek troops in the city of Andijan in May 2005. The brutality of the Uzbek regime became clear to the world when troops shot and killed hundreds of demonstrators protesting against Karimov's rule.[71] The US State Department joined European nations in their call for an independent inquiry into the massacre. When Karimov responded to the State Department's position by again preventing US military flights from using the Khanabad airbase, the Bush administration quickly changed its position and even blocked a NATO demand for an international probe into the massacre. Nevertheless, Karimov remained unhappy with the State Department's response to the massacre and demanded that US forces leave Uzbekistan within six months. One Pentagon official made the military's position clear: 'We want to get back the ability to use that base fully.'

US military ties to neighbouring Kyrgyzstan also grew stronger following the 9/11 terrorist attacks. Despite a human rights record only marginally better than Uzbekistan's, the Bush administration and Kyrgyzstan's President Askar Akayev became close allies in the war on terror. Akayev allowed the US military to use the Manas airfield for its war against Afghanistan. In return for use of the airfield, the Bush administration provided the Akayev government with $49.9 million in assistance in 2002, of which $12 million was military aid with no human rights conditions attached.[72] As of July 2004, there were still 1,150 US troops based in Manas and the military was erecting more permanent buildings, clearly illustrating that it had no intention of leaving in the near future.[73] Meanwhile, according to Human Rights Watch, 'With its increasingly close relationship to the US and heightened international profile, the government appeared confident that repressive measures would have no diplomatic consequence.'[74] But while the government's repressive measures did not reap any negative reaction from the Bush administration, the people of Kyrgyzstan rose up and overthrew Akayev in March 2005 after opposition parties were barred from participating in parliamentary elections. Shortly after the uprising, Rumsfeld visited the country to ensure that the interim government had no intention of requesting that US military forces leave Kyrgyzstan.

While Kazakhstan did not permit the United States to establish a military base on its soil, it nevertheless developed close military ties with Washington. The Bush administration signed a five-year military cooperation agreement with the Nazarbayev regime in September 2003 which called for the supply of helicopters, planes and ships to Kazakhstan. The deal was signed one month after Kazakh troops were deployed to Iraq to help the US war effort in that country. After visiting Kazakh officials in February 2004, Rumsfeld stated: 'We talked about the US support for Kazakhstan's sovereignty and independence, and our important military-to-military relationship.'[75] Undoubtedly, Rumsfeld was referring to the Bush administration's desire to ensure Kazakhstan's 'independence' from Russian and Chinese influence, not Washington's.

The escalating US military presence in Central Asia has created tensions between Washington and both Moscow and Beijing, which consider the region their back yard. Russian troops remain stationed in Kyrgyzstan, while China has conducted joint military exercises with that country. Additionally, in July 2004 Tajikistan agreed to permanently host 20,000 Russian troops. US- and Russian-led military alliances are also competing for influence in the region. Washington is eagerly recruiting Central Asian nations to participate in the NATO Partnership for Peace programme in an attempt to extend the security alliance's influence far beyond the North Atlantic. Meanwhile, members of the Russian-led Collective Security Treaty Organization – Russia, Kazakhstan, Kyrgyzstan and Tajikistan – held military exercises in August 2004. Perhaps even more troubling for Washington was the fact that Russia and China held their first ever joint military exercises in August 2005.

*Conclusion*

The US military presence and Washington's support for secular governments marked by repression, corruption and nepotism have increased anti-American sentiments among the region's Muslim population and have fuelled terrorism. Washington's Silk Road strategy has been reminiscent of cold-war-era policies in which the United States supported repressive dictatorships in Asia in order to protect its political and economic interests from the designs of Russia and China. For the newly independent republics, their desire to avoid being dominated by long-time nemesis Russia has made them vulnerable to Washington's machinations. But with governments in the region slowing the pace of neo-liberal reforms and maintaining close military ties to Russia and China, it remains unclear who will ultimately prevail in the new Great Game.

# 3 | West Africa: exploiting the other gulf

The Bush administration's quest for alternative sources of oil has led it to develop closer ties with resource-rich nations in West Africa. While three countries in the region – Nigeria, Angola and Gabon – were among the top suppliers of crude oil to the United States during the 1990s, the area was not a foreign policy priority for Washington. The terrorist attacks on 11 September 2001, however, led to a re-evaluation of US policy in West Africa, which the US Department of Energy forecasts will become increasingly important over the next decade. The United States gets 15 per cent of its oil from sub-Saharan Africa – most of it from the Gulf of Guinea, which runs from Nigeria to Gabon – but that amount is expected to increase dramatically. As Republican Senator Chuck Hagel, chairman of the Senate International Economic Policy Subcommittee, noted in 2004: 'We could be importing as much as 25–30 per cent of our oil imports from the Gulf of Guinea over the next few years. That certainly would rival the Persian Gulf as a supplier of crude oil.'[1]

Some of the countries in West Africa, particularly Angola, have endured brutal decades-long civil wars. Nigeria has spent most of its independence under military dictatorships and most recently returned to civilian rule in 1999. Repressive dictators still hold power in other oil-rich countries in the region. President Omar Bongo has ruled Gabon with an iron fist since 1967, while President Teodoro Obiang Nguema came to power in Equatorial Guinea in a 1979 military coup. Despite the region's history of civil conflict, ruthless dictatorships and ongoing ethnic clashes, foreign oil companies, including US energy giants ChevronTexaco and ExxonMobil, have continued to operate in West Africa. Foreign oil companies have worked closely with corrupt regimes in the region and benefited from human rights violations committed by national military apparatuses responsible for protecting oil operations. The Bush administration's escalating involvement in the region in order to secure new sources of oil has led to increasingly close ties with repressive regimes under a foreign policy reminiscent of the US engagement in Africa during the cold war.

## Nigeria: the land of no tomorrow

Like many African nations, Nigeria has struggled to come to terms with its colonial past since gaining independence from Britain in 1960 and becoming a republic in 1963. The British had arbitrarily established the country's borders in 1907 with little regard for historical ethnic divisions. Today, Nigeria is Africa's most populous nation with 137 million people drawn from more than 250 ethnic groups, the most dominant being the Hausa in the north, the Yoruba in the west and the Igbo in the east. Another legacy of colonialism has been religious strife between the half of the country's population that is Muslim and the 40 per cent that is Christian. A crisis of governance following independence also led to Nigeria being ruled by brutal military dictatorships for much of its first forty years as a nation-state. Even after Nigeria returned to civilian rule in 1999, the country remained the third most corrupt in the world.[2] As a result of corrupt and inefficient governments, foreign exploitation of its vast oil reserves, economic mismanagement and religious and ethnic strife, many consider Nigeria to be a failed state struggling to survive these seemingly endemic problems that threaten to break the country into several smaller ethnic-based nations. According to Bobo Brown, a Nigerian public relations official for Shell, 'Nigeria is the land of no tomorrow' (Maier 2002: xviii).

Few Nigerians have benefited from the country's discovery of

West Africa

oil in the 1950s. While Nigeria is one of the world's leading oil producers – the valuable resource accounts for 95 per cent of Nigeria's export earnings – poverty is worsening in a country that is already one of the world's poorest nations. The battle over control of Nigeria's more than 30 billion barrels of proven oil reserves has led to massive government repression and ethnic conflict, particularly in the Niger river delta region.[3] As is common among people in oil-rich nations of the South, many Nigerians view oil as more of a curse than a blessing. Nigeria is the fifth-largest supplier of crude oil to the United States, but it ranks a lowly 151st out of 177 nations on the UN's Human Development Index, which measures the quality of life of a country's citizens (UNDP 2004: 141). In 2004, according to the World Bank, 66 per cent of Nigerians lived in absolute poverty – subsisting on less than $1 a day – compared with 43 per cent in 1986.[4] Additionally, more than 3.5 million Nigerians are living with HIV/Aids, while the life expectancy for a Nigerian born in 2004 is barely fifty years.[5]

Oil was first discovered in Nigeria by Shell in 1956 while the country was still a British colony. That same year, Mobil also received a concession to conduct oil exploration in the country. Despite the Mobil concession, the Shell Petroleum Development Corporation (SPDC) maintained a virtual monopoly over Nigerian oil exploration until the country's independence in 1960. Following independence, other foreign companies including Gulf, which became Chevron in 1984, also began operating in Nigeria. Shell's principal operations were in the Niger river delta region, while Mobil's operations were primarily located offshore. Gulf/ Chevron operated in both the Delta region and offshore. In the early 1970s, Shell, Mobil and Gulf/Chevron were all required to participate in joint venture partnerships with the state-owned Nigerian National Oil Corporation (NNOC), which became the Nigerian National Petroleum Corporation (NNPC) in 1977.

Government revenues increased dramatically during the global

*3  West Africa*

oil boom initiated by the 1973 Arab–Israeli war. Unfortunately, the corruption and clientelistic policies of the government prevented most Nigerians from benefiting from the country's oil wealth. In the 1980s, Nigeria paid dearly for its hyper-dependence on oil exports when global oil prices plummeted and the government could no longer service its $19 billion foreign debt. The country's floundering economy led to a coup that brought General Ibrahim Babangida to power in August 1985.

President Babangida wanted to restructure the country's debt, but private lenders would not consider it unless Nigeria received the IMF's stamp of approval, which required implementing a structural adjustment programme (SAP). The previous dictator, General Muhamadu Buhari, had refused to negotiate with the IMF for fear that widespread public distrust of the international financial institution and the neo-liberal reforms upon which its loans were conditioned would lead to civil unrest. Fully aware of public sentiment, Babangida announced in early 1986 that the Nigerian people would not accept IMF conditionalities; therefore, the country would apply its own 'home-grown' remedies. Thus, the president appealed to the nationalist concerns of Nigerians by rejecting the IMF. He neglected to tell the Nigerian people, however, that his 'home-grown' remedy was virtually identical to an IMF-imposed structural adjustment programme. Furthermore, the IMF monitored the structural adjustment programme because Nigeria's creditors and other international financial institutions such as the World Bank still required an IMF stamp of approval before they would authorize new loans to the country.

In early 1986, as part of Babangida's economic reforms, Nigeria offered more attractive terms to foreign oil companies willing to sign a memorandum of understanding (MOU) with the government. An MOU defined the overall structure of a joint venture between the NNPC and a foreign company, including establishing oil rents – royalty and income tax rates. In Nigeria, it also guaranteed minimum profit margins of $2 a barrel for oil companies. In 1991, the MOUs were modified to offer even more favourable terms for foreign companies, guaranteeing them a minimum profit of $3 per barrel.[6] The liberalization of the foreign exchange market was another of the reforms that Babangida implemented. It immediately resulted in a 66 per cent depreciation of the Nigerian currency (the naira), which further impoverished millions of Nigerians.

There was enormous public opposition to the neo-liberal

reforms, particularly from university students and workers, who rioted in 1988 and 1989. Babangida responded to the unrest by easing the reform regime, but also by using repression against opposition groups. According to a 1991 Human Rights Watch report, 'Throughout its six-year tenure, the military government of General Ibrahim Babangida ... relied on force to ensure its stay in power. In the process, the Babangida government [was] responsible for the deaths of hundreds of students and others who demonstrated against its policies, the detention without trial of thousands of government critics, the silencing of opposition organizations and the erosion of the rule of law.'[7]

Following a series of coups and short-lived military dictatorships between 1993 and 1998, Nigeria was poised to return to civilian rule. In August 1998, three new political parties – the People's Democratic Party (PDP), the All People's Party (APP) and the Alliance for Democracy (AD) – were formed to participate in elections. The PDP won a majority of seats in the senate and its presidential candidate, former army general Olusegun Obasanjo, who had ruled the country as a military dictator during the 1970s, won the presidency amid claims of fraud. Nearly sixteen years of military rule finally came to an end when Obasanjo was inaugurated in May 1999.

Almost immediately after assuming office, Obasanjo had to contend with new outbreaks of violence as confrontations between ethnic groups flared up throughout the country. The new president responded by ordering the army to shoot ethnic militants on sight. The arbitrary executions led human rights groups to accuse the civilian government of perpetrating the same abuses that had routinely occurred under military rule. Tragically, during more than forty years of independence, the only consistent behaviour that Nigerians had come to expect from their government consisted of corruption, inefficiency and repression.

In Nigeria, as in many oil-rich nations of the South, foreign companies and the central government are the principal recipients of the country's oil wealth, while local communities suffer the environmental consequences of oil production. Such is the case in the Niger delta region where there exists a history of conflict between Shell, supported by the Nigerian military, and the relatively small Ogoni ethnic group. Since 1990, the Ogoni, who number half a million and depend on agriculture, have sought greater autonomy and compensation for the environmental damage caused to their lands by gas flaring, chronic oil spills, unlined toxic waste pits and pipeline construction.

In January 1993, a locally based organization called Movement for the Survival of the Ogoni People (MOSOP) held the first 'Ogoni Day' rally to focus attention on the extensive environmental devastation wrought by Shell, which was responsible for half of Nigeria's oil production. In April, more than ten thousand Ogonis demonstrated when US contractor Willbros began constructing an oil pipeline for Shell on Ogoni farmland. Nigerian military and police, responsible for protecting the oil operations of foreign companies active in the country, opened fire on the demonstrators, killing one and wounding ten.[8]

Several months after the military crackdown on the demonstrators, MOSOP leader Kenule Saro-Wiwa was arrested and imprisoned for thirty-one days. The government also transferred Ogoni police officers away from the region, replacing them with officers from different ethnic groups, who then launched attacks against Ogoni villages. According to Human Rights Watch, during the last five months of 1993 'approximately 1,000 Ogonis were killed in attacks believed to be sanctioned by governmental authorities. Villages were destroyed, and thousands of Ogonis were displaced.'[9] Meanwhile, the civil unrest forced Shell to suspend its drilling operations on Ogoni lands, although frequent oil spills from Shell pipelines running through Ogoni territory continued to occur. In all of Nigeria, between 1976 and 1996, more than 1.8 million barrels of oil from 4,835 spills despoiled the environment (Human Rights Watch 1999: 59).

Both Shell and the Nigerian government were concerned about the shutdown of oil operations in Ogoni territory. In May 1994, a memo signed by Major Paul Okuntimo, commander of a regional security task force, declared: 'Shell operations still impossible unless ruthless military operations are undertaken for smooth economic activities to commence.'[10] The same day, Saro-Wiwa publicly displayed a copy of a memo issued by the regional police commissioner entitled 'Operation Order No. 4/94 – Restoration of Law and Order in Ogoni Land'. Order 4/94 contained the plans for a massive military operation in Ogoni territory intended to protect the operations of foreign companies. As Saro-Wiwa pointed out: 'The drafting of such a large force into the small Ogoni area [404 square miles] is meant to intimidate and terrorize the Ogoni people in order to allow Shell to recommence its operations in the area without carrying out the environmental, health, and social impact studies which the Ogoni people have demanded since 1992.'[11]

Two weeks later, state security forces again arrested Saro-Wiwa. The Ogoni leader and nine other Ogoni activists were held in prison for eight months before each of them was finally charged with four counts of murder. The charges alleged that they were responsible for the deaths of four pro-government Ogonis at the hands of a mob the previous year. They were tried before a special tribunal that included active members of the Nigerian military in a case fraught with irregularities. In October 1995, the tribunal convicted Saro-Wiwa and eight of the other activists, while freeing Ledum Mitee, then deputy president of MOSOP. On 10 November, all nine convicted Ogonis were executed by hanging in Port Harcourt.

The executions spurred an international outcry against the

dictatorship of General Sani Abacha. The United States, Britain and other countries recalled their ambassadors from Nigeria in protest. Additionally, the British Commonwealth suspended Nigeria's membership, Britain announced a total ban on arms sales to General Abacha's regime and the World Bank decided not to provide $100 million in funding to Shell for a new pipeline through the Niger delta region. The United States also withheld military aid to Nigeria.

Six months before he was executed, Saro-Wiwa wrote a letter in prison which was published by South Africa's *Mail & Guardian.* In the letter, the Ogoni leader made it clear that the struggle would continue even if he was killed:

> Whether I live or die is immaterial. It is enough to know that there are people who commit time, money and energy to fight this one evil among so many others predominating worldwide. If they do not succeed today, they will succeed tomorrow. We must keep on striving to make the world a better place for all of mankind – each one contributing his bit, in his or her own way.[12]

The struggle did indeed continue during the ensuing years, but so did the military repression. In 1996, more than a thousand Ogonis fled military crackdowns and became refugees in Benin. Tragically, more than two thousand Ogonis were killed by the Nigerian military during the 1990s.[13] Nevertheless, 20,000 people took to the streets of Bori to commemorate Saro-Wiwa's death in 1998, and in May of the following year some two thousand Ogonis marched on Shell's headquarters in Port Harcourt to protest against the environmental devastation wrought upon their lands by the oil company's past operations.

For years, Shell had publicly denied Ogoni claims that the company paid Nigeria's brutal military to protect its oil facilities, denying any collusion with the country's security forces. According to Human Rights Watch, however, Shell eventually 'admitted having made direct payments to the Nigerian security forces, on at least one occasion in 1993, under duress' (Human Rights Watch 1993: 3). In 1996, Shell admitted to purchasing weapons for the Nigerian police force, known as the 'Shell police', responsible for guarding the company's oil facilities. Company spokesperson Eric Nickson stated: 'Shell has purchased sidearms handguns on behalf of the Nigerian police force who guard Shell's facilities. But once imported, the arms remain the property of the Nigerian police, who store, guard and use them.'[14] And 'use them' they did, according to the Ogonis, who claimed that the Shell police routinely turned these weapons against villagers.

In 1996, a suit filed in the US Federal Court accused Shell of complicity in human rights abuses against the Ogoni people, including the death of Saro-Wiwa. Shell's lawyers tried to have the case dismissed by claiming that the United States did not have jurisdiction because the company was based in Britain. Finally, in February 2002, US Federal Court judge Kimba Wood ruled that the case had legal merit and could proceed because part of the Shell Oil group was based in the United States. Judge Wood stated that the charges by the plaintiffs accusing Shell of conspiring with Nigerian security forces to commit crimes against humanity, summary executions, arbitrary detentions and other violations of international law met the requirements for charges filed under the 1789 Alien Tort Claims Act.[15]

Since 1979, foreign victims of human rights abuses committed by US corporations operating overseas and brutal regimes supported by the United States have been filing civil suits in US federal courts under the Alien Tort Claims Act. Beginning in July 2002, however, the Bush administration sought to curtail the ability of foreign nationals to seek justice in US courts because some of the suits targeted governments allied with Washington in its war on terror. On 29 July 2002, the State Department's legal adviser, William H. Taft IV, sent a letter to the judge presiding over a case against ExxonMobil for human rights abuses in the Indonesian province of Aceh. The letter requested that the judge dismiss the case because it could compromise US interests by dissuading the Indonesian government from helping in the war on terror.[16] The case had been filed on 11 June 2001 on behalf of eleven Acehneses claiming that their human rights had been violated by Indonesian troops responsible for protecting ExxonMobil's facilities in Aceh. The suit claimed that ExxonMobil – then Mobil Oil – had provided logistical and material support to Indonesian military units that committed murder, torture, sexual abuse and kidnapping.

The Bush White House again attempted to undermine the Alien Tort Claims Act in May 2003 when it had the US Department of Justice file a thirty-page brief in the 9th Circuit Court of Appeals in a case brought by Burmese citizens against the California-based Unocal Corporation. The brief called on the court to limit the ability of foreign citizens to seek justice in US courts for human rights violations committed abroad because such lawsuits were seen to be harming US foreign policy. The Burmese plaintiffs alleged that during the building of a $1.2 billion gas pipeline, Unocal and its partner in the project, Burma's brutal military regime, were responsible for human rights abuses committed against workers, including the use of forced labour, rape and murder.[17] So far, the Bush administration's attempts to redefine the Alien Tort Claims Act have not proved successful and cases such as the Shell suit remain active. Consequently, notes Judith Chomsky of the New York-based Center for Constitutional Rights: 'Multinational corporations can't shield themselves from liability in the violation of international law by hiring foreign armies to do what they know they shouldn't do themselves.'[18]

Shell has also failed to effectively address the extensive environmental damage caused by its operations in the Niger delta region. Gas flaring, a process used to burn unwanted gases, has proven particularly hazardous as it often occurs in communities, spewing acrid plumes of black smoke over villages around the clock. In November 2005, villagers achieved a rare victory when the country's Federal High Court ordered oil companies to stop engaging in the outdated process of gas flaring.[19] The ruling, however, did not address the issue of oil spills. According to community leader Clifford Enyinda: 'Our only source of drinking water, fishing stream, and farm-lands covering over 300 hectares of land with aquatic lives, fishing nets and traps, farm crops, animals, and economic trees worth several billions of naira (equivalent to millions of US dollars) are completely destroyed by the spillage and was made worse by the three separate fires that broke out of the spill site.'[20]

In June 1999, Michael Fleshman, human rights coordinator for the New York-based organization Africa Fund, visited the site of a Shell oil spill in a remote part of the Niger delta region which had resulted from a ruptured pipeline the previous year. According to Fleshman:

> Without benefit of the required investigation, Shell declared that the cause of the spill was sabotage and refused to pay compensation. The impact of the spill on the community has been devastating, as the oil has poisoned their water supply and fishing ponds, and is steadily killing the raffia palms that are the community's economic mainstay. ... The sight that greeted us when we finally arrived at the spill was horrendous. A thick brownish film of crude oil stained the entire area, collecting in clumps along the shoreline and covering the surface of the still water. The humid air was thick with oil fumes ... quickly making me nauseous. ... A sheet of oil covered the water in all directions, extending out into the creek and spreading throughout the region's waterways.[21]

Residents of the delta region also refute Shell's claims that it invests heavily in community development projects. According to a 2004 report issued by the environmental organization Friends of the Earth, 'Oil-producing communities in Nigeria want to know how Shell can spend US$69 million a year of shareholders' money on social development projects in the Niger Delta, with no visible benefits for the majority of people who own the land which contains the oil and gas.'[22]

Shell has used the announcement and construction of community projects for public relations purposes, but has failed to provide the funding necessary to maintain them. In one example, according to an investigation conducted by the California Global Corporate Accountability Project, 'Shell established a hospital in Gokana (Rivers State) but has since failed to fund its upkeep; it has deteriorated to the point that patients must return home to recuperate from illnesses caught at the hospital.'[23] While the oil companies do provide some good jobs and social benefits to communities, says Emeka Duruigbo, who conducts research on corporate responsibility for the San Francisco-based Natural Heritage Institute, corporate corruption often diminishes the effectiveness of development projects. According to Duruigbo, 'It is not only the government that is corrupt in Nigeria; oil company officials are also corrupt with regard to distributing benefits to the communities. For example, if the company provides $10 million to a community project, $1 million might actually be delivered. Company officials steal the money, as do community chiefs and contractors. There is a lot of corruption at the corporate level.'[24] In March 2005, Chris Finlayson, Shell's chief executive for exploration and production in Africa, acknowledged that the company had experienced significant corruption among its employees with regard to funding local community projects.[25]

At the end of 2004, Shell's drilling operations on Ogoni lands remained suspended. The company continued, however, to maintain its pipelines throughout the territory with the support of the Nigerian military. For their part, the Ogoni people in the delta region continue to demand that the oil giant clean up the environmental damage caused by its drilling and pipeline spills. Meanwhile, thousands of miles away in a courtroom in New York, Shell is defending itself against charges of gross violations of human rights against the Ogoni people.

With 12 million people, the Ijaw is the largest ethnic group in the Niger river delta region. During the 1990s, violence between Ijaw groups seeking independence and the Nigerian military escalated. The oil operations of Chevron, which became ChevronTexaco following its 2001 merger with Texaco, lay at the heart of the Ijaw struggles.

In May 1998, more than one hundred unarmed Ijaw Youth Council protesters occupied Chevron's Parabe offshore oil platform, demanding that the company hire more local workers and clean up oil pollution. After three days of negotiations, the protesters announced that they would leave the platform the next day. Chevron, however, decided to make a strong statement that would deter future occupations of its oil platforms. The company called in Nigerian military forces that were on Chevron's payroll and the company's pilots transported the troops and Chevron's security chief to the oil platform in company-leased helicopters. In the ensuing confrontation to retake the platform, the military killed two protesters and wounded several others.[26]

Eight months later, Chevron's pilots in company-leased helicopters and boats again transported Nigerian forces in an attack against two Ijaw villages after residents demanded that the company pay compensation for oil-related environmental damage. Four villagers were killed in the attack and sixty more went missing and were presumed dead. Nigerian troops then burned down most of the homes in the two villages.[27] Chevron has admitted that it controls the actions of Nigerian forces deployed to protect the company's facilities in times of crisis. According to the company, Chevron security 'insists on exercising reasonable control over those deployed to assist, ensuring that no more than the minimum force required to bring the situation under control is applied' (Human Rights Watch 1999: 119). In May 1999, survivors of the attacks filed a suit against Chevron in the US Federal Court under the Alien Tort Claims Act, charging the company with violating their human rights.

Ijaw youth activists, meanwhile, issued a declaration in December 1998 demanding that the federal government immediately withdraw all military forces from Ijaw territories and suspend all oil operations in the delta region. The declaration also stated that any oil company using Nigerian military personnel to protect its operations would be viewed as an enemy of the Ijaw people. The government responded by declaring a state of emergency and in the ensuing weeks the military killed some thirty-five Ijaw.[28]

According to Human Rights Watch, the return of civilian rule in 1999 led to a further deterioration of the situation in the delta region. Unscrupulous politicians began to hire youth gangs to intimidate political opponents during electoral campaigns in 1999 and 2003. The region's extreme poverty and high youth unemployment made recruitment easy for Ijaw youth gangs, particularly for the region's two largest gangs: the Niger Delta People's Volunteer Force (NDPVF) and the Niger Delta Vigilante (NDV). Local government leaders provided logistical support to gang leaders to enable them to influence elections. In reference to NDV leader Ateke Tom, Human Rights Watch reported that 'Tom was given free rein to carry out profitable bunkering [oil smuggling] activities in exchange for his group's violent services during the 2003 elections'.[29]

In 2003, violence escalated in the delta region's Rivers State and its capital Port Harcourt, leading Shell and ChevronTexaco to shut down a third of Nigeria's oil production. Hundreds of people were killed and tens of thousands displaced as the NDPVF and the NDV vied for control of villages throughout the region in an attempt to control the oil smuggling trade, known as 'oil bunkering'. Oil bunkering conglomerates often included local politicians, businesspeople and military personnel, who paid armed youth groups such as the NDPVF and the NDV to protect their illegal business interests. Using populist rhetoric to justify his actions, NDPVF leader Alhaji Dokubo Asari claimed: 'I don't engage in bunkering, I take that which belongs to me. It is not theft; the oil belongs to our people.'[30]

State security forces rarely attempted to protect the civilian population from fighting between the NDPVF and the NDV. On the rare occasions on which they did intervene, security forces targeted supporters of the NDPVF, since Asari had fallen out of favour with Rivers State governor Peter Odili. On 3 September 2004, Nigerian troops launched an offensive against the NDPVF that resulted in the destruction of several fishing villages in Rivers State. Asari responded by threatening to wage 'all-out war' if the federal government did not cede greater control of the region's vast oil resources to the Ijaw ethnic group. While the government considered Asari a common criminal, many locals viewed him as a hero who was trying to redistribute the region's oil wealth. According to one Port Harcourt resident, 'You can say he is like Robin Hood. Our own government is corrupt, and they hate us.'[31]

In October 2004, President Obasanjo met with Asari and NDV leader Ateke Tom and reached a ceasefire agreement that called for the disbandment of the armed groups in return for negotiations. The peace, however, remained fragile because the agreement failed to address the underlying causes of the violence: extreme poverty and unemployment, corrupt politicians and military personnel, and oil bunkering.

Foreign oil companies contributed to the escalation of youth gangs and violence in the delta region. Companies routinely made compensation payments to communities located in areas where the companies wanted to drill for oil. Companies also promised oil and security jobs to members of local communities. According to Human Rights Watch, 'The oil companies negotiate such agreements and contracts with individuals whom they identify as community representatives, notably the top traditional leaders or chiefs.'[32] These often corrupt community representatives routinely use the money to fund armed gangs to consolidate their control over the region. Those youth gangs not receiving oil money from community leaders compete for control over communities situated on oil-rich lands. As a result, says Human Rights Watch, 'Oil companies have in turn been forced to make cash payments to the youth for access to facilities or to ensure the security of their business operations.'[33]

Nigerian women have also organized against foreign oil companies. In July 2002, some six hundred women occupied Chevron-Texaco's Escravos export terminal for ten days and demanded that the company leave the delta region. Following ChevronTexaco's refusal to discuss the demand that it abandon its operations, the Itsekiri women negotiated an agreement with the company requiring, among other things, that the company establish a permanent body to resolve oil-related problems in rural communities and hire local people. The company failed to follow through on its promises and future demonstrations by the women were met with military repression. According to one Nigerian woman involved in the protests, 'We want Chevron to employ our children. If Chevron does that we the mothers will survive, we will see food to eat. Our farms are all gone due to Chevron's pollution of our water. We used to farm cassava, okra, pepper and others. Now all the places we've farmed are sinking, we cannot farm' (Turner and Brownhill 2003: 8).

In its report on Chevron's performance in Nigeria, the California Global Corporate Accountability Project examined how the oil industry as a whole has affected development in this West African nation:

> Oil development has arguably deepened the poverty of many Nigerians. It has bankrolled a series of corrupt and authoritarian governments; it has destroyed agricultural lands, drinking water, and fisheries on which subsistence economies depend; it has deprived local peoples of ownership and control of their lands; it has supported and abetted egregious human rights abuses. These are not merely regrettable offshoots or periodic abuses of the development process; they *are* the development process.[34]

## Angola and the corrupting commodity

As bad as poverty is in Nigeria, the situation is even worse in Angola, the seventh-largest supplier of oil to the United States. Despite vast reserves of oil and diamonds, Angola remains a social and economic disaster. Eighty-two per cent of Angolans live in poverty and more than half of the population is unemployed.[35] Most of Angola's thirty years of independence have been dominated by war and massive governmental corruption. Angola is Africa's second-largest oil producer and the valuable commodity is responsible for 90 per cent of the government's revenues.[36] The state-owned oil company, Sonangol, has entered into production-sharing agreements with numerous foreign oil companies including US-based ChevronTexaco and ExxonMobil, and British oil giants BP and Shell, in order to exploit the country's 5.4 billion barrels of proven oil reserves, most of which lie offshore.[37]

In 1974, an armed insurgency finally liberated Angola from almost five centuries of colonial rule, only to see the country plunge into a civil war that would rage for more than twenty-seven years and result in 300,000 deaths. The war for independence and the ensuing civil conflict devastated Angola's economy and infrastructure, and displaced almost a third of the country's 13 million people. The country's dire situation was reflected in the 2004 UN Human Development Index, which ranked Angola 166th out of 177 nations and noted that life expectancy for Angolans was a mere forty years (UNDP 2004: 142).

Although the Portuguese abandoned Angola in 1974, the country did not officially become an independent nation until November 1975. Following the departure of the Portuguese, a civil war broke out, pitting the Popular Movement for the Liberation of Angola (MPLA) against the National Front for the Liberation of Angola (FNLA) and the National Union for the Total Independence of Angola (UNITA). The MPLA was supported by the Soviet Union and Cuba and was prominent in the country's capital, Luanda. Fearful that the pro-Soviet and socialist MPLA would prove victorious in Angola, South African troops invaded the country. With the Soviets providing the weaponry and Cuba the soldiers – 30,000 Cuban troops would eventually be deployed to Angola – the MPLA pushed back the South African offensive and consolidated its control over the government. By 1979, the FNLA had been defeated, but UNITA continued to fight in south-eastern Angola with support from South Africa and the United States. Over the next decade, the country's oil revenues were primarily used to fund the government's war effort against UNITA's forces. Not surprisingly, the country's economy collapsed as a result of the conflict and a lack of social and economic investment.

In 1988, a US-brokered peace deal led to the withdrawal of Cuban and South African troops from Angola. The deal failed to achieve a lasting peace as fighting again broke out between the MPLA government and UNITA. In 1991, President José Eduardo Dos Santos and UNITA leader Jonas Savimbi signed a ceasefire agreement that called for multi-party elections the following year. Dos Santos won the September 1992 elections, certified by UN monitors as generally free and fair. Unwilling to accept the results, Savimbi and UNITA again resumed their armed struggle. The war continued for another ten years until government troops killed Savimbi in February 2002. Two months later, UNITA signed a ceasefire and its forces began demobilizing shortly thereafter. In return, Dos Santos pledged to hold new elections in 2006. The 700,000 Angolans who remained displaced by the conflict began the process of returning to their homes.

While the civil war was finally over, a separatist struggle in the northern coastal enclave of Cabinda continued. The demobilization of UNITA's fighters in southern Angola in 2002 allowed the government to deploy 30,000 troops to Cabinda in an attempt to finally defeat 2,000 separatists who had been fighting for more than twenty-five years. The small enclave of Cabinda and its 300,000 residents are separated from Angola by a narrow strip of territory belonging to the Congo. Because Cabinda accounts for more than half of the country's oil production, the Angolan government is not willing to contemplate secession by the renegade enclave. Rebels from the Front for the Liberation of the Enclave of Cabinda (FLEC) have called for the government to increase the amount of oil revenues it disperses to Cabinda, which currently receives 20 per cent of the funding disseminated to the country's eighteen provinces.[38]

Before the 2002 army offensive, the FLEC wrought havoc with oil operations. It viewed employees of ChevronTexaco and other foreign companies as military targets, forcing them to take refuge in walled compounds. Because of constant attacks against workers travelling by road, ChevronTexaco began transporting its employees to and from its facilities by helicopter.[39] By mid-2003, however, the Angolan army had drastically weakened the FLEC and gained control over Cabinda. According to Human Rights Watch, the army maintained control of the enclave by committing 'violations against the civilian population, including killing, arbitrary detention, torture, sexual violence, and the denial of access to agricultural areas, rivers, and hunting grounds through restrictions on civilians' freedom of movement'.[40]

Military control of Cabinda resulted in safer working conditions for employees of ChevronTexaco and other oil companies. Cabindans, however, lived in fear of the Angolan troops and continued to subsist in extreme poverty. A mere 100 metres from ChevronTexaco's compound, which is called 'Little America' and is protected by landmines, shanty-town dwellers are forced to scavenge for firewood for cooking owing to a lack of kerosene. Father Jorge Congo, a Catholic priest who has been critical of the military repression, noted that 'you can walk around and you won't see real signs that tell you that Chevron is here and making life better for Cabindans'. Father Congo's sentiments were echoed by Cabindan resident Raul Danda: 'You don't have gas for cooking, yet if you look at the sea, you can see gas being burned.'[41]

One of the principal reasons that so little of the country's oil wealth has reached impoverished Angolans is the deeply entrenched system of corruption that benefits Angola's political leaders and foreign oil companies. During the late 1990s, a decrease in the intensity of the civil war led foreign oil companies BP, ExxonMobil and French energy giant Total to expand their Angolan operations. As a result, state revenues increased dramatically between 1997 and 2002, totalling $17.8 billion. An IMF Oil Diagnostic Study of Angola, however, revealed that $4.22 billion of this fiscal revenue had gone missing. Considering that the government's social spending totalled $4.27 billion during those years, the missing funds could have doubled the amount spent on much-needed social programmes.[42]

The realization that Angolan oil funds had disappeared resulted from the 'Angolagate' scandal that broke in France in 2000. Angolagate involved a scheme in which French officials used intermediaries to illegally supply arms to the Angolan government in 1993 and 1994. The sales were conducted covertly because President François Mitterrand knew that members of his government who sympathized with the UNITA rebels would block such a deal. France delivered weapons and equipment to the Angolan government at highly inflated prices. The government of President Dos Santos mortgaged the country's future oil revenues in order to obtain loans to pay for the armaments. A significant portion of the money ended up in the secret Caribbean bank account of businessman Pierre Falcone, who, along with the French president's son, Jean-Christophe Mitterrand, and others, was eventually arrested for influence-peddling and illegal arms trafficking.

Falcone helped orchestrate French arms deals worth well over half a billion dollars with high-ranking Angolan officials. According to the court testimony of one participant in the arms deal scheme, Falcone and Russian businessman Arkadi Gaydamac earned $300 million from one April 1994 deal alone. The two arms dealers then used some of this money to pay kickbacks to Angolan officials who had helped facilitate the deal.[43]

Falcone also had ties to President George W. Bush. In 1994, Falcone and his wife formed a cosmetics company in the United States called Essanté. The company made a $100,000 contribution to Bush's first election campaign in 2000.[44] Bush campaign officials eventually returned the money, claiming that they did not want to create the impression that a foreign arms dealer was buying influence with the future president of the United States. The money, however, was not returned until after the election, and only after Falcone's arrest in France for illegal arms trading and influence-peddling became public knowledge. When French police raided the Paris apartment of Falcone's secretary, they discovered a letter inviting then presidential candidate George W. Bush to meet Angolan president Dos Santos at Falcone's ranch in Arizona. It appears that Falcone believed his campaign contribution would indeed buy influence with the soon-to-be-elected president.

A 2002 special report by the British NGO Global Witness compared Falcone's contribution to the funding the Bush campaign received from the Enron Corporation, one of the world's largest energy companies. According to Global Witness, Enron's influence with the Bush administration 'clearly bought a substantial reformulation of national energy policy and diminished regulatory oversight'.[45] At the same time that now bankrupt Enron was using its influence with the Bush administration to diminish regulatory oversight of the energy industry, it was taking advantage of existing regulatory loopholes to defraud its stockholders of tens of billions of dollars. As the Global Witness report noted:

> Interestingly, Enron CEO Kenneth Lay's US$100,000 donation to the Bush campaign is strikingly similar to Falcone's US$100,000. We have seen what Enron managed to achieve through its 'donations' – what was Falcone hoping to achieve, and perhaps more to the point, what would he have achieved, had the embarrassment of his arrest not facilitated the belated return of his money?[46]

Falcone was also linked to US oil companies operating in Angola. Among the pay-offs for his role in facilitating the covert arms deals, the Angolan government gave Falcone's Panama-based firm Falcon Oil Holdings a minority share of the oil consortium that operates Angola's offshore Block 33. The consortium includes the Angolan state oil company Sonangol and ExxonMobil. Falcone also met officials of Oklahoma-based Phillips Petroleum on three separate occasions during 2000, at the same time that the US oil giant was negotiating a deal with the Angolan government for offshore Block 34. The deal was signed the following year, although it remains unclear exactly what role Falcone played in securing it.[47]

After the Angolagate investigation had shed light on the Angolan government's corrupt business practices, the IMF demanded that the government make its books available to independent auditors before it would consider approving a loan to the troubled country. It was this audit that discovered that the Angolan government could not account for more than $4 billion in oil revenues between 1997 and 2002. The sort of covert international dealings and political influence-peddling that Angolagate revealed have played a prominent role in fostering an environment of secrecy and corruption with regard to the government's handling of Angola's oil revenues.

Clearly, the Angolan government is ultimately responsible for the manner in which it manages the nation's fiscal revenues. The behaviour of multinational oil companies, however, has contributed to the lack of transparency in Angola. While the Angolan government reluctantly opened its books for review, most multinational oil companies have not been so accommodating. Consequently, the figure of $4.22 billion in missing oil revenues was based only on the government's accounting numbers. The amount could be higher, but it is impossible to verify the accuracy of Angola's revenue figures as long as foreign oil companies refuse to make public their royalty payments to the government.

Part of the problem lies in the decision by foreign oil companies, including ExxonMobil, ChevronTexaco, BP-Amoco, Shell and Total, to sign confidentiality deals as part of their production-sharing agreements with Sonangol. While companies often claim that these confidentiality agreements do not allow them to be more transparent, it remains unclear whether or not these agreements include confidentiality protection for the amount of revenue paid to the government.

In 2001, BP-Amoco became the first major oil company to agree to publicize information pertaining to its operations in Angola.

The company agreed to make public its payments to Sonangol under its production-sharing agreements and to disclose how much in taxes it was paying to the Angolan government. Sonangol responded to BP-Amoco's announcement by sending the company a letter threatening to terminate its contract if it divulged financial information pertaining to its Angolan oil operations. Sonangol also sent copies of the letter to the other foreign oil companies operating in Angola, clearly meant as a warning against following BP-Amoco's example. Sonangol's concern about oil revenues being made public stemmed from the fact that it was illegally managing the country's oil earnings with no accountability to the government. According to a 2002 IMF report, released one year after Sonangol's threat to BP-Amoco, the state oil company 'assumed some time ago complete control of foreign currency receipts from the oil sector and stopped channelling them through the central bank as mandated by law'.[48]

Most governments in the North require that oil companies operating in their countries publicly declare the amount they pay in royalties and taxes. Global Witness has suggested that Northern governments go a step farther and also require that oil companies based in their countries make public all royalty and tax payments made to overseas governments. The fact that the oil companies follow one set of rules in countries of the North and another in nations of the South makes them complicit in the lack of transparency with regard to the mismanagement of oil revenues by corrupt governments. With the exception of BP-Amoco, the major foreign oil companies in Angola are contributing to the undermining of democracy in that country by not providing citizens with the information they need in order to hold their government accountable for its management of the nation's wealth.

Increased transparency could contribute to ensuring that more of Angola's oil wealth benefits the country's impoverished population. The value of that wealth, however, is declining owing to the establishment of a favourable investment climate for foreign companies. Between 2000 and 2003, the government's share of total oil receipts declined from 53 per cent to 43 per cent. According to the IMF, 'Possible factors behind these changes include differences in tax regimes' as well as the 'structure of the profit-sharing agreements'.[49] As a result of corruption and oil contract terms that favour multinationals, millions of impoverished Angolans continue to depend on huge amounts of foreign humanitarian aid while corrupt government officials and foreign oil companies get rich from the country's oil reserves.

## Washington's role in West Africa

The US quest to diversify its oil sources has led the Bush administration to focus an increasing amount of attention on West Africa's Gulf of Guinea. As David Goldwyn, a former assistant energy secretary in the Clinton administration, noted in 2004: 'We are in no position to endure a serious oil supply disruption from the Gulf of Guinea today. The global oil market is stretched to capacity.'[50]

Because of Nigeria's large Muslim population, the United States has viewed the country as a key ally in the war on terror and the Bush administration continues to provide it with military aid despite rampant human rights abuses by the Nigerian armed forces. According to Human Rights Watch, 'These political considerations led to a reluctance to criticize Nigeria's human rights record.'[51] The Bush White House also considers Nigeria an important oil supplier and has become increasingly concerned about attacks by activists and armed ethnic groups against oil facilities both in the Niger river delta region and offshore. US Air Force general Charles Wald, deputy commander of the US military's European Command for Europe and Africa, visited Nigeria in July 2004 to discuss security in oil-producing regions. Referring to the possibility of the US military being deployed to help protect oil operations in Nigeria, Wald declared: 'Wherever there's evil, we want to get there and fight it. ... Where you have wealth, if you don't protect it, you are vulnerable to terrorists and illegal arms dealers and so you are not safe.'[52] In December 2004, the Bush administration agreed to supply the Nigerian Navy with fifteen patrol boats to be used to protect oil installations in the Niger delta and along the country's coast. While Wald claimed the navy vessels were to protect oil facilities from terrorist attacks, there is a high probability that they will be used against delta villagers protesting against the activities of foreign oil companies.[53]

Perhaps more troubling than Washington's relatively limited military role in West Africa is its escalating political and economic influence in the region. In the late 1990s, the US Export-Import Bank issued loans and loan guarantees to Angola that have benefited US oil companies operating in that country. In June 1998, the US Export-Import Bank guaranteed an $87 million loan by the SocGen Bank in New York to the Angolan government to cover Sonangol's share of the development of an oil well in partnership with foreign oil companies in the troubled enclave of Cabinda. The Export-Import Bank's 'loan guarantee' means that the SocGen Bank bears no risk in loaning millions of dollars to a corrupt and repressive regime in Angola. If the already heavily indebted Angolan government fails to pay back the loan, then the Export-Import Bank, or to be more accurate US taxpayers, will simply make good on the $87 million debt to SocGen. The following year, the Export-Import Bank provided a $64 million direct loan to the Angolan state oil company Sonangol for the purchase of equipment and services from more than twenty US energy companies, including Halliburton.[54] In this case, if Sonangol fails to repay the loan, then US taxpayers will have subsidized over twenty US corporations.

In Equatorial Guinea, the repressive government of General Teodoro Obiang Nguema has ruled since it seized power in a 1979 coup. Obiang Nguema has held several elections during his rule which have been far from free and fair. The US State Department noted that Equatorial Guinea's leader was 're-elected in a December 2002 election marred by extensive fraud and intimidation'.[55] Obiang Nguema has used a repressive hand to maintain control over the mostly impoverished population. In 2004, according to the US State Department, 'The Government's human rights record remained poor, and the Government continued to commit serious abuses. ... Security forces committed numerous abuses, including torture, beating, and other physical abuse of prisoners and suspects, which at times resulted in deaths.'[56] In 1995, the Clinton administration had responded to Obiang Nguema's horrendous human rights record by closing the US embassy in Equatorial Guinea, which at that time did not possess substantial proven oil reserves.

During the latter part of the 1990s, several foreign companies, including ExxonMobil, ChevronTexaco and Amerada Hess from the United States, made significant oil discoveries in Equatorial Guinea. The US desire to secure alternative sources of oil led to a renewal of ties between Washington and the repressive Obiang Nguema regime. In 2000, the US government's Overseas Private Investment Company (OPIC) provided $373 million in loan guarantees for the construction of a methanol plant partly owned by two US companies – Noble Affiliates and Marathon.[57] Like the Export-Import Bank, OPIC often funds the 'development' projects of US companies acting in partnership with repressive regimes. Obiang Nguema welcomed his government's new friendship with the United States. During a February 2002 trip to Washington, DC, he reciprocated the increasing US goodwill towards his oil-rich nation by declaring: 'We can promise American companies that their investments are guaranteed.'[58]

Questions have been raised about the relationship between foreign oil companies and the Obiang Nguema government.

According to the State Department, 'There has been some concern regarding the use of irregular payments made by oil companies into bank accounts controlled personally by the President and the ruling elite. Most of the oil wealth remained in the control of the Government with little being distributed to the majority of the population, which remained poor.'[59] In fact, Equatorial Guinea has had the fastest-growing GDP in the world since it became a major oil producer in the late 1990s and yet 65 per cent of its half-million people remain mired in poverty.[60]

Perhaps the clearest illustration of the Bush administration's willingness to overlook Equatorial Guinea's lack of democracy and Obiang Nguema's human rights abuses was its opening of a new US embassy in the oil-rich nation in October 2003. Even the US government-owned media outlet Voice of America noted how the Bush administration avoided bringing attention to the country's human rights situation by quietly opening the embassy 'with little fanfare and no formal announcement'.[61]

A similar situation exists in the oil-rich country of Gabon – among the top fifteen oil suppliers to the United States – where the Bush administration has provided training to the Gabonese military, despite the government's democratic shortcomings and its history of human rights abuses. The US State Department's 2005 human rights report stated that President Omar Bongo, who has ruled since 1967, 'was reelected for a 7 year term in a 1998 election marred by irregularities'. The report also noted that the 'Government's human rights record remained poor. ... Security forces sometimes beat and tortured prisoners and detainees, prison conditions remained harsh, and security forces sometimes violently dispersed demonstrations. Arbitrary arrest and detention were problems.'[62] Despite admitting to a clear lack of democracy and blatant human rights violations in Gabon, the State Department declared: 'Relations between the United States and Gabon are excellent.'[63]

In 2004, US ambassador to Gabon Kenneth Morefield suggested that the country should diversify its economy away from its hyper-dependence on oil by following IMF-prescribed neo-liberal policies. Morefield, apparently oblivious to his own State Department's human rights reports, claimed that by implementing neo-liberal reforms Gabon could 'maintain the admirable stability and respect for human rights that they have managed to sustain here'.[64]

There is little doubt that the Bush administration prefers the stability that exists in Gabon to the public disorder that frequently disrupts oil production in nearby Nigeria. Gabon is an important source of oil for the United States, which receives more than half of the country's oil exports. Gabon's proven oil reserves have increased from 1.3 billion barrels in 1996 to 2.5 billion barrels in 2004 – the third-largest reserves in sub-Saharan Africa.[65] While the country's oil production has been declining since 1996, new discoveries and contracts with foreign companies promise to reverse that trend in the near future.

Among the foreign companies operating both onshore and offshore in Gabon are Shell, Total and Houston-based VAALCO Energy. On 13 June 2005, VAALCO announced that it had signed a $30 million revolving credit loan with the World Bank's International Finance Corporation (IFC), the division of the bank that funds private investment projects in the global South. According to VAALCO, 'The loan facility will support the Company's multiyear oil exploration, development and production programs ... assisting the Company's effort to find additional reserves.'[66] The revolving credit line is good until October 2009 and can be extended for a further two years.

It is clear that Gabon has been a profitable investment for VAALCO. In May 2005, the company announced that its first quarter earnings were up 223 per cent over the same period the previous year. The company's oil sales almost doubled, owing in part to increased production in its Gabon operations.[67] As in other oil-rich countries in the region, there is a grossly inequitable distribution of wealth in Gabon with 5 per cent of the population owning more than 90 per cent of the nation's wealth.[68] Clearly, national economic elites and foreign oil companies are getting rich from Gabon's oil reserves while the majority of the country's 1.2 million people continue to suffer under Bongo's repressive regime. For its part, the Bush administration has defended the political and economic status quo in Gabon by maintaining close ties to the Gabonese government, providing military training to its armed forces and supporting World Bank funding for a Houston-based oil company operating in the small African nation.

The United States is not the only oil-consuming giant seeking to escalate its presence in West Africa; China has also become more actively engaged in the region. In 2004, in an attempt to help quench China's rapidly growing thirst for oil, the communist country's state-owned oil company Sinopec signed an agreement with the Bongo administration which called for Gabon to supply Beijing with 20,000 barrels of oil a day. The deal also allows Sinopec to explore for oil and to build a refinery in Gabon.[69] Also in 2004, Chinese companies reached a deal with the Nigerian government to develop two oilfields and to build refineries and pipelines in that country.[70] At the same time in Angola, Beijing agreed to provide the country with $2 billion in aid in exchange for 10,000 barrels of oil a day.[71]

*Conclusion*

The Bush administration has made securing present and future oil supplies from West Africa's Gulf of Guinea a foreign policy priority. US political, economic and military influence in the region is increasing in order to protect US economic interests and the operations of US oil companies. Meanwhile, foreign oil companies, particularly ChevronTexaco, ExxonMobil and Shell, have profited greatly from a long history of working closely with corrupt and repressive regimes throughout the region. As a result, Nigerians in the Niger river delta region have been subjected to repeated attacks by military forces protecting the operations of foreign oil companies. They have also had their ability to support themselves through subsistence farming seriously jeopardized by the environmental destruction wrought by oil spills. The majority of people in Nigeria, as well as in Angola, Gabon and Equatorial Guinea, continue to endure extreme poverty while their corrupt political leaders and foreign companies pocket much of the oil wealth. The Bush administration's policies have sought to defend the status quo through the provision of support to US oil companies and the region's repressive regimes. Despite President Bush's claims that his administration's foreign policy seeks to spread freedom and democracy around the globe, there is little evidence that the US role in West Africa is advancing these noble objectives.

# 4 | Colombia: feeding Washington's addiction

In December 2000, US-trained counter-narcotics battalions, US-supplied Black Hawk helicopters and US-piloted spray planes descended on southern Colombia to initiate the counter-narcotics programme known as Plan Colombia. During the first four years of Plan Colombia's aerial fumigation campaign, coca-growing areas in Putumayo and other southern departments were repeatedly sprayed. Although the US government claimed its fumigation prescriptions finally began decreasing coca cultivation in 2002 and 2003, there was still no evidence that Plan Colombia was achieving its primary stated objective of reducing the flow of cocaine to the United States. But while Plan Colombia failed to affect the price, purity and availability of cocaine in US cities, its militarization of Putumayo contributed significantly to increased oil exploration by multinational companies in that resource-rich region. Following 9/11, the US war on drugs evolved into a war on terror, under which the Bush administration expanded US military intervention throughout Colombia to protect the operations of US oil companies. Neo-liberal economic reforms that constituted the economic component of Plan Colombia further sweetened the pot for foreign oil companies.

Oil is Colombia's leading export earner and the South American country is among the top dozen suppliers to the United States despite the fact that it possesses only 1.54 billion barrels of proven oil reserves.[1] It is estimated that Colombia could possess as many as 40 billion barrels of oil, although many of these potential reserves are difficult to access because they are situated in territory controlled by the country's leftist guerrillas.[2]

Washington's desire to diminish its reliance on Middle Eastern oil has led the United States to escalate its military intervention in Colombia's civil conflict as part of its global war on terror. A major objective of the US military role in Colombia is to protect the operations of multinational oil companies, which have been repeatedly attacked by the country's two leftist rebel groups: the Revolutionary Armed Forces of Colombia (FARC) and the National Liberation Army (ELN).

## *The roots of the conflict*

The US State Department placed the FARC and the ELN on its list of terrorist organizations in 1997. The State Department claims that the guerrilla groups are responsible for kidnappings, bombings, assassinations and forced displacement.[3] Both the FARC and the ELN have been waging guerrilla warfare against the Colombian government for more than forty years. The FARC evolved out of peasant self-defence groups that fought the Colombian army during the chaotic sectarian violence of the 1940s and 1950s, known as *La Violencia*, which pitted supporters of the country's Conservative Party against those of the Liberal Party and communists. In 1958, the elites of both political parties united to form the National Front government, which replaced the military dictatorship of General Gustavo Rojas Pinilla. Under the National Front, the Conservative and Liberal parties agreed to alternate four-year terms in the presidency and divide all government positions evenly between themselves. This limited democracy lasted until 1974, when the two parties again fielded candidates against each other. The National Front government unified the country's oligarchy in its struggle against the growing threat of armed insurgencies that no longer recognized the legitimacy of the two dominant parties or the political and economic system that had preserved the grossly unequal distribution of Colombia's wealth.

In 1964, a group of armed peasants officially became the FARC. Espousing Marxist ideology and calling for radical political, social, economic and agrarian reforms, they sought to overthrow the government. By the end of the 1990s, owing to lucrative ransoms from kidnappings, its extortion of businesses and taxation of coca growers, the FARC had become a well-armed force of 18,000 fighters that controlled some 40 per cent of the national territory.[4] The FARC's political, social and economic agenda has been especially visible in remote areas of Colombia, where the rebels have acted as the de facto government for decades. One example of the rebel group's agrarian reform policy can be seen in Meta department, a long-time guerrilla stronghold in eastern Colombia. During 2002 and 2003, the FARC broke up ten large ranches in the southern part of Meta. The smaller properties were then redistributed to subsistence farmers.[5]

In May 2003, UN special envoy to Colombia James LeMoyne warned that, in a country where the inequitable wealth distribution has left 64 per cent of the population living in poverty, it would be 'a mistake to think that the FARC members are only drug traffickers and terrorists'.[6] Despite its social agenda, however, the FARC appears to have compromised ideology in certain regions of the country in order to implement a strategy emphasizing military control over resources and territory. One consequence of this shift has been a rise since the early 1990s in its targeting of civilians through selective assassinations, bombings and kidnappings – tactics that have been condemned by human rights groups.

The ELN was also formed in 1964, but unlike those of the peasant-based FARC, its founders were middle-class intellectuals recently returned from Cuba. The ELN, influenced by the Cuban revolution and liberation theology, also called for socialist revolution. For the most part, the 4,000-strong ELN has not profited from the drug trade. Instead, the group has funded itself primarily through kidnapping and extortion of the oil industry

*4 Colombia*

in northern and eastern Colombia. Like the FARC, the ELN has been critical of the neo-liberal reforms implemented by the government since the early 1990s. In August 2000, ELN commander Antonio García claimed that 'any project that changes society must include the idea that we need an economic model that serves the people and society, not the other way around'.[7] The rebel group's role as the de facto government in one rural region neglected by the state was witnessed by photojournalist Scott Dalton while riding with an ELN commander in Arauca department in eastern Colombia:

We drove for more than two hours, stopping in many small towns. People approached the car and talked to the commander, asking favors and exchanging information. It occurred to me that the government had a difficult task ahead. To win over these areas from rebel control, it would also have to win the confidence of the people who live here – people who have never had any contact with the police or military, people who have no faith in the government and people who have always turned to the rebels for help.[8]

In its war against the FARC and the ELN, the Colombian military has worked closely with illegal right-wing paramilitary groups. These militia groups were established in the 1980s by the Colombian military, drug traffickers and wealthy landowners to combat the guerrilla threat. The ideology of the paramilitaries is fiercely anti-communist, while their tactics have served to protect and further the interests of Colombia's economic elite and multinational corporations. Over the years, paramilitaries have been responsible for the majority of Colombia's human rights abuses, particularly massacres and forced displacement. During the late 1980s, they virtually eradicated the leftist political party Patriotic Union (UP) by killing more than two thousand members, including two presidential candidates and four elected congressmen. In 1997, regional paramilitary groups unified under an umbrella organization called the United Self-Defence Forces of Colombia (AUC). In its dirty war, the AUC worked closely with the Colombian military as it targeted suspected guerrilla sympathizers, including peasant leaders, community organizers, trade unionists, human rights workers and teachers. While the FARC and the ELN were placed on the US State Department's foreign terrorist list in 1997, the AUC didn't make it on to the list until four years later, even though it was Colombia's principal violator of human rights during that period.[9] In 2003, the AUC began peace talks with the government with the goal of demobilizing its 12,000 fighters by the end of 2005. Several dissident factions refused to participate in negotiations, however, until the guerrillas also agreed to cease hostilities.

## From drugs to terror

The United States had been providing relatively low levels of military aid and training to Colombia since the 1950s, but US assistance escalated dramatically in 1989. In the late 1980s, drug traffickers – primarily Pablo Escobar and other leaders of the Medellín cocaine cartel – launched an urban bombing campaign in an attempt to force the Colombian government to end the practice of extraditing drug lords to the United States to stand trial. Bogotá turned to the administration of President George H. W. Bush for military aid to combat the narco-traffickers. Bush was more than happy to provide the necessary aid, albeit with certain strings attached. In return for Colombia's share of the $2.2 billion Andean Initiative counter-narcotics aid package, Bush called for the dismantling of Colombia's protectionist system and the implementation of economic reforms 'on the basis of market-driven policies'.[10] Shortly after receiving the aid, the Gaviria administration initiated *la apertura*, the opening of the Colombian economy, which led to an increased flow of foreign investment and goods.

The economy soon began to deteriorate as lower tariffs resulted in lower prices for imported goods, driving many small and medium-sized domestic producers that could not compete with multinational corporations out of business. Colombia's trade surplus of more than $1 billion in 1989 had become a deficit of close to $4 billion by 1998.[11] Meanwhile, unemployment rose to almost 20 per cent and increasing numbers of those who were working were forced to subsist in the informal sector. Additionally, according to the World Bank, the poverty level increased during the second half of the 1990s from 60 per cent to 64 per cent of the population.[12] By 1999, Colombia's economy had sunk into its worst recession in more than half a century. While US and Colombian officials blamed the country's deteriorating economic performance during the 1990s on the civil conflict, responsibility can be more accurately placed on the neo-liberal policies introduced during the decade. After all, the intensity of Colombia's conflict during the late 1940s and 1950s far exceeded that experienced during the 1990s, and yet the economy grew during that period. In fact, this economic growth continued until the 1990s, making Colombia one of the more economically stable countries in Latin America during the second half of the twentieth century. Only a minority of Colombians, however, benefited from this growth.

More worrying than the economic crisis as far as Washington and Bogotá were concerned was the growing military strength of the FARC. For the first time in more than thirty years of insurgency, Colombia's rebels were capable of seriously threatening the country's urban elite through kidnapping and bombings. Rebel attacks were also wreaking havoc on the activities of foreign oil companies, whose operations were located in vulnerable rural regions. The FARC's increased military capabilities had largely resulted from the 'successes' of the US drug war in the Andean region. While eradication efforts in neighbouring Peru and Bolivia during the 1990s dramatically reduced the amount of coca – the plant that provides the raw ingredient for cocaine – in those countries, cultivation in Colombia doubled between 1995 and 2000, offsetting the Peruvian and Bolivian decline.[13] Furthermore, most of this increase occurred in Putumayo and other southern departments controlled by the FARC, who profited by taxing coca-growing farmers. Also, Colombia's two largest cocaine cartels – Medellín and Cali – responsible for most of the cocaine production and trafficking, had been dismantled by the mid-1990s. This led to a decentralization of drug trafficking activities as scores of smaller cartels, many of which were closely linked to right-wing paramilitaries, filled the vacuum.

In the late 1990s, as it had done a decade earlier when confronted with the Medellín cartel's urban bombing campaign, Bogotá once again turned to Washington for increased aid. On this occasion, Colombia's president Andrés Pastrana sought to defend the country from the escalating insurgency by requesting development aid in order to address some of the socio-economic problems that were fuelling the conflict. In 1999, the Pastrana administration devised Plan Colombia, which called for massive amounts of foreign aid to fund social and economic development. The original plan did not request significant amounts of counter-narcotics or military aid. The Clinton administration, however, rewrote Plan Colombia, turning it into a mostly military programme intended to dramatically diminish drug trafficking, boost Colombia's economy and end the civil conflict.

In January 2000, President Bill Clinton proposed $1.6 billion in mostly military aid for Plan Colombia. The economic component of the plan simply consisted of IMF-imposed neo-liberal reforms agreed to by the Pastrana administration one month earlier in return for a three-year $2.7 billion loan. The terms of the loan called for Colombia to further lower tariffs, privatize state-owned companies and reduce government spending. For the most part, despite resistance from unions, guerrillas and even Colombia's Constitutional Court, Bogotá satisfied the IMF's loan conditions.

In the summer of 2000, the US Congress approved $1.3 billion over two years as the initial US contribution to Plan Colombia, making Colombia the third-largest recipient of US military aid behind Israel and Egypt. Military aid constituted more than 70 per cent of the aid package, which was to be used to fund the aerial fumigation of illicit coca crops in FARC-controlled southern

Colombia, create a Colombian army counter-narcotics brigade to be trained by US Army special forces troops, and provide Colombia's security forces with more than sixty Black Hawk and Huey helicopter gunships.

The FARC were viewed as the principal drug war enemy even though the paramilitaries were far more involved in drug trafficking. The FARC taxed coca growers and traffickers in the regions it controlled and sometimes acted as a middleman by purchasing coca paste from farmers and selling it to traffickers for processing into cocaine. The AUC paramilitary group, on the other hand, was far more involved in the processing and trafficking of cocaine. In 2001, AUC leader Carlos Castaño admitted that a substantial portion of his group's income was derived from narco-trafficking (Aranguren Molina 2001: 205).

Plan Colombia's initial six-week spraying campaign was launched in the oil-rich Putumayo department in December 2000. Over the next two years, tens of thousands of hectares in Putumayo and surrounding departments were fumigated. But the spraying not only destroyed coca crops, it also devastated food crops, adversely affected the health of local children and displaced thousands of families.[14] The devastation wrought by the spraying led to protests by thousands of peasants and the governors of the six southern departments affected by the fumigations.

There were widespread accusations of corruption and waste with regard to the 8 per cent of US aid earmarked for alternative crop programmes. Jair Giovani Ruiz, an agro-industrial engineer with the Ministry of the Environment's Corpoamazonia (Corporation for Sustainable Development in the Southern Amazon), claimed that peasants had received little of the alternative crop funding: 'Maybe a cow or three chickens, but the farmers can't live off of these. Maybe the money got lost on the way, or maybe [the government] contracted a lot of experts in order to supply a cow.' The bottom line, according to Ruiz, was that 'there was bad management of Plan Colombia's resources'.[15] Meanwhile, the more than 70 per cent of the aid that constituted Plan Colombia's military component had proved very effective in destroying the livelihoods of impoverished farmers. Mario Cabal of PLANTE, the government agency in charge of the under-funded alternative crop programme, complained: 'We have money for helicopters and arms for war, but we don't have money for social programmes.'[16]

The Plan Colombia aid bill included a requirement that some of the funding be used to create, train and arm a 3,000-strong Colombian army counter-narcotics brigade, which would function independently from the Colombian army's counter-insurgency troops. The purpose of creating the new brigade was to appease members of the US Congress concerned with aid going to Colombian army units that routinely collaborate with right-wing paramilitaries in the country's dirty war. It soon became evident, however, that this strategy had failed. According to Catalina Diaz of the human rights group Colombian Commission of Jurists (CCJ), 'It is very clear that there is a tolerance and acceptance of the paramilitaries by this [US-trained counter-narcotics] brigade.' Diaz said that she had received information about collaboration between the US-trained counter-narcotics brigade and paramilitaries in Putumayo, which was then passed on to the US embassy in Bogotá.[17]

Another incidence of collusion occurred on 17 August 2002, a few miles up the Putumayo river from the town of Puerto Asís. Late that afternoon, some fifteen soldiers from the US-trained counter-narcotics brigade allowed four AUC paramilitaries armed with AK-47s and walkie-talkies to pass by their patrol unhindered. The soldiers then stood and watched the right-wing militiamen openly brandish their weapons as they boarded canoes and made their way downriver in the direction of Puerto Asís.[18] Several hours later, an alleged paramilitary death squad killed three unarmed civilians in Puerto Asís. Two of the victims were shot in the head, while the third was hacked open with a machete from the neck to the belly.[19]

One and a half years after its initial implementation, Plan Colombia was clearly failing to achieve its stated objectives. Colombia's economy remained stagnant, the conflict still raged and, despite record numbers of hectares having been fumigated, the price, purity and availability of cocaine in US cities remained unaffected. The militarized nature of Plan Colombia was being condemned by Colombian and international NGOs, as well as by some politicians in both Colombia and the United States. Colombia's neighbours were also criticizing the US drug war strategy; Brazil, Venezuela, Panama and Ecuador were all concerned about drug traffickers, armed groups and displaced people seeking refuge in their countries. Venezuelan president Hugo Chávez suggested that Plan Colombia 'could lead us to a Vietnamization of the whole Amazon region'.[20] Meanwhile, in February 2001, the European Union's Parliament voted 474–1 against contributing to Plan Colombia because of its emphasis on a military solution.[21] With its drug war policies under fire from all sides, 9/11 and the ensuing global war on terror provided Washington with a new, more popular and emotive justification for escalating its military involvement in Colombia.

Less than three weeks after 9/11, Democratic senator Bob Graham of Florida, chairman of the Senate Select Committee on Intelligence, launched a campaign to portray the FARC as a major international terrorist threat: 'The FARC are doing the same thing as global level terrorists, that is organizing in small cells that don't have contact with each other and depend on a central command to organize attacks, in terms of logistics and finance. It is the same style of operation as Bin Laden.'[22]

In October 2001, the State Department's top counter-terrorism official, Francis X. Taylor, declared that Washington's strategy for fighting terrorism in the western hemisphere would include, 'where appropriate, as we are doing in Afghanistan, the use of military power'.[23] Taylor left little doubt about the 'appropriate' target when he stated that the FARC 'is the most dangerous international terrorist group based in this hemisphere'.[24] Meanwhile, Taylor's boss, US Secretary of State Colin Powell, told the Senate Foreign Relations Committee that the FARC belonged in the same category as al-Qaeda: 'There is no difficulty in identifying [Osama bin Laden] as a terrorist and getting everybody to rally against him. Now, there are other organizations that probably meet a similar standard. The FARC in Colombia comes to mind.'[25]

In the last week of October, Senator Graham ramped up his accusations, declaring that Colombia should be the principal battlefield in the global war on terror. According to the Florida senator, there were almost 500 incidents of terrorism committed worldwide against US citizens and interests in 2000, and 'of those almost five hundred incidents, 44 per cent were in one country. Was that country Egypt? No. Israel? No. Afghanistan? Hardly a tick. Forty-four per cent were in Colombia. That's where the terrorist war has been raging.'[26]

What Graham failed to mention was that the huge majority of 'terrorist' attacks against the United States by Colombian guerrillas consisted of bombing oil pipelines used by US companies – they were designed to hurt corporate profit margins, not US civilians. In fact, the Florida senator neglected to point out that these attacks did not kill a single US citizen in 2000, the year to which Graham was referring. Nevertheless, the propaganda campaign vilifying the FARC successfully laid the groundwork for US ambassador Anne Patterson's announcement at the end of October that the United States would provide counter-terrorism aid to Colombia as part of Washington's new global war on terror.

Given the widespread public support in the United States for a global war on terror, it was no surprise that the US Congress approved a \$28 billion counter-terrorism bill in July 2002 which included \$35 million in supplemental aid for Colombia. More important than the additional funds, however, was the fact that the new bill also eliminated the conditions restricting US drug war funding for Colombia to counter-narcotics programmes. This change allowed the military aid that had constituted more than 70 per cent of the \$2 billion in counter-narcotics funding since 2000 – as well as future drug war funding – to be used for counter-insurgency operations as part of the war on terror.[27] The Bush administration worked hard to link drugs to terrorism by convincing the US public and Congress that the habits of illegal drug users were bankrolling terrorist groups. In June 2003, the Bush administration's propaganda campaign made the ultimate claim linking illegal drug use to terrorism when General James Hill, commander of the US Army's Southern Command, told the Senate Caucus on International Narcotics Control that drugs were a 'weapon of mass destruction'.[28] Despite repeated claims by US officials in 2000 that the Clinton administration's \$1.3 billion contribution to Plan Colombia did not mark an expansion of the US military role in Colombia beyond the drug war, the mission creep that critics feared had now occurred. The line between Washington's war on drugs and Colombia's civil conflict, as thin as it was, had been completely erased.

At least one US oil company operating in Colombia had sought to erase that line during the original congressional debates over funding for Plan Colombia more than two years earlier. On 15 February 2000, Los Angeles-based Occidental Petroleum's vice-president Lawrence Meriage, testifying before a congressional subcommittee debating the Plan Colombia aid package, recom-mended a supplemental aid package to protect oil regions in northern and eastern Colombia. Meriage told Congress: 'This will help augment security for oil development operations, which, as noted earlier, are fundamental to the success of Plan Colombia.'[29] From Meriage's perspective, providing security for Occidental's oil operations may well have been fundamental to the economic success of Plan Colombia, but the problem for Occidental lay in the fact that Plan Colombia was touted as a counter-narcotics programme and there was little coca cultivation in the region in which Occidental operated.

Following the lifting of the conditions that limited US military aid to counter-narcotics operations, Occidental finally got its supplemental aid package as part of the 2002 counter-terrorism bill. The following year, the Bush administration provided Colombia with $439 million in drug war funding, an additional $93 million in counter-terrorism aid and deployed US Army special forces troops to provide counter-insurgency training to the Colombian army's 18th Brigade.[30] The 18th Brigade's primary mission is the defence of the Caño Limón oil pipeline, which is partly owned and operated by Occidental.

Foreign oil companies operating in Colombia have long been enmeshed in the country's civil conflict. Oil companies make payments to the Colombian government to help cover the cost of using the Colombian military to protect their facilities and infrastructure. Companies also provide logistical support, including the use of company helicopters and vehicles, to Colombian army units responsible for protecting their operations. The agreements between foreign companies and specific Colombian military units remain confidential, but a few details have emerged from past deals. In the mid-1990s, according to Human Rights Watch, British Petroleum made payments totalling $11 million over three years to the Colombian army's 16th Brigade for the protection of its operations in Casanare department. Likewise, Occidental Petroleum paid $2 million to the Colombian army's 18th Brigade in 1997 for the protection of its facilities in Arauca department. Human Rights Watch claims that both these brigades were responsible for gross violations of human rights during the time they were receiving these direct payments from the oil companies.[31]

Occidental has a history of links to Colombian military units involved in human rights abuses. In the mid-1990s, the company began exploring for oil in the traditional territory of the indigenous U'wa in North Santander department. When more than three hundred U'wa blockaded an access road to Occidental's exploration site on 11 February 2000, the Colombian army attacked the unarmed U'wa protesters and three indigenous children died in the resulting mêlée.[32] Another tragic incident involving Occidental occurred on 13 December 1998. On that day, a Colombian air force helicopter dropped a US-made cluster bomb on the village of Santo Domingo in Arauca, killing eighteen civilians, including seven children. The helicopter's Colombian pilot and crewman told investigators that they had planned the operation at an Occidental oil facility in Arauca. They also claimed that a plane operated by Florida-based security firm AirScan supported the Colombian military in the attack against alleged guerrillas and that the three US crew members of the AirScan plane provided the coordinates for the fatal bombing. At the time, AirScan was a private security company contracted to help protect Occidental Petroleum's operations, including the Caño Limón oil pipeline.[33]

On 24 April 2003, the Washington, DC-based International Labor Rights Fund and the Center for Human Rights at the Northwestern University School of Law filed a suit in the US District Court on behalf of the families of the victims of the Santo Domingo bombing. The suit, filed under the Alien Tort Claims Act, claimed that Occidental and AirScan were complicit in the violation of the human rights of the victims. As it had done in similar cases filed against US oil companies operating in Nigeria, Indonesia and Burma, the Bush administration sent a letter to the presiding judge requesting that the charges be dismissed because the case could adversely affect US foreign policy.[34] The Bush administration clearly did not want human rights concerns to interfere with its provision of counter-terrorism aid to the Colombian military and deployment of US Army special forces troops to help protect Occidental Petroleum's oil operations in Arauca.

## The national security state

The US military escalation coincided with the military solution to Colombia's conflict sought by the country's newly elected president, Alvaro Uribe. During the 2002 presidential campaign, Uribe's hard-line stance towards the guerrillas appealed to those Colombians disillusioned by the collapse of President Andrés Pastrana's peace talks with the FARC. The right-wing Uribe declared that he would not negotiate with the FARC or any other armed group unless they first agreed to a ceasefire. The new Colombian president's aggressive approach also resonated with the Bush administration, which desperately wanted a hard-line ally in Bogotá.

Upon assuming office in August 2002, Uribe began implementing his Democratic Security and Defence Strategy. According to Minister of Defence Marta Lucía Ramírez, the strategy's objective was 'nothing more nor less than security for every citizen, whatever his condition may be. And the best guarantee of each citizen's security is the strengthening of the rule of law.'[35] Uribe's first step in strengthening the 'rule of law' came on 11 August in the form of a presidential decree declaring a 'state of internal unrest', tantamount to announcing a state of emergency. The military and police were granted increased powers, allowing them to 'preventively' arrest people without warrants and providing the security forces with greater flexibility to conduct searches and phone taps.

On 21 September, also as part of his democratic security strategy, Uribe established two so-called Rehabilitation and Consolidation Zones, in which far greater military powers existed than under the state of internal unrest. The zones were established to help consolidate government control over economically important areas of the country, particularly oil-producing regions. One of the rehabilitation zones included parts of Sucre and Bolívar departments in northern Colombia, while the other encompassed a section of Arauca department on the country's eastern plains. The common thread between the two zones was the 478-mile-long Caño Limón oil pipeline, which originated at Occidental Petroleum's Caño Limón oilfield in Arauca, traversed the eastern range of the Andes mountains and ran through Bolívar and Sucre to the Caribbean port of Coveñas.

Uribe endowed military commanders in the rehabilitation zones with authority that superseded that of local elected officials. The military could restrict the movement of civilians and impose curfews. All foreigners, including journalists and human rights workers, had to request permission from the Interior Ministry eight days in advance to enter the zones. Foreign reporters were required to declare for whom they worked, where they were going and for how long. Critics claimed that forcing foreign journalists to obtain permission to enter the zones provided the Uribe administration with the opportunity to censor those it deemed to be critical of government policies. On 26 November 2002, however, Uribe's democratic security strategy was dealt a setback when Colombia's Constitutional Court ruled that the suspension of civil liberties in the two Rehabilitation and Consolidation Zones was unconstitutional. Justice Alfredo Beltrán summed up the court's ruling: 'Uribe can't go above the constitution; that's a dictator.'[36]

Among the many repressive actions undertaken while the rehabilitation zones existed was the rounding up of more than two thousand residents in Saravena, Arauca, which is located near the Caño Limón oil pipeline and was where US Army special forces troops would be deployed two months later. The mass arrests by the Colombian military took place during the night of 12 November and, according to Amnesty International, 'By the end of the night more than 2,000 people had been rounded up at gunpoint and taken to Saravena's stadium where they were photographed, videotaped, questioned, their background checked, and their arms marked with indelible ink. ... Most of Saravena's human rights community, as well as many known trade unionists and other social leaders were among the 2,000 people detained that night.'[37]

The Bush administration openly endorsed Uribe's democratic security strategy, despite the repressive nature of the government's tactics, which targeted trade unionists and other sectors of civil society critical of the president's policies. On a December 2002 visit to Bogotá, US Secretary of State Colin Powell met with Uribe and declared: 'We support your new national security strategy. It is a comprehensive plan to build a healthy democracy. A key part of that strategy, indeed, the part that makes everything else possible, is that element of the plan directed towards defeating the deadly combination of terrorism and drugs.'[38]

One year after Uribe assumed office, officials in Washington and Bogotá were applauding the efforts and 'successes' of his democratic security strategy. Officials in both countries emphasized the 16 per cent drop in homicides during Uribe's first year in office, but neglected to mention that the decrease in murders was the result of fewer common homicides; the number of political killings remained stable. According to the human rights group CCJ, 6,978 people were killed for socio-political reasons during Uribe's first year in office, which amounted to nineteen people a day, the same rate as the previous two years. The CCJ determined that paramilitaries were responsible for at least 62 per cent of the killings, more than double the number committed by the guerrillas.[39] Colombian and US officials more accurately highlighted a 23 per cent drop in kidnappings, which was partly due to Uribe's strategy of increased military protection for the country's highways, from which the guerrillas routinely abducted citizens.[40]

While the security situation for people in Colombia's cities had largely improved, the conflict still raged in many of the country's rural regions. While touting Uribe's successes, officials ignored the record numbers of Colombians that were being 'disappeared' and the ongoing crisis of forced displacement. During 2002 and 2003, 3,593 people were 'disappeared', according to the Association of Family Members of the Detained and Disappeared (ASFADDES), a Colombian NGO. This number represents a dramatic increase over the 3,413 people who were disappeared between 1994 and 2001.[41] In a trend eerily reminiscent of the dirty war in Argentina, paramilitaries and state security forces were responsible for the majority of the disappearances, according to the United Nations.[42] As Gloria Gomez of ASFADDES noted: 'In Argentina, their tragedy happened in a short space of time, and the image of the junta in their military uniforms made it easy to generate international antipathy. Our authoritarianism wears a suit and tie and was democratically elected.'[43]

While the Uribe administration's security policies achieved a decrease in forced displacement in 2003, the number of Colombians forced from their homes and land by violence increased dramatically the following year. The Human Rights and Displacement Consultancy (CODHES), a Colombian human rights organization, reported that 287,581 people were forcibly displaced in 2004 – an average of 780 people per day and a 38 per cent increase over the previous year.[44] In all, 2.9 million people, or 7 per cent of Colombia's population, have been forcibly displaced since 1985, making it the country with the second-largest internally displaced population in the world behind the Sudan.[45]

The displacement crisis has been compounded by a reduction in government funding to aid the country's internal refugees. In 2001, government aid amounted to $60 per displaced person, but by 2003 it had plummeted to $14 per person as Uribe gutted social programmes in order to meet IMF structural adjustment demands.[46] Some of Colombia's displaced were forced off their lands for being suspected of harbouring sympathies for one or another of the armed groups, but many were displaced by paramilitaries because their lands contained valuable resources coveted by Colombia's economic elite and multinational corporations. According to Harvey Suarez Morales, director of CODHES, 'Displacement isn't a collateral effect of the war – it's a central strategy of the war. It is entirely functional.'[47]

Despite announcing a unilateral ceasefire in December 2002 in order to engage in demobilization talks with the Uribe government, paramilitaries continued to be responsible for much of the violence perpetrated against the civilian population. According to Amnesty International, 'Despite the declared cease-fire, paramilitaries were still responsible for massacres, targeted killings, "disappearances", torture, kidnappings and threats. They were allegedly responsible for the killing or "disappearance" of at least 1,300 people in 2003, over 70 per cent of all attributable, non-combat, politically related killings and "disappearances".'[48] Despite this reality, the Bush administration kept its counter-terrorist sights firmly placed on the FARC and provided aid to a military closely allied to paramilitaries on the State Department's foreign terrorist list. In 2003, the US State Department's own annual human rights report acknowledged the links between the Colombian military and the paramilitaries: 'Some members of the security forces actively collaborated with members of paramilitary groups – passing them through roadblocks, sharing intelligence, providing them with ammunition, and allegedly even joining their ranks while off duty.' The report added: 'Impunity

Colombia

141

for military personnel who collaborated with members of para-military groups remained common.'[49]

Uribe's democratic security strategy also led to a dramatic increase in arbitrary arrests by state security forces. On 24 August 2003, some six hundred soldiers and police raided homes in Cajamarca in central Colombia and arrested fifty-six people. Among those detained were an elderly paraplegic and the local priest. The same month, 128 people were arrested in the north-western city of Sincelejo for alleged ties to the FARC. They were all imprisoned for three months before being released owing to a lack of evidence.[50] The round-ups in Cajamarca and Sincelejo were just two examples of the Uribe administration's crackdowns on civil society groups critical of the president's security and economic policies. During Uribe's first year in office, the CCJ claims that 4,362 people were subjects of arbitrary arrests; almost double the total for the previous six years.[51] According to the Colombian human rights group José Alvear Restrepo Lawyers' Collective, most of those detained were arrested 'for their social activity, or simply for living in areas that authorities consider "suspect"'.[52]

On 8 September, two weeks after the mass arrests in Caja-marca, Sincelejo and other parts of the country, Uribe launched a verbal attack against NGOs during a nationally televised speech at a military ceremony in Bogotá. During his speech, the president accused human rights groups of being terrorists. The accusations were made in response to a 172-page report issued earlier that day by a coalition of eighty NGOs criticizing the president's security policies. The NGO report claimed that the human rights situation had worsened under Uribe because of 'indiscriminate military operations' that sought to achieve 'social control and to implant terror in the population'. As a result, according to the report, the number of people whose human rights were violated owing to extra-judicial executions, forced disappearances, torture and arbitrary detentions had increased dramatically during Uribe's first year in office.[53]

During his speech, in what was clearly a reference to the eighty organizations that issued the report, Uribe claimed there was a group of NGOs that were 'politicking at the service of terrorism'. He went on to say that the NGOs 'cowardly shield themselves behind the human rights banner to try to give back to terrorism the space that public forces and citizens have taken from them'. The president then directly linked human rights groups to the guerrillas when he stated: 'Every time a security policy is carried out in Colombia to defeat terrorism, when terrorists start feeling weak, they immediately send their spokesmen to talk about human rights.'[54]

Uribe's speech contradicted statements he had made a few months earlier in June 2003 while explaining his democratic security strategy: 'This Government rejects the idea of "National Security" of bygone eras in Latin America, which considered certain ideological groups or political parties as the "enemies within".' The president had also declared: 'Security and democracy are not mutually exclusive. On the contrary, security guarantees the room for debate and dissent – the oxygen of all democracies – so that differences of opinion are not also risks to one's personal security.'[55]

Three weeks after his verbal attack on NGOs, Uribe visited the United States, where he spoke at the United Nations and met with US Secretary of State Colin Powell. Not only did Powell fail to criticize the Colombian leader for his recent verbal tirade against human rights defenders, he actually affirmed his support for Uribe. Following the Colombian president's claims at the UN that his government respected the work of human rights groups, Powell said he was impressed by Uribe's 'clear commitment to human rights in the prosecution of this war that he is fighting against terrorists and against drug lords in Colombia'.[56]

Uribe's accusations against NGOs did more than just illustrate the Colombian president's attitude towards human rights; they endangered the lives of human rights workers. Right-wing paramilitaries, who also view human rights defenders as guerrilla sympathizers, likely perceived Uribe's message to be a 'green light' for targeting NGO workers. The symmetry between Uribe's and the paramilitaries' attitudes towards NGOs was clearly evident in comments made by an AUC paramilitary commander in Putumayo: 'It is not a secret that the NGOs are managed by guerrillas. NGOs are giving money to certain people so they'll make claims against army generals. ... The NGOs are managed by the subversives.'[57]

Uribe and the paramilitaries were not the only ones linking NGOs to Colombia's guerrillas. In February 2000, Occidental Petroleum's vice-president Lawrence Meriage testified before the US Congress in support of Plan Colombia. During his testimony, Meriage addressed opposition to an Occidental oil project in northern Colombia by telling Congress: 'Only two groups are intent on blocking the project – leftist guerrillas who seek to undermine the country's democratically elected government and several fringe non-governmental organizations (NGOs) in the US. Both groups are united in their opposition to oil exploration and development.'[58]

The obstacles and dangers faced by NGO workers, particularly human rights defenders, in Colombia have been enormous. According to Adam Isacson of the Washington, DC-based Center for International Policy, 'In a country where more than 95 per cent of crimes go unpunished and the powerful go to great lengths to protect their impunity, this is challenging and often dangerous work. A human rights defender is assassinated about once every month. Dozens of the country's most effective activists and experts have been forced into exile in recent years.'[59]

While Uribe's security strategy was proving somewhat successful against Colombian civil society groups, it was struggling on the battlefield. After some initial gains against the rebels during Uribe's first two years in office, the Colombian military suddenly found itself on the defensive in 2005. A series of FARC attacks against Colombian military units throughout the country illustrated that more than two years of Uribe's democratic security policies had failed to seriously undermine the military strength of the guerrillas. In some of its boldest attacks since Uribe assumed the presidency, the FARC launched large-scale assaults against military bases and convoys in the departments of Antioquia, Arauca, North Santander, Putumayo and Nariño during the first six months of the year. The attacks left more than two hundred soldiers dead and led to the resignation of Colombia's minister of defence, Jorge Alberto Uribe – no relation to President Uribe.

In February 2005, the Colombian army's 17th Brigade responded to a FARC attack that had killed twenty-one of its troops in the Urabá region of Antioquia by targeting the peace community San José de Apartadó. The residents of San José de Apartadó declared their municipality a peace community in 1997, stating that it was off limits to all armed actors in the conflict – guerrillas, paramilitaries and state security forces. The community's demand that government soldiers or police not enter its territory led to repeated accusations by the military and paramilitaries that San José's residents were guerrilla sympathizers. On 21 February 2005, soldiers from the 17th Brigade entered the hamlet of Mulatos in the municipality of San José de Apartadó and murdered five adults and four children, including community founder and leader Luis Eduardo Guerra-Guerra. According to witnesses, the soldiers threatened to bring in paramilitaries to kill the remaining residents and even joked about decapitating one little girl.[60]

Uribe's democratic security strategy was clearly targeting those

Colombians, such as the residents of San José de Apartadó, who were actively seeking alternative solutions to Colombia's conflict. As sociologist James Brittain noted: 'The grotesque activities carried out by the 17th Brigade, as stated and witnessed by inhabitants of the region, are another example of the counterinsurgent efforts of the Colombian state to inhibit the support and further expansion of social movements struggling for change within Colombia.'[61]

At the same time the Uribe administration was targeting civilians critical of the government's policies, it was offering a virtual amnesty to the country's right-wing paramilitaries. The AUC announced a ceasefire in December 2002 in order to enter into demobilization talks with the government. The ceasefire proved to be a charade as, according to the CCJ, paramilitaries participating in the talks killed at least 1,899 civilians in the twenty-one-month period following the ceasefire announcement.[62] Despite the blatant ceasefire violations, the government continued negotiating with the AUC while simultaneously demobilizing paramilitary units, despite the lack of any legal guidelines. In June 2005, the Colombian Congress finally passed the Peace and Justice law, which defined a legal framework for the demobilization process. Under the law, AUC leaders guilty of gross violations of human rights, including massacres, could serve as little as twenty-two months of jail time. The demobilization process also failed to ensure that paramilitary leaders dismantled their drug trafficking networks.[63]

Uribe's negotiations led to only a partial demobilization of the country's right-wing paramilitaries as the estimated three thousand fighters of several dissident groups that had refused to participate in the process remained active. Furthermore, in some cases the demobilization process actually failed to demobilize paramilitary units. The November 2003 'demobilization' of the AUC's Cacique Nutibara Bloc in Medellín, for example, did not end that group's paramilitary activities in Colombia's second-largest city. According to Amnesty International, two years after their demobilization:

> Paramilitaries continue to operate as a military force, to kill and threaten human rights defenders and local community activists, to recruit and to act jointly with the security forces. However, rather than operating in large, heavily-armed and uniformed groups as they did in the past, they are now increasingly cloaking their activities by posing as members of private security firms or by acting as informants for the security forces.[64]

## The great oil giveaway

At the same time that Uribe was negotiating with the paramilitaries and intensifying the war against the guerrillas and the political opposition, he sought to make the nation's economy function more efficiently. His economic policies were dictated primarily by the IMF and called for, among other things, the restructuring and privatization of state-owned companies.

In January 2003, an increase in US military aid to Colombia again coincided with demands to implement neo-liberal economic reforms. The IMF provided a two-year, $2.1 billion loan to Colombia only months after the Bush administration had agreed to provide counter-terrorism aid and deploy US Army special forces troops to Colombia. According to the IMF, in return for the loan the Colombian 'authorities intend to take the measures needed to ensure public debt sustainability and maintain Colombia's record of servicing its debt. Accordingly, the program calls for … key structural reforms and administrative improvements in the public sector.' The loan agreement also required that the country's fiscal deficit be 'reduced to 2.5 per cent of GDP in 2003 and 2.1 per cent in 2004 from an estimated 4 per cent in 2002'.[65] In order to implement these neo-liberal reforms and to make money available to pay the country's foreign debt

– the $39.4 billion owed to international lending institutions in 2002 constituted 46.2 per cent of the country's GDP – the Uribe administration agreed to privatize and restructure state-owned companies and to cut thousands of public sector jobs.[66]

The Uribe administration's two agendas – security and economy – were not mutually exclusive. Members of civil society who criticized Uribe's neo-liberal economic policies soon found themselves labelled as 'terrorists' or 'subversives' by the government. One critic of Uribe's economic policies, Hernando Hernandez, international affairs secretary for the powerful Oil Workers Union (USO), was accused of maintaining links to terrorist organizations. Hernandez was arrested in January 2003 and remained incarcerated until March 2004, despite never being charged with a crime.

Hernandez and other USO members were fierce critics of Colombia's implementation of neo-liberal reforms, particularly those applied to the oil sector. In 2001, in order to comply with IMF structural adjustment demands, the Colombian government established new regulations that permitted foreign companies to keep up to 70 per cent of the oil extracted from new fields. The new 70–30 split in favour of foreign oil companies replaced the 50–50 split in oil rights that had previously existed in association contracts between multinational corporations and the state oil company Ecopetrol. The new regulations also extended the length of time for which foreign companies retained production rights and dramatically lowered the amount they had to pay the government in royalties on their share of oil production. Before the new regulations, Colombia had demanded a Latin American high of 20 per cent in royalties, but the new rules included a sliding scale under which most of Colombia's oilfields – those producing under 5,000 barrels a day – required only an 8 per cent royalty payment. The government claimed that these changes were necessary to make the country more competitive, encourage foreign investment and maintain oil self-sufficiency. While Colombia raised its corporate tax rate from 35 per cent to 38.5 per cent in late 2002, the additional tax revenues did not begin to offset the decline in oil royalties and the lost revenues from Ecopetrol's reduced share of production.[67]

On 26 June 2003, in order to meet IMF demands under the latest loan agreement, Uribe issued Executive Decree No. 1760 announcing the liquidation of the state-owned oil company Ecopetrol, which had made $558 million in profit the previous year.[68] The government, in anticipation of worker resistance to the upcoming restructuring, had deployed troops to all of Ecopetrol's facilities three weeks earlier to prevent unionized workers from protesting. Under the restructuring, Ecopetrol was split into three companies: a new company, the National Hydrocarbon Agency, was established to administer and allocate hydrocarbon exploration areas; another new company called the Colombian Energy Promotion Association was created to handle promotional duties; and a truncated Ecopetrol was to manage production and refining.

While it was not a privatization of the state oil company per se, the restructuring ultimately had the same effect when Colombia's energy minister, Luis Ernesto Mejía, announced further reforms eight months later in Houston, Texas. Under the new regulations, foreign companies could negotiate contracts with the National Hydrocarbon Agency without entering into partnership with Ecopetrol. For its part, Ecopetrol would have to begin competing for contracts with foreign oil companies. The new terms also eliminated time limits on production rights by allowing foreign companies to keep 100 per cent of the oil for as long as a field remained productive.[69] Most foreign oil companies would continue to pay only an 8 per cent royalty rate. Clearly, the terms had shifted dramatically in favour of foreign companies, considering that contracts signed four years earlier called for equal partnership with Ecopetrol, 20 per cent royalty payments and a time limit on production, after which all the remaining oil and drilling assets had to be turned over to Ecopetrol.

The Uribe administration justified its oil policies to the Colombian people by claiming that they were necessary to prevent the country from becoming a net oil importer. In order to meet its growing domestic demand and still remain a net exporter, Colombia needed to produce more oil. While Uribe's reforms will likely increase oil production in the future, the fact that Colombia might retain self-sufficiency or its position as a net exporter is merely a technicality. Ecopetrol does not actually produce all the oil the country consumes and exports; it buys much of it at market rates from foreign companies operating in Colombia, because some contracts allow these companies to sell their share of oil production to Ecopetrol. In Putumayo department, for example, both Canada's Petrobank and Houston-based Argosy Energy sell all their oil at market price to Ecopetrol as soon as it leaves the ground. Ecopetrol then transports the oil through the Transandino pipeline to the Pacific coast for export to the United States.[70]

One of the first companies to benefit from the new contract terms was Texas-based Harken Energy. On 4 November 2004, Harken announced that its subsidiary Global Energy Development had signed a contract with Colombia's National Hydrocarbon Agency. As a result, says Harken, the company 'will own 100% of the contract subject only to an initial 8% royalty payable to the Colombian Ministry of Energy'. In other words, because Harken was not required to enter into partnership with Ecopetrol, it owned the rights to 100 per cent of the oil. Harken goes on to note that the 'contract grants Global exclusive exploration and production rights to 85,000 acres which adjoin the established, producing Palo Blanco field' and its 'proved reserves of approximately 1.8 million net barrels'.[71]

While contracts such as the one signed by Harken will help increase Colombian oil production in the coming years, the oil will be primarily produced by foreign companies. Furthermore, as noted earlier, Colombia will then purchase much of this oil at the same global market prices it would pay for overseas crude. Oil extracted by foreign companies, however, is not classified as imported because it is produced in Colombia. Therefore, even though Colombia is paying global rates for its own oil, technically the country will remain a net exporter. Despite the favourable terms for foreign oil companies and the diminished financial benefits to Colombia under the terms of the new contracts, José Armando Zamora, director of the National Hydrocarbon Agency, insisted that the contract concessions 'do not represent a loss of sovereignty or the sale of the nation's resources'.[72]

## *The oil war in Arauca*

While foreign oil companies operating in Colombia were poised to benefit financially from IMF-imposed structural reforms, they still faced the problem of a lack of security in oil-producing regions. Shortly after assuming office, Uribe responded to these and other security concerns by implementing his Democratic Security and Defence Strategy. Meanwhile, the Bush administration responded to Occidental Petroleum's security concerns in Arauca by providing Colombia with counter-terrorism aid and deploying seventy US Army special forces troops to help protect the Caño Limón oil pipeline and the Caño Limón oilfield, one of only fifty billion-barrel fields in the world. Oil is the principal US economic interest in Colombia. It is also Colombia's number-one legal export. The eastern departments of Arauca and Casanare contain the bulk of Colombia's proven oil reserves. The other key oil-producing region is Putumayo department, the primary target of the US war on drugs in Colombia.

In January 2003, seventy US soldiers – thirty based in the

departmental capital, Arauca City, and forty in the town of Sara-vena – were deployed to a region that had long been under the influence of the FARC and the ELN. The guerrillas profited from the discovery of oil in the early 1980s by extorting contractors working for Occidental and local municipalities that received a percentage of the oil revenues. While the ELN had been promoting its Marxist ideology in the region since the mid-1960s, the FARC did not establish a presence until the 1980s.

In 2001, rebels demanding that the government fully nationalize the oil industry bombed the Caño Limón oil pipeline a record 170 times, shutting it down for 240 days during the year and costing Occidental $100 million in lost earnings.[73] The oil company's persistent lobbying in support of US military aid to Colombia paid off in early 2003 when the Bush administration deployed US troops to Arauca and Congress approved $93 million in counter-terrorism aid for the protection of the pipeline. With the aid package, US taxpayers began paying $3.55 in security costs for every barrel of Occidental oil that flowed through the pipeline. This figure contrasted sharply with the 50 cents per barrel that the company was contributing to its own security costs.[74] With a war in Iraq looming on the horizon and instability in Venezuela, Colombia had become an important alternative source of oil. Colombia was already among the top suppliers of oil to the United States when, following 9/11, US ambassador to Colombia Anne Patterson stated: 'Colombia has the potential to export more oil to the United States, and now more than ever, it's important for us to diversify our sources of oil.'[75]

In 2002, Occidental Petroleum was extracting 100,000 barrels of oil a day from the Caño Limón oilfield and it was estimated that some 120 million barrels of oil still remained in the reservoir that straddled the Colombia–Venezuela border.[76] The problem for Occidental was that every time pumping on the Colombian side was shut down by a rebel attack, production on the Venezuela side continued. Because there was no agreement between Occidental and Venezuela's national oil company PDVSA regarding the extraction of oil from the Caño Limón field, the Venezuelans benefited from increased production every time Occidental was forced to stop pumping.

The forty US Army special forces soldiers stationed near the pipeline in Saravena were billeted in the army base on the outskirts of town. While the US soldiers carried out their mission of providing counter-insurgency training to Colombian troops in the relatively safe confines of the army base, Saravena's citizens remained defenceless in the face of a military and police crackdown and frequent rebel attacks. Substantial popular support in the town's poor barrios allowed the rebels to attack the centre of Saravena with bombs, mortars, grenades or gunfire on eighty different days in 2002.[77]

Shortly after his arrival in Saravena in July 2002, the commander of the town's national police unit, Major Joaquín Enrique Aldana, received a detachment of 100 *carabineros* (militarized police) who had been specially trained under a programme run by the US Army's 7th Special Forces Group at a base in Tolemaida in central Colombia – the country's national police force is administered by Colombia's Department of Defence. This programme provided US military training to heavily armed police units with the intention of dispatching them to rural towns throughout Colombia. Saravena was one of the first towns to receive a detachment of *carabineros* and their presence caused Major Aldana to boast: 'We have started to defeat the terrorists who hide behind the fear they instil in the people.'[78] Like all Colombia's police and military officials since 9/11, the politically savvy commander repeatedly used the word 'terrorists' when referring to the guerrillas.

While the mayor of Saravena, José Trinidad Sierra, welcomed the increased military and police presence in his battered town,

**Colombia**

he also criticized the national government's failure to address the region's social and economic ills. According to Trinidad, 'The inhabitants of Saravena have been asking the government for social investment. We believe that the public order problem is not going to be solved with the presence of the public forces. It must be complemented with social investment. We have asked the national government to help us generate employment. And we also require investment in education and health.'[79]

In addition to Bogotá and Washington failing to provide effective social and economic assistance to Arauca, the Uribe administration began withholding the department's 9.5 per cent share of the nation's oil revenues. The local municipalities that sat atop the Caño Limón oilfield were also deprived of the additional 2.5 per cent of oil proceeds that they normally received. According to Uribe, too much of the oil money was ending up in the hands of the rebels through extortion and sympathetic local politicians.

Meanwhile, the US soldiers provided counter-insurgency training to units of the Colombian army's 18th Brigade. The US military advisers were teaching Colombian troops how to conduct reconnaissance missions and wage unconventional warfare, among other things. The insignia of the 18th Brigade includes an oil derrick, and its commander, Brigadier General Carlos Lemus, directed operations from an office inundated with souvenirs bearing the name of the company whose oil it was his mission to protect. Occidental Petroleum contributes both money and logistical support, including transport helicopters, to the 18th Brigade to assist with protection of the pipeline. General Lemus explained the need for the US military aid and training: 'We need some of these things to help protect the pipeline and provide troop mobility, training, and more intelligence capacity to allow our troops to be able to respond to attacks more efficiently and faster.'[80] The training programme marked a significant shift in

US military policy in Colombia from focusing exclusively on coca crops, poppy fields and drug processing labs to a new emphasis on counter-insurgency.

The new US counter-insurgency role meant that US soldiers were working with Colombian troops closely allied with paramilitaries responsible for gross violations of human rights. In 2001, paramilitaries were responsible for 70 per cent of the more than 420 political killings – including the assassinations of two local congressmen – in the vicinity of Arauca City.[81] While General Lemus denied there were links between his troops and paramilitaries, Amnesty International claimed to have 'received information indicating strong collusion between units of the 18th Brigade of the Colombian Army and paramilitaries, including reports of joint military–paramilitary operations or army units wearing paramilitary armbands and identifying themselves as paramilitaries'.[82] In one such incident in May 2003, paramilitaries and soldiers from the 18th Brigade entered the Betoyes indigenous reserve in the municipality of Tame as part of an offensive called Operation Colosso. The gunmen raped and killed a pregnant sixteen-year-old indigenous girl and then cut the fetus out of her stomach before disposing of her body in a river.[83] When asked about the paramilitary strategy of entering villages and massacring unarmed civilians accused of being guerrilla collaborators, one US Army special forces soldier in Saravena replied: 'Sometimes that's what you have to do, I guess.'[84]

While the paramilitaries were prominent in Tame and Arauca City, where thirty of the US Army special forces troops were based, they were only beginning to gain a foothold in Saravena. Consequently, it was primarily the army that was challenging the rebels' decades-long rule of Saravena's barrios. The 18th Brigade regularly deployed its psychological operations unit into marginalized neighbourhoods, ostensibly to wage a battle to win over the 'hearts and minds' of local residents. One of its psychological warfare strategies specifically targeted children. In a programme dubbed 'Soldier for a Day', children between three and seventeen years of age were brought to the army base every Thursday to play soldier. The activities included Colombian troops and uniformed army psychologists placing camouflage headbands on the children and painting their faces with camouflage make-up. At the same time, two soldiers dressed in clown suits entertained the children. Throughout the experience, the 'little soldiers' were continuously bombarded with the requisite pro-army and anti-rebel propaganda. Finally, after a dip in the camp's swimming pool, the children were trucked around the base on top of an armoured personnel carrier equipped with a 50-calibre machine gun.[85]

Paola Alzate Acosta, an army psychologist dressed in camouflage combat fatigues, claimed that the programme helped children cope with traumas caused by the violence they frequently experienced in Saravena. According to Alzate, the children 'dream about learning how to handle a gun to kill the bad guy in the neighbourhood. They dream about learning how to drive a tank to be able to destroy the cylinder bombs.'[86] But the programme had another, more immediate, military benefit: counselling children from marginalized barrios controlled by the rebels provided the army with valuable intelligence on activities not only within the barrios, but also within the children's own homes and families. When asked whether some of these kids were children of guerrillas, Alzate responded: 'In many cases these are children whose parents are in the militias and those children become conflicted about what is right and what is wrong.' She then added: 'In some cases when we put camouflage headbands on them, they say that they can't take them home because their fathers will yell at them. When those kinds of things happen we try to talk to them to find out what is happening at home.'[87]

Local human rights groups have questioned the tactics used by the army to entice children to attend these programmes. According to one Saravena woman who requested anonymity for security reasons, she was watching her friend's children at their house one afternoon when soldiers arrived and said they were taking the kids to see the clowns. The soldiers gave money and candy to the children and accused the woman of being a guerrilla when she refused to let the children go. She said the soldiers 'were asking the children about their mother and father' and then 'they came in and checked the house, looking at everything'.[88]

While some of the psychological warfare and intelligence-gathering tactics appeared to contravene the Geneva Convention with regard to the involvement of civilians, particularly children, in an armed conflict, they had the support of US military advisers in Colombia. One US Army special forces soldier stationed in Saravena emphasized the importance of psychological operations when he stated: 'This war is not going to be won with bullets. It's going to be won by winning the people over to the side of the Colombian army. You are not going to defeat the guerrillas by humping through the jungle like in Vietnam.'[89]

The Colombian army's 18th Brigade has not only used its newly acquired unconventional warfare skills against the guerrillas, it has also targeted civilians critical of the government's policies. During 2003, there were numerous mass arrests of trade union leaders, human rights defenders and opposition politicians, who were accused of maintaining ties to 'terrorist' groups, namely the guerrillas. On 21 August in Saravena, soldiers from the 18th Brigade raided homes and arrested forty-two trade unionists, social activists and human rights defenders. Among those arrested and accused of being 'subversives' were Alonso Campiño Bedoya, leader of the regional branch of the country's largest union, the Central Workers Union (CUT), and José Murillo Tobo, president of the Joel Sierra Regional Human Rights Committee. Murillo had recently criticized the collusion between the

Colombian army and paramilitaries in Saravena.[90] The round-up was carried out by Colombian soldiers from the same base that housed the US Army special forces troops.

According to Amnesty International, 'The arrests also follow a spate of accusations against the [Joel Sierra Regional Human Rights] Committee made by the security forces in recent months that they were subversive collaborators.'[91] Only two months earlier in nearby Tame – a heavily militarized town with a prominent paramilitary presence – the deputy mayor had claimed that the Joel Sierra Regional Human Rights Committee and the guerrillas were one and the same. When asked about the activities of the human rights organization, the deputy mayor held up a FARC death threat faxed to Mayor Jorge Bernal and declared: 'This is from them, this is from an illegal group, from the FARC-ELN – that's the "human rights group".'[92]

In October 2003, soldiers from the Colombian army's 18th Brigade rounded up more than twenty-five politicians in Arauca department less than a week before local elections. Among those arrested for suspected ties to guerrillas were the mayor of Arauca City, the president of the regional assembly, a candidate for governor, and five mayoral candidates. Defence Minister Marta Lucía Ramírez explained the arrests: 'Unfortunately, terrorist groups have infiltrated the Department of Arauca at every level.'[93] But Amnesty International accused the Uribe administration of politicizing human rights, claiming, 'A lot of it has to do with silencing those who campaign for human and socio-economic rights.' The timing of the arrests, only days before local elections, also led an Amnesty spokesperson to declare: 'It is part of a strategy to undermine the opposition's credibility.'[94] In March 2002, AUC paramilitary leader Salvatore Mancuso had claimed that the AUC controlled 35 per cent of the Colombian Congress. While the government acknowledged the presence of paramilitary sympathizers in Congress, none of these AUC-linked politicians was arrested, nor were there any statements issued by high-ranking government officials claiming that 'terrorists have infiltrated' the national government 'at every level'.[95]

On 5 August 2004, Colombian soldiers from the base housing the US military advisers again ventured out into Saravena's barrios. This time, the soldiers dragged three union leaders out of their beds in the middle of the night and executed them. The Colombian army initially claimed that the three trade unionists were armed guerrillas killed in battle. An investigation conducted by local and international human rights groups led to Colombia's attorney general's office opening its own investigation. One month after the killings, Deputy Attorney General Luis Alberto Santana announced: 'The evidence shows that a homicide was committed. We have ruled out that there was combat.'[96] In a rare case of justice being carried out in Colombia's dirty war, one army officer and two Colombian soldiers were arrested and charged with the murder of the three union leaders.

Almost a year after the arrest of the soldiers, it remained evident that members of Colombia's political elite still supported the military's dirty war. In a July 2005 editorial published in the country's largest daily, *El Tiempo*, former minister of the interior and justice Fernando Londoño defended the patriotism of the army officer charged with killing the union leaders: 'Nobody will remember the second lieutenant who killed three ELN guerrillas in Arauca, who were disguised as union leaders like all the guerrillas who break the law in that zone. Now, in prison, he pays the price of his burning love for Colombia.'[97]

The deployment of US Army special forces troops to Arauca illustrates how 9/11 dramatically changed the political landscape, allowing the Bush administration to send US troops to one of the hottest regions in Colombia as part of the global war on terror. The Bush administration's expansion of the US role in Colombia effectively turned US soldiers into Occidental Petroleum's personal security trainers. The efforts of the US Army special forces soldiers, who trained more than two thousand Colombian troops in two years, appeared to be paying dividends for the US oil company as the Caño Limón pipeline was bombed only seventeen times in 2004.[98] The US advisers, however, had helped secure Occidental's operations by providing counter-insurgency training to a Colombian army brigade directly responsible for gross violations of human rights.

## The oil war in Putumayo

The implementation of the $1.3 billion Plan Colombia in Putumayo followed on the heels of a dramatic increase in the number of attacks against the department's oil infrastructure, from forty-eight in 1999 to 110 the following year. According to the Colombian army commander responsible for protecting Putumayo's oil operations, Lieutenant Colonel Francisco Javier Cruz, US drug war aid made the region safer for conducting oil operations because the army was able to use 'helicopters, troops and training provided in large part by Plan Colombia'.[99]

The escalation of the civil conflict in Putumayo department in southern Colombia during the 1990s had made foreign oil companies hesitant to exploit the vast oil reserves that existed mostly in rebel-controlled regions. The situation changed with the arrival of right-wing paramilitaries in the late 1990s and the implementation of Plan Colombia in 2000, both of which resulted in greater security for oil operations. At the outset of Plan Colombia, oil production in this remote Amazon region had been declining for twenty years after reaching a high of some 80,000 barrels a day in 1980. And while production still remained at the relatively anaemic level of 9,626 barrels a day in 2003, a slew of new contracts signed between multinational companies and the Colombian government since 2002 promise dramatic increases.

The remote municipality of Orito, where four oil pipelines interconnect, is the hub of Putumayo's oil operations. Two pipelines carry oil from nearby fields being exploited by the state oil company Ecopetrol, Houston-based Argosy Energy and Petrominerales, a subsidiary of Canada's Petrobank. Another pipeline brings oil across the border from the Ecuadorian Amazon where US-based Occidental Petroleum and Canada's EnCana have operations. The fourth is the Transandino pipeline, which transports oil from the other three pipelines across the Andes to the port of Tumaco on Colombia's Pacific coast, from where it is shipped to the United States.

Ecopetrol's Orito facility contains an army base housing the Ninth Special Battalion, which consists of 1,200 specially trained troops whose mission is to protect Putumayo's oil infrastructure. Leftist guerrillas have repeatedly targeted oil pipelines in the region to protest against the exploitation of the country's resources by multinational companies. In a seeming contradiction, the rebels have also profited from not targeting the operations of foreign oil companies that meet the extortion demands of the guerrillas. Though none of the foreign oil companies admits to directly paying off the guerrillas, Occidental vice-president Lawrence Merriage has admitted that, in the past, contractors hired by his company have met extortion demands in Arauca. When asked about FARC threats and demands in Putumayo, Argosy Energy's Colombia representative, Edgar Dyes, acknowledged that there had been threats to kidnap employees, but claimed he had no knowledge of whether or not the company's contractors had made extortion payments to the rebels. Interestingly, the FARC left Argosy's Putumayo operations untouched during a wave of attacks in 2003 that damaged pipelines and storage tanks and set oil wells ablaze.[100]

The militarization of Putumayo under Plan Colombia had reduced the number of attacks to forty-three by 2002, but the following year they leapt to a record 144. More than half the 2003 attacks occurred in November, when FARC guerrillas launched a major offensive against Putumayo's oil infrastructure. To help it protect oil operations, Lieutenant Colonel Cruz's Ninth Special Battalion has two helicopters – owned by the state oil company Ecopetrol and Canada's Petrobank – at its disposal for transporting troops on counter-insurgency operations. Lieutenant Colonel Cruz is clear regarding his mission: 'Security is the most important thing to me. Oil companies need to work without worrying and international investors need to feel calm.'[101]

Foreign oil companies clearly have a vested interest in Cruz's troops being able to maintain security in Putumayo. According to Steven Benedetti, a Petrobank representative in Bogotá, the company began operations in the region in June 2002 because 'we believe there is a big prize in Putumayo'. That 'prize' is the estimated 1.1 billion barrels of oil in the Orito field, of which 80 per cent remains untouched. In order to begin accessing the region's untapped reserves, Petrobank invested $50 million in its Putumayo oil operations in 2003. The investment immediately began paying dividends for the company when, despite several of its drilling sites having been targeted in the FARC's November 2003 offensive, Petrobank increased production by 18 per cent over the previous year.[102]

According to Cruz, the army alone cannot prevent guerrilla attacks against the oil infrastructure. His men often rely on civilian informers working as part of the informant network created under Uribe's democratic security programme. Cruz noted that, in order to accomplish his mission, it was very important that the army 'make the people understand that when they collaborate to avoid terrorist attacks, everybody wins'.[103] Cruz was referring to the fact that when attacks halt oil production, there is a corresponding reduction in royalties paid by foreign companies to the Colombian government. Colombian law stipulates that these oil royalties be used for social and economic programmes, but it is difficult to find the benefits of the royalties in Orito. Orito municipality is Putumayo department's largest recipient of oil revenue, but the degree of poverty and underdevelopment is no less stark than in other comparably sized Colombian towns that receive no oil funds. Within the town, however, the dramatic contrast between the lifestyle of the oil workers and other local residents is reminiscent of famous Colombian novelist Gabriel García Márquez's portrayal of the foreign fruit company's presence in the mythical town of Macondo. Near the centre of the town of Orito sits a huge recreation complex for the employees of Petrobank and Ecopetrol. The complex contains basketball courts, picnic and games areas, a hall for social gatherings and a huge swimming pool with a winding waterslide. A tall wire-and-steel fence ensures that the residents of nearby shanty towns don't stray into the fortress-like compound.

The reason why Orito has not benefited from royalty payments, according to one local resident, is that 'the oil leaves Putumayo and the royalties go into the wallets of the administrators'.[104] Another states it even more bluntly: 'The politicians steal the money.'[105] In contrast to his decision to cut off royalty payments to the oil-rich Arauca department because corrupt municipal governments are allegedly sympathetic to leftist guerrillas, President Uribe allowed the money to continue flowing to corrupt local officials in Putumayan towns controlled by right-wing paramilitaries.

Despite – or perhaps because of – the presence of the Colombian army and the national police, the town of Orito is controlled by AUC paramilitaries. The paramilitaries arrived in Putumayo in the late 1990s and after a series of massacres successfully seized control of many towns, including Orito. Even though the FARC regained control of several towns in 2003, and despite Cruz's claims that the army is fighting the paramilitaries as well as the rebels, the AUC's ruthless tactics helped it retain control of Orito. According to Javier, a local who requested that only his first name be used for security reasons, 'They kill innocent campesinos just because they *might* be guerrillas.'[106] As if to illustrate Javier's claim, paramilitaries assassinated local peasant leader Alirio Silva in Orito on the same day this writer met with Lieutenant Colonel Cruz.

US policy in Putumayo shifted the focus of the conflict over resources from coca to oil. Plan Colombia's aerial fumigation campaign decreased coca cultivation in Putumayo, shifting it to other departments throughout the country. At the same time, the militarization of the region provided a more secure environment for foreign oil companies to expand their operations. As a result, the military, the guerrillas and the paramilitaries continue to make Putumayo a focal point of their armed struggle. On 25 June 2005, as many as three hundred FARC guerrillas launched another series of attacks against oil installations which left twenty-one soldiers dead.[107] Uribe responded to the attacks by deploying an additional 1,000 troops backed by helicopter gunships to the region. Many in Putumayo believe that oil production is only sustaining a conflict in which most of the victims are civilians. As one Putumayo resident candidly stated: 'Everyone knows the conflict in the Middle East is because of oil, and Colombia's problems are no different. Maybe the coca is going, but there's still oil. And if there's oil, then the armed groups won't leave because they are interested in places where there are money and power.'[108]

### Conclusion

Despite the FARC's resurgence in 2005, Uribe maintained approval ratings near 70 per cent, according to opinion polls conducted by telephone in the country's four largest cities. The methodology used to conduct polls in Colombia means that they mostly reflect the views of the middle and upper classes – the principal beneficiaries of reductions in crime and kidnappings. In the war-torn countryside, Uribe found it far more difficult to win the hearts and minds of the country's peasant population. The president's democratic security strategy focused almost exclusively on military actions; the government built few roads, schools and medical clinics for the 85 per cent of rural Colombians who live in poverty.[109]

By mid-2005, the FARC's spate of attacks throughout Colombia had made it clear that almost five years of Plan Colombia and three years of Uribe's democratic security strategy had failed to diminish the military capacity of the guerrillas. While security had improved for much of the urban population, life for rural Colombians continued to be plagued by violence and poverty. Meanwhile, US military aid and IMF-imposed economic reforms had improved the security and economic situation for foreign oil companies operating in Colombia. Under Uribe, Colombia became a neo-liberal poster child, increasing foreign investment and achieving respectable economic growth. But as had occurred throughout the country's history, the majority of Colombians did not benefit from the new-found prosperity. Furthermore, Uribe's macroeconomic successes were partly a result of state repression, including the waging of a dirty war against those sectors of civil society opposed to neo-liberalism.

In August 2005, the United Nations criticized the Uribe administration for its practice of using arbitrary detentions to target those critical of the government's policies. The director of the UN High Commissioner for Human Rights office in Colombia, Michael Frühling, announced that his office 'has noted with concern that illegal or arbitrary detentions constitute, both in number and frequency, one of the most worrying violations of human rights reported in the country'. Frühling further noted that the UN 'is also concerned that mass-scale detentions and

165

individual seizures with no juridical basis frequently affect members of vulnerable groups such as human rights advocates, community leaders, trade union activists and people living in areas where illegal armed groups are active'.[110] For its part, the Bush administration has mostly turned a blind eye to the Colombian government's poor human rights record. Instead, in order to secure the flow of Colombian oil to the United States, Washington has used the wars on drugs and terror to justify providing vast amounts of aid to a military apparatus closely linked to right-wing paramilitaries on the State Department's foreign terrorist list.

# 5 | Venezuela: an alternative for the twenty-first century?

On 2 February 1999, Hugo Chávez became president of Venezuela. With his inauguration, more than seventy years of close ties between the United States and Venezuela began to unravel. The new president harshly criticized Washington's global neo-liberal project and implemented social and economic policies that prioritized the needs of the poor. As a result, Chávez became the symbol of resistance, first for impoverished Venezuelans, and then for millions of marginalized people throughout Latin America, to US hegemony in the region. The Venezuelan leader soon replaced Cuban president Fidel Castro as Washington's public enemy number one in Latin America. Some in the United States, such as former White House and Pentagon official Douglas McKinnon, went so far as to declare that 'Chávez posed a greater threat to our national security than Osama bin Laden or any terrorist operating out of the Middle East'.[1]

In 1997, one year before Hugo Chávez was elected president, Venezuela was the top supplier of oil to the United States, accounting for 17 per cent of US petroleum imports that year. In the ensuing years, Venezuela remained among the top four suppliers of oil to its northern neighbour.[2] From Washington's perspective, the 'threat' to US national security lay in Chávez's efforts to ensure that a greater percentage of Venezuela's oil wealth benefited impoverished Venezuelans rather than national elites, foreign companies and US energy needs.

## Oil in the back yard

Like most oil-rich nations of the South, Venezuela's economy has been heavily dependent on the highly sought-after resource. The country has proven reserves of 78 billion barrels of oil, the largest reserves outside the Middle East. Oil exports account for 50 per cent of the government's revenues and 80 per cent of export earnings.[3] The first significant oil discovery in Venezuela occurred in 1914 on the eastern shore of Lake Maracaibo. By the 1930s, the country had become the world's largest oil exporter. The presence of US oil companies in Venezuela brought the country increasingly into the US sphere of influence. In 1927, former US diplomat Jordan Herbert Stabler reported to the State Department: 'The advent of great numbers of Americans connected with the oil industry has had a decided effect and Venezuela looks towards the United States much more than ever before for imports and any financial needs it might have' (Ewell 1996: 122). In the 1920s and early 1930s, Washington was more than happy to support the dictator Juan Vicente Gómez, particularly in light of the fact that the 'tyrant of the Andes' allowed lawyers for US oil companies to write the country's petroleum legislation in 1921.

During the 1920s, several former State Department officials worked for the largest US oil companies – Exxon, Gulf and Standard – operating in Venezuela and, by 1929, these companies dominated the country's oil production. Meanwhile, the companies implemented a system of segregation in Venezuela's oil-producing regions in which foreign workers were paid in dollars and Venezuelan workers were not permitted to enter the companies' social facilities, such as movie theatres and clubs. The racist attitude of the oil companies was also apparent in comments by company officials. William T. Wallace, vice-president of Gulf in Venezuela, stated: 'It is impossible to expect the native mind to conform to the accepted method of

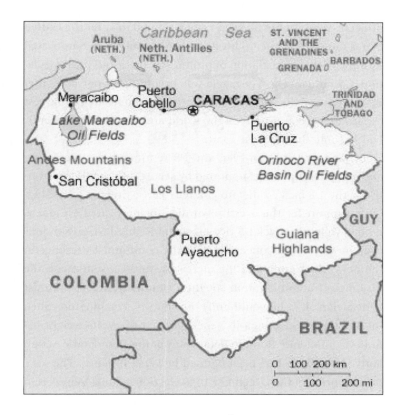

5  *Venezuela*

living in highly developed countries after centuries of dirt and unsanitary living' (ibid.: 140).

During the ensuing decades, US foreign policy towards Venezuela was rooted in protecting the interests of multinational oil companies operating in its 'own back yard'. Nevertheless, the Venezuelan government did succeed in 1943 in implementing partly nationalistic petroleum policies that extended foreign concessions in return for 50 per cent of oil revenues. During the 1940s and 1950s, the Venezuelan government oversaw a rapid industrialization of the country by US companies and state-funded projects. Washington allowed Venezuelan oil to enter the United States duty free, while US investors in Venezuela were motivated by unrestricted repatriation of profits, low taxes and little regulation. US influence in Venezuela was becoming so pervasive that by the end of the 1950s the country was home to the largest expatriate US community in the world and baseball, not soccer, had become the national sport.

By January 1958, however, anti-US sentiment was increasing and a popular uprising supported by sectors of the military overthrew the US-backed dictator Marcos Pérez Jiménez. Washington's support for the overthrown dictator motivated a Caracas mob to violently attack US vice-president Richard Nixon's motorcade in May 1958. Concerned with the communist presence in the new ruling junta and the increasing anti-US sentiment, the Eisenhower administration sought a staunchly anti-communist Venezuelan ally who could unify the country. Washington called for democratic elections in Venezuela and threw its weight behind the moderate Rómulo Betancourt of the Democratic Action Party (AD), which had been banned by Pérez Jiménez. The AD's Betancourt won the December 1958 election against Venezuelan Christian Democratic Party (COPEI) candidate Rafael Caldera, another moderate.

In 1959, following Washington's imposition of import quotas on Venezuelan oil, President Betancourt's minister of mines and hydrocarbons, Juan Pablo Pérez Alfonzo, met with representatives of Saudi Arabia, Iran, Iraq and Kuwait. The group laid the groundwork for the establishment of the Organization of Petroleum Exporting Countries (OPEC) the following year, with the objective of shifting control of the world's oil supply from consuming countries to producing nations. Venezuela also established a state oil company, the Venezuelan Petroleum Corporation (CVP). Successive AD and COPEI governments used the country's increasing oil revenues to fund development throughout the 1960s and 1970s. While the country's economic elites were the principal beneficiaries of the oil wealth, a sizeable middle class also developed as the country industrialized.

In the early 1970s, the Venezuelan government, much to the chagrin of Washington, followed the example of its OPEC partners in the Middle East and announced that it was increasing its share of oil revenues to 60 per cent. Caracas also declared its intention to nationalize the oil sector when existing contracts with multinationals expired.

Following the 1973 Arab–Israeli war, Venezuela found itself caught in the middle of an economic conflagration between its oil-producing partners in the Middle East and the United States, its long-time hemispheric ally and largest trading partner. The Venezuelan government chose to defy the OPEC oil embargo rather than further antagonize its northern neighbour. The United States showed little gratitude for Venezuela's defiance of the embargo when, in 1974, the US Congress excluded OPEC countries, including Venezuela, from tariff preferences granted to nations of the South. The ensuing political battle between Washington and Caracas brought relations between the two countries to a new low. In 1976, by which time multinational companies were paying 80 per cent of their earnings in royalties and taxes, Venezuela nationalized the petroleum sector.

The nationalization of the oil industry and establishment of a new state company, Petroleos de Venezuela, Sociedad Anónima (PDVSA), was supposed to lead to even greater wealth for Venezuelans. By the end of the 1970s, however, it had become apparent that this would not be the case as declining oil prices contributed to the economy entering a downward spiral that would continue for the next twenty years. Still, the newly established PDVSA remained both profitable and the principal generator of government revenue despite the decline in global oil prices. The company, however, responded to the country's economic crisis as though it were a private corporation rather than a state-owned entity. Instead of increasing the amount of oil revenue flowing into the state's coffers, nationalization actually resulted in a decrease in government fiscal revenues.

Prior to nationalization, the government had stipulated that the Venezuelan operations of foreign oil companies be managed by Venezuelans. When the government nationalized the oil sector, it placed the Venezuelan executives that headed the three major foreign companies in Venezuela – Exxon, Shell and Gulf – in charge of the newly formed PDVSA. Rather than earning revenue for the state, PDVSA's corporate-trained executives sought to distance the company from the government. They were able to achieve their objective because the Ministry of Energy and Mines (MEM) failed to monitor PDVSA's activities with the same degree of vigilance that it had applied to foreign oil companies prior to nationalization. The company's executives, seeing no reason to maximize profits simply to provide the government with fiscal revenue, decided instead to reinvest PDVSA's profits in the company's operations. OPEC, meanwhile, had responded to falling oil prices by introducing production quotas for member countries. Production cutbacks due to OPEC quotas made it difficult for PDVSA to reinvest its profits in the company's domestic operations. So, in 1983, PDVSA began implementing a policy of 'internationalization', which called for the company to reinvest its profits in overseas projects. Venezuela's state oil company purchased refineries in Germany, Sweden, Belgium and the United States, and developed a retail chain of more than fourteen thousand gasoline stations in the latter country under the name of its wholly owned subsidiary Citgo. According to political scientist César Baena, PDVSA's executives decided 'to create an international network of operations that would enhance their capacity to perform, farther away from the government's unexpected fiscal demands and from Congress' meddling'.[4]

In order to further restrict the Venezuelan government's access to its earnings, PDVSA implemented a policy of 'transfer pricing'. PDVSA sold oil at discounted prices to its overseas subsidiaries, which then benefited from increased profit margins. The subsidiaries retained these profits overseas so that PDVSA would show lower domestic earnings. In the eighteen years of internationalization and transfer pricing, the overseas subsidiaries never paid dividends to PDVSA. According to Venezuelan social scientist Bernard Mommer, 'By the second half of the 1990s, PDVSA was remitting through transfer pricing an average of about $500 million annually from its domestic accounts to its foreign affiliates' (Mommer 2003: 134–5). Simply put, much of Venezuela's oil revenue was in the hands of PDVSA's overseas subsidiaries, where it was benefiting the economies of the host nations, particularly the United States.

PDVSA's executives ran the state oil company as though it were their own private company rather than representing the interests of its sole shareholder: the national government. Instead of generating revenue for the state, and by extension the Venezuelan people, PDVSA reinvested its profits in order to expand its operations as an end in itself. The damage that PDVSA – in conjunction with IMF-imposed neo-liberal reforms – inflicted on the Venezuelan economy was evidenced by the dramatic decline in the government's share of oil revenues. In 1981, the country's oil production generated $19.7 billion in earnings and PDVSA paid $13.9 billion in fiscal revenues to the government. In 2000, oil earnings had increased dramatically to $29.3 billion, but PDVSA paid only $11.3 billion to the government (ibid.: 137). In percentage terms, between 1976 and 1992 the government received an annual average of 71 per cent of PDVSA's export revenues; between 1993 and 2000, this plummeted to only 36 per cent.[5]

During the 1980s, PDVSA also sought ways to bypass OPEC quotas. The company manipulated the definition of crude by claiming that its production of extra-heavy crude – which, when processed, is known as Orimulsion – and its production of synthetic crude were not in fact crude oil and therefore not subject to the quota system. As a result, PDVSA undermined OPEC's goal of restricting production in order to boost the global price of oil. Venezuelan overproduction was a contributing factor to global oil prices falling below $11 a barrel in the late 1990s.

The AD and COPEI governments had not only used oil revenues to fund the country's development, they had also borrowed heavily against future oil revenues. While some of this money funded development projects, much of it wound up in the pockets of wealthy Venezuelans connected to the AD and COPEI. When the global price of oil fell in the early 1980s, the economy stalled and the government found itself in a severe fiscal crisis owing to its increased debt load. Capital flight ensued as the country's wealthy protected themselves by sending their money abroad. In 1982 alone, some $8 billion left the country. At the same time, corruption in the AD and COPEI facilitated the disappearance of $11 billion of hard-currency reserves from the government's coffers (Buxton 2003: 116).

The number of Venezuelans living in poverty increased during the 1980s, reaching 43.9 per cent of the population by the end of the decade. Meanwhile, the nation's elites continued to invest the wealth they had obtained through corruption overseas. In 1989, economist Paul Krugman noted:

Venezuelan citizens have more assets abroad than those of any other debtor nation and all of Venezuela's foreign debt buildup was used to finance capital flight. Over the past 15 years the overseas assets purchased by Venezuelan residents have actually exceeded the country's foreign borrowing by about US$20 billion. In other words, if the Venezuelan government could lay claim to all the New York bank accounts and Miami condominiums owned by wealthy Venezuelan citizens, it could pay off the foreign debt and still have funds to spare.[6]

Shortly after assuming office on 2 February 1989, President Carlos Andrés Pérez of the AD announced that he had reached an agreement with the IMF to address the country's fiscal crisis. Pérez agreed to implement neo-liberal economic reforms in return for a $3.8 billion loan from the international financial institution.[7] The announcement contradicted his campaign promise that he would not introduce free market reforms. Feeling betrayed by Pérez, thousands of poor Venezuelans responded to a reduction in fuel subsidies and the implementation of other neo-liberal reforms by taking to the streets of Caracas on 27 February 1989. The popular uprising spread to nine other cities before the army succeeded in quelling the revolt. The official death toll was 287, but other estimates claim that more than a thousand died in what became known as the *Caracazo*. The protests represented the first class-based uprising in Venezuela since the 1930s.

Despite the obvious dissatisfaction expressed by thousands of Venezuelans during the *Caracazo*, Pérez moved ahead with his implementation of neo-liberal reforms. The government cut public spending at a time when increasing numbers of Venezuelans were in need of a social safety net. The Pérez administration also privatized state companies and opened up the oil sector to foreign companies for the first time since nationalization. The cuts in social spending, lay-offs resulting from privatization, the opening of the petroleum sector and PDVSA's policy of transfer pricing all contributed to poverty levels skyrocketing from 43.9 per cent in 1988 to 66.5 per cent by the end of 1989 (Buxton 2003: 118).

In the petroleum sector, the Pérez government, under PDVSA's urging, implemented low royalty and income tax rates in order to entice foreign companies to enter into joint ventures with the state company in extra-heavy oil projects. It also permitted foreign companies, including Chevron, BP and Shell, to sign operating services agreements with PDVSA for exploration and production in marginal oilfields. Perhaps most insulting to Venezuela's national pride was PDVSA agreeing, for the first time in the country's history, that contractual disputes would be made subject to international arbitration. According to Mommer, PDVSA's liberal policies, which benefited foreign companies, were 'antithetical to everything that Venezuelan oil nationalism has ever achieved, including the founding of OPEC and nationalization. It is imperialism in its most ancient of definitions: the conquest of foreign land and its mineral resources' (Mommer 2003: 137–9).

On 4 February 1992, Lieutenant Colonel Hugo Chávez led a coup attempt against the increasingly unpopular Pérez. Although the coup failed and Chávez was imprisoned, it brought the young army officer to the public's attention. In addition to receiving a traditional military education, Chávez and his coup accomplices had also attended social studies classes at the more progressive public universities. As a result of their lower-middle-class backgrounds and broader education, some members of this new generation of Venezuelan political officers were more sympathetic to the plight of the poor than many of their counterparts in other Latin American military apparatuses.

As the 1993 presidential elections neared, Venezuela was in the throes of a political crisis brought on by declining living standards for most Venezuelans, the *Caracazo*, the Chávez coup attempt, a second failed military coup in November 1992, and the impeachment of Pérez in 1993 for corruption. Rafael Caldera, a founder of COPEI, abandoned his party to take advantage of the growing popular discontent with the traditional political parties and institutions. Running as the candidate of a coalition of small independent parties, he was elected president in 1993.

In reality, he still represented the traditional political establishment. Caldera promised during his campaign that he would not implement neo-liberal reforms. Two years into his term, however, Caldera followed in the footsteps of his predecessor Pérez and negotiated an agreement with the IMF. In 1996, the Venezuelan president agreed to implement neo-liberal reforms in return for a $975 million loan.[8]

By the end of Caldera's term in 1998, the degree of inequality with regard to income and land ownership had reached staggering proportions. According to the IMF, the richest 20 per cent of Venezuelans received 84 per cent of the national income, while the poorest 20 per cent earned only 3 per cent. Meanwhile, 3 per cent of the country's landowners owned 76.5 per cent of the national territory.[9] The UNDP reported that between 1990 and 1998 poverty increased to 68 per cent of the population, while 69 per cent of poor households were unable to meet their basic needs. Furthermore, 70 per cent of all new jobs were created in the informal sector, the average real wage of all workers in 1998 represented only 58.8 per cent of its value in 1990, 44 per cent of youths lacked access to education and the same percentage of Venezuelan households had at least one family member suffering from a chronic illness.[10]

Venezuela's economy continued to deteriorate as global oil prices slipped below $11 a barrel in 1998, the lowest level in more than fifty years. The country was polarized along class lines with the poor majority among Venezuela's 24 million people no longer willing to support any presidential candidate linked to the traditional political parties and institutions. On 6 December 1998, with widespread support from the 68 per cent of Venezuelans mired in poverty, Chávez won the presidential election with 57 per cent of the vote – the largest percentage total in four decades of Venezuelan democracy.[11]

Venezuela had followed the same neo-liberal path during the

previous decade as other oil-rich nations such as Kazakhstan, Azerbaijan, Nigeria and Colombia. And as in those nations, the social and economic consequences for the majority of the population had proved devastating. Unlike those nations, however, Venezuela was on the verge of implementing a dramatic ideological shift with regard to the management of its vast oil reserves.

## The political reformation

Following his release from prison in March 1994, Chávez began promoting the Bolivarian Revolutionary Movement 200 (MBR-200), which was named after Venezuelan independence hero Simón Bolívar, who had sought to establish a unified Latin America. Military officers had initially formed the MBR-200 in the early 1980s, but after 1994 Chávez and other members sought to transform it into a national political organization. They began establishing committees in municipalities throughout the country called Bolivarian Circles, which then organized at the local level. Despite some friction between the military members and the ever increasing numbers of civilian participants, the MBR-200 soon evolved into a national movement.

The MBR-200 decided to compete in the 1998 municipal, congressional and presidential elections. Chávez established an official political party as the electoral front of the MBR-200. The party was called the Fifth Republic Movement (MVR) because the Venezuelan constitution prohibited political parties from using Simón Bolívar's name. The MVR formed a coalition with several other small alternative parties with the goal of obtaining enough seats in Congress to force the establishment of a Constituent Assembly in order to rewrite the country's constitution and restructure the political institutions. Chávez easily won the presidential election after campaigning on a platform that condemned past AD and COPEI governments for ruling in the interests of Venezuela's rich minority and foreign oil companies. For its part, the mostly middle- and upper-class white opposition, which constituted only 23 per cent of the population, were horrified that the country's new leader was a dark-skinned 'Indian' from the ranks of the lower middle class. The opposition soon began blaming Chávez's revolutionary policies for the country's polarization along class lines. In actuality, the corruption of the AD and COPEI and the implementation of neo-liberal economic policies had polarized the nation almost a decade before Chávez was elected, as the *Caracazo* had illustrated.

After his inauguration on 2 February 1999, Chávez immediately set about fulfilling his campaign promise to hold elections for a Constituent Assembly. In April, Venezuelans approved Chávez's procedural plans for the assembly in a national referendum and three months later the president's governing alliance won 125 seats in the 131-member assembly. The newly elected Constituent Assembly drafted a new constitution in only three months, and it was approved by more than 70 per cent of voters in another national referendum held in December. The new constitution renamed the country the Bolivarian Republic of Venezuela, increased the presidential term from five to six years and allowed re-election for a second term. It also, among other things, replaced the bicameral Congress with a unicameral National Assembly, allowed for the recall of all elected officials as a means of combating corruption, gave the military more autonomy, and enshrined indigenous and environmental rights. With regard to the oil sector, the new constitution prohibited the privatization of PDVSA, although this did not apply to the company's subsidiaries. Critics of the new constitution claimed that establishing a unicameral assembly and extending the presidential term by one year gave disproportionate power to the executive. Chávez's supporters, on the other hand, emphasized the constitution's democratic aspects, including increased direct public participation in decision-making, the codification of human rights and mechanisms for recalling elected officials, including the president.

While Chávez was focused on implementing political reforms during his first year in office, the economy continued to deteriorate and poverty increased. To make matters worse, in December 1999 the country experienced its worst ever natural disaster when heavy rains caused serious flooding and mudslides in ten northern states, which left more than twenty thousand dead. The increase in poverty rates over the previous two decades had left tens of thousands of Venezuelans living in shanty towns built on steep hillsides. These precarious living conditions proved fatal when the rains came in December 1999. Chávez responded to the disaster by deploying Venezuelan troops to help with rescue efforts, an experience that led to his continued use of the military in the implementation of social projects throughout the country, particularly the building of infrastructure.

At the same time he was dealing with the national emergency caused by the flooding, Chávez was also campaigning for elections called for under the new constitution. On 30 July 2000, Chávez was again elected president, this time with 59 per cent of the vote. His closest rival, Francisco Arias of the centre-left Causa R party, garnered only 37 per cent of the ballots cast.

In 2000, having completed his constitutional reforms, Chávez began focusing on his social and economic revolution with the goal of ensuring that Venezuela's oil wealth benefited the majority of Venezuelans instead of the country's elites and foreign oil companies. In order to properly fund his 'revolution for the poor', Chávez needed to rein in PDVSA, which he claimed functioned like a 'state within a state'. Chávez appointed Alí Rodríguez Araque as head of the Ministry of Energy and Mines (MEM) in a first step to regaining control of the country's hydrocarbon resources and increasing the fiscal revenues derived from those resources. First, Rodríguez Araque reasserted MEM authority over

PDVSA, forcing the company to strictly adhere to OPEC quotas for the first time in more than a decade and revising the method of determining royalty payments to improve revenue collection from the state company. Venezuela also considered selling some of its US-based Citgo refineries, because the PDVSA subsidiary was selling oil to the United States for $2 a barrel below market price under an agreement signed before Chávez came to power. As Chávez noted: 'We are subsidizing the US budget.'[12]

In an effort to increase the global price of oil, Chávez and Rodríguez Araque – who would became secretary-general of OPEC the following year – convinced OPEC members to adopt a price band system in March 2000. The objective was to maintain the global price of oil at between $22 and $28 a barrel, with member nations automatically increasing or decreasing production accordingly if the price moved out of this range. In September 2000, Chávez hosted a summit meeting for OPEC heads of state with the objective of further strengthening the cartel and defending global oil prices. Fully aware that increased oil prices would hurt not only the economies of wealthy industrial nations but also those of poor nations, Chávez called on oil-rich countries to work regionally in order to alleviate the harm done to their impoverished neighbours. In 2000, Venezuela began providing oil to Central American and Caribbean nations under preferential financing terms that included allowing them up to fifteen years to pay for the oil.[13]

The following year, the Chávez government enacted the new Organic Law of Hydrocarbons, which states that the oil sector must serve the 'sustainable development of the country' by using its revenues to finance 'health, education, a macro-economic stabilization fund and productive investment … for the welfare of the people'.[14] The law also decreed that PDVSA must hold a majority share in all joint ventures with foreign companies. Additionally, it raised the royalty rates that foreign oil companies had to pay to the Venezuelan government. The royalty rate increased from 16.6 per cent a barrel to between 20 and 30 per cent for conventional oil and from 1 per cent to 16.6 per cent for extra-heavy crude. At the same time, the income tax rate on conventional crude was lowered from 59 to 50 per cent, while the tax rate on extra-heavy crude remained the same at 32 per cent. Ultimately, the new law ensured increased revenue for the government because of the higher royalty rates, which were much easier to determine and collect than income taxes (Mommer 2003: 141). Critics claimed that the new law would deter foreign investment and drive multinational oil companies out of Venezuela. In the ensuing years, however, companies reluctantly began renegotiating their contracts with PDVSA. After eight companies signed new deals, industry analyst Roger Tissot of PFC Energy in Washington, DC, noted: 'This is a victory for the Venezuelan government because these eight companies have agreed to tougher terms. The remaining companies may be trying to negotiate a better deal, but I don't see anyone disputing what appears to be a *fait accompli*, and I certainly don't see a stampede out of Venezuela.'[15]

In February 2002, Chávez replaced PDVSA president General Guaicaipuro Lameda with Gastón Parra, a former president of the Venezuelan National Bank and a nationalist whose views were more in line with MEM policy. Chávez also appointed five new members to PDVSA's board of directors. Historically, board members had been selected from within the company's upper management, but the new appointees were from outside the company. Upper management responded to the removal of Lameda and the new board appointees by accusing Chávez of politicizing PDVSA. They demanded that Chávez remove the new board members and threatened to join the upcoming April strike called by Venezuela's largest business association, the Venezuelan Federation of Chambers of Commerce (Fedecamaras), and the country's largest union, the Confederation of Venezuelan Workers (CTV).

Unlike most leftist leaders in Latin America, Chávez did not command widespread backing among organized labour. He did, however, have the support of many of the more than 50 per cent of Venezuelans who worked in the country's informal sector. Most of these workers had suffered under neo-liberal reforms and now lacked job security, healthcare and pension plans. The CTV, which had failed to vigorously oppose the neo-liberal agenda of the Pérez and Caldera governments, was closely aligned with the AD and was reluctant to allow informal workers and unions not affiliated with the AD to join the confederation. Following the election of Chávez, the CTV's close affiliation with the AD and its frequent alliances with Fedecamaras, which represented the interests of the country's business elite, placed the union firmly in the camp of the opposition.

PDVSA management joined CTV and Fedecamaras in a general strike launched on 9 April 2002. The following day, Venezuelan army general Néstor González appeared on the country's five private television networks and demanded that Chávez resign. Shortly afterwards, the head of Fedecamaras, Pedro Carmona, appeared on television and called on all those opposed to Chávez to march to PDVSA's headquarters the next day. Venezuela's private television networks, which controlled 95 per cent of the country's airwaves and were highly critical of the government, repeatedly promoted the anti-Chávez demonstration throughout the day. On the morning of 11 April, tens of thousands of anti-Chavistas marched from the wealthy neighbourhoods of Caracas to PDVSA's headquarters. Opposition leader Carlos Ortega, president of the CTV, then addressed the crowd and urged them to march to the president's residence at Miraflores Palace to 'get him out'. A government official immediately appeared on the state-owned television channel and pleaded with opposition leaders, who knew that pro-Chávez demonstrators were outside the palace, to end their march and avoid a confrontation.[16]

Despite the government's pleas, a confrontation ensued involving both groups of demonstrators, the National Guard and Caracas police officers, who were controlled by the city's anti-Chávez mayor. By the end of the day, at least ten demonstrators had been killed and dozens injured. According to the eyewitness account of journalist Gregory Wilpert, 'Shots were fired into the crowds and I clearly saw that there were three parties involved in the shooting: the city police, Chávez supporters, and snipers from buildings above. Again, who shot first has become a moot and probably impossible to resolve question.'[17] The private television networks unequivocally blamed Chávez's supporters for the violence and broadcast film footage that had been deliberately edited to show them firing handguns while not allowing viewers to see that snipers were shooting at the pro-Chávez crowd.[18]

Military officers sympathetic to the opposition used the unrest to justify seizing control of the presidential palace. Chávez, members of his government and soldiers from the National Honour Guard, whose mission was to protect the palace, took refuge in the interior of Miraflores Palace. Only when the coup leaders threatened to bomb the palace did Chávez surrender.

On the morning of 12 April, Venezuelans awoke to television and radio broadcasts announcing that a coup had taken place and Chávez had resigned. They were also witness to an astounding admission by the opposition that the coup was premeditated. During the Venevisión television network's morning show *24 Hours*, opposition leader Victor Manuel Garcia thanked all the private television networks for the role they had played in the coup. He then explained how General González's televised demand two days earlier that Chávez resign was intended to suggest that a coup was in the offing. The objective, said Garcia, was to prevent the Venezuelan president from leaving the country to attend a scheduled meeting of the Organization of American States

(OAS) in Costa Rica: 'We needed Chávez here in Venezuela. ... So when Chávez didn't go to Costa Rica and stayed here in Venezuela, we activated the plan.' Venezuelan navy admiral Carlos Molina Tamayo, also a guest on *24 Hours*, then described the plan: 'The plan was to get masses of people into the streets; to get this social support before deploying the armed forces.'[19]

Several hours after Venevisión's morning broadcast, the military swore in the head of Fedecamaras, Pedro Carmona, as president. Carmona immediately began issuing decrees that dissolved the National Assembly, dismissed the attorney general, declared the constitution null and void, and revoked forty-nine laws passed by the Chávez government. The coup leader then changed the country's name back to the Republic of Venezuela, dropping the word Bolivarian, and restored Lameda to his post as president of PDVSA.

At first, Chávez's supporters were stunned by the resignation of their leader. But over the next twenty-four hours, they learned from community radio stations and foreign cable news broadcasts that the Venezuelan private media's assertions that Chávez had resigned were not true. Hundreds of thousands of Chávez supporters took to the streets of Caracas and other cities to demand that the country's democratically elected leader be returned to power. They fought pitched battles with the police in Caracas and finally seized the state-run television station on the night of 12 April. Meanwhile, 3,000 soldiers from the National Honour Guard still loyal to Chávez retook the presidential palace. Finally, to cap off an incredible reversal of events, Carmona went into hiding and Chávez was restored to the presidency on 14 April. The coup and its aftermath had left more than one hundred Venezuelans dead.

Questions immediately arose about US involvement in the coup. Since coming to power in January 2001, the Bush administration had assumed a far more confrontational stance towards the Chávez government than had the Clinton administration. Stocked with cold war ideologues from the Reagan years, the Bush White House was not about to let Chávez's plans to manipulate global oil prices and create a new 'socialism for the twenty-first century' go unopposed. The administration, however, held little economic leverage over Venezuela. First, the rise in oil prices after Chávez came to power made it easier for Venezuela to service its foreign debt, which was relatively low by Latin American standards. Consequently, Chávez did not need to borrow money from the IMF; therefore the international financial institution held little sway over the country. And second, imposing sanctions was out of the question because the US economy was heavily dependent on Venezuelan oil, which accounted for approximately 15 per cent of all US petroleum imports. In addition to Chávez's oil policies and socialist tendencies, the Bush administration was also critical of the Venezuelan leader's close relationship with Cuba's President Fidel Castro and unhappy with Chávez's scathing critiques of US 'imperialism', particularly Washington's neo-liberal agenda.

Assistant Secretary of State Otto Reich, a key figure in the Reagan administration's attempts to overthrow the Sandinista government in Nicaragua, had met with coup leader Carmona and other Venezuelan opposition leaders on numerous occasions in the months and weeks leading up to the coup. The very same day that Carmona was sworn in as president by the military, Reich summoned ambassadors from Latin America to his office, where he blamed the coup on Chávez's policies and informed them that the United States would support the new Venezuelan government.[20] The Bush administration's support for the coup regime stood in stark contrast to the reaction of most Latin American governments, which categorically condemned the overthrow of Venezuela's democratically elected leader. In addition, the vast majority of governments from outside the region, conspicuously ignoring the US cue, refrained from sending any early signal of support to the coup leaders.

It may be years before declassified documents shed light on the full extent of US involvement in the coup. In the meantime, a handful of heavily redacted CIA documents obtained through the Freedom of Information Act in October 2004 by lawyer Eva Golinger and journalist Jeremy Bigwood show that the Bush administration had advance knowledge of a coup attempt. A top-secret CIA intelligence brief dated 11 March 2002, one month before the coup, noted: 'There are increased signs that Venezuelan business leaders and military leaders are becoming dissatisfied with President Chávez ... the military might move to overthrow him.'[21] Another classified CIA intelligence brief issued on 6 April 2002, only five days before the coup, contained the heading 'Venezuela: Conditions ripening for coup attempt'. The brief was eerily accurate in its prediction of the coup:

> Dissident military factions, including some senior officers and a group of radical junior officers, are stepping up efforts to organize a coup against President Chávez, possibly as early as this month, [censored] the level of detail in the reported plans [censored] targets Chávez and 10 other senior officials for arrest. ... To promote military action, the plotters may try to exploit unrest stemming from opposition demonstrations slated for later this month.[22]

The Bush administration had funded opposition groups prior to the coup through the National Endowment for Democracy (NED) and the United States Agency for International Development (USAID). The NED, which is funded by the US Congress, had been used in the past to support pro-neo-liberal groups closely allied with US interests in Latin America and around the world. The Reagan administration used the NED during the 1980s as a key component of its policy to remove Nicaragua's Sandinista government from power. The NED provided millions of dollars to anti-Sandinista groups and also played a vital role in the neo-liberal restructuring of post-Sandinista Nicaragua.

In Venezuela, the Bush administration also used the NED as an instrument for achieving regime change. Not only did the NED fund opposition groups prior to their involvement in the coup, it continued funding them afterwards. The heads of two Venezuelan organizations that continued to receive post-coup funding from the NED had been appointed by Carmona to cabinet positions in the coup government – Leopoldo Martínez as finance minister and Leonardo Carvajal as education minister. A State Department report that examined the period leading up to the coup stated: 'It is clear that, during the six month period, NED, the [State] Department, and DOD [US Department of Defense] provided training, institution building, and other support under programmes totalling about $3.3 million to Venezuelan organizations and individuals, some of whom are understood to have been involved in the events of 12–14 April.'[23]

Another significant illustration of the political role played by both the NED and USAID, which falls under the jurisdiction of the State Department, was their funding of Venezuelan 'democracy promotion' programmes managed by the International Republican Institute (IRI). The day after the coup, IRI president George Folsom made his partisan position clear when he declared: 'Last night, led by every sector of civil society, the Venezuelan people rose up to defend democracy in their country. Venezuelans were provoked into action as a result of systematic repression by the Government of Hugo Chávez.'[24] Folsom evidently did not consider the majority of poor Venezuelans who supported Chávez to be part of civil society.

While there is not yet any indisputable evidence proving that the United States was involved in planning and orchestrating the coup, it is clear that US taxpayer dollars were funding opposition groups involved in the ousting of Chávez. Furthermore, the Bush administration's advanced knowledge of the coup and its refusal to warn the Venezuelan government made it, at the very least, an accomplice in the overthrow of a democratically elected leader.

Not surprisingly, the US mainstream media echoed the Bush administration's official anti-Chávez line and exhibited an equally troubling concept of democracy. A 13 April *New York Times* editorial stated: 'With yesterday's resignation of President Hugo Chávez, Venezuelan democracy is no longer threatened by a would-be dictator. Mr Chávez, a ruinous demagogue, stepped down after the military intervened and handed power to a respected business leader, Pedro Carmona.'[25] Meanwhile, the *Chicago Tribune* declared: 'It's not every day that a democracy benefits from the military's intervention to force out an elected president.'[26] Apparently, it was of little concern to the Bush administration and the US mainstream media that Chávez had been democratically elected twice with 57 and 59 per cent of the vote respectively. Nor did it seem to matter that Chávez, as the CIA had noted in an intelligence brief only days prior to the coup, maintained widespread support among poor Venezuelans who accounted for the vast majority of the population.[27]

There were two principal reasons why the Bush administration was eager to see Chávez removed from power. One was Venezuelan oil policies, which had increased global prices and hurt the interests of US oil companies. The other reason was Washington's growing concern that Chávez's 'revolution for the poor' and anti-neo-liberal rhetoric were influencing others in Latin America, thereby posing a threat to US political and economic interests throughout the region. CIA director George Tenet had laid bare the Bush administration's attitude towards Venezuela in testimony before a Senate Intelligence Committee two months prior to the coup: 'Venezuela is important because they're the third-largest supplier of petroleum. I would say that

Mr Chávez – and the State Department may say this – probably doesn't have the interests of the United States at heart.'[28] Tenet's statement vividly encapsulated the essence of US policy towards Latin America: that first and foremost, governments in the region should serve the interests of the United States, not their citizens.

Despite the failure of the coup, Venezuela's opposition persisted in their attempts to remove Chávez from power. On 2 December 2002, Fedecamaras and CTV again launched a general strike in which PDVSA's management participated. In reality, the national work stoppage was more a lockout by management than a strike by workers. While a significant portion of the workforce initially participated in the strike, increasing numbers soon began returning to their jobs, although many found themselves locked out.

The lockout crippled Venezuela's oil industry, and by extension the national economy, as management personnel and technicians shut down much of the petroleum sector. On the eighth day of the strike, Chávez deployed the military to occupy vital oil installations in an attempt to keep the industry operating. Many blue-collar oil workers began returning to work, but management and most technicians vowed to continue the work stoppage until Chávez resigned and new elections were called. The Bush White House openly sided with the opposition by calling for an 'electoral solution to Venezuela's crisis'.[29]

On 3 February 2003, with the strikers becoming increasingly divided, opposition leaders ended the lockout. During the sixty-three-day work stoppage, Chávez had fired some eighteen thousand oil workers, mostly management, and replaced them with retirees and new appointees. After years of struggle, Chávez had succeeded in gaining control of PDVSA. The Venezuelan leader was finally in a position to ensure that a substantial portion of the state oil company's revenues would be used to fund social and economic programmes that benefited the majority of Venezuelans as called for in the country's new constitution.

Three months after the strike ended, primarily pro-Chávez workers established the National Union of Venezuelan Workers (UNT). Members of the UNT have repeatedly debated how closely they should ally themselves with the Chávez government, given the co-optation of the CTV that resulted from its close ties to the AD. In the meantime, the UNT replaced the CTV as the country's most prominent union federation, accounting for more than 75 per cent of collective bargaining agreements signed in 2003 and 2004, compared to only 20 per cent for the CTV.[30]

Having failed to remove Chávez from power through two elections, a coup and a general strike, the opposition decided to use the new constitution to try to achieve its goal. Article 72 of the constitution allows for the recall of elected officials after the mid-point of their term of office has been reached. The constitution requires that a petition be signed by at least 20 per cent of the country's registered voters in order to trigger a recall referendum. The signed petitions must then be submitted to the National Elections Council (NEC) for counting and verification before a recall referendum vote can be held. In order for an elected official to be recalled in a referendum authorized by the NEC, at least 25 per cent of registered voters must participate and a number of voters equal to or greater than the number that had elected the official must vote in favour of the recall.[31]

After the halfway point of Chávez's term, the opposition successfully collected enough signatures to meet the constitutional requirement that 20 per cent of the country's registered voters sign the petition. The NEC verified the signatures and the referendum was scheduled for 15 August 2004. Voters in the referendum simply had to vote yes if they wanted Chávez recalled and no if they wanted him to finish his term. An astounding 73 per cent of registered voters turned out to cast a vote in the referendum.

Once again, Chávez won convincingly with 59 per cent of the vote; he proved victorious in twenty-two of the country's twenty-four states. International observers from the Carter Center and the Organization of American States (OAS) confirmed the validity of the process and the results.[32]

Meanwhile, questions were raised about whether the US role in the referendum process constituted an intervention into Venezuela's domestic political affairs. In 2002, Maria Corina Machado formed the non-governmental organization Súmate to organize and promote the recall referendum. From the beginning it was clear that Súmate was not the non-partisan organization it claimed to be. Machado was a prominent member of the opposition, who had signed the decree issued by coup leader Carmona dissolving the country's democratic institutions. Even former president Jimmy Carter referred to Súmate as an opposition group in his post-referendum report, stating that he had met with 'Súmate and other opposition groups'.[33]

The Bush administration, which was already funding various opposition groups, began funding Súmate through the NED and USAID. The NED provided Súmate with a $53,400 grant in September 2003. According to the NED, Súmate was to use the funding to undertake a campaign that would 'encourage participation in the referendum voting process'.[34] In a general election pitting opposing candidates against each other, such an objective could be considered commendable. But the referendum process was unique because the constitution required that at least 25 per cent of registered voters go to the polls or the opposition's attempt to remove the president from power would automatically fail. Therefore, in the context of the referendum, encouraging participation was a partisan political act. The NED further demonstrated its partisan nature by editorializing about Venezuela's political polarization in the grant's text. The NED laid the blame for Venezuela's troubles squarely on Chávez's shoulders: 'Once in office, Chávez's revolutionary rhetoric, public disregard for democratic processes and institutions and vitriolic attacks on his opponents, escalated political and social tensions and hardened the opposition.'[35]

On 20 August 2003, USAID provided $84,840 to a Súmate programme to organize the recall referendum. The political nature of USAID was clearly apparent in language contained in the funding contract stating: 'If at any time USAID determines that continuation of all or part of the funding for a program should be suspended or terminated because such assistance would not be in the national interest of the United States ... then USAID may directly ... terminate this award.'[36] Given that the Bush administration's preference was to see regime change in Venezuela, there was no question that supporting Súmate's drive to oust Chávez was clearly a political act conducted, not in the name of democracy, but in the 'national interest of the United States'.

The Bush administration had unsuccessfully applied several strategies used in the past to oust Latin American governments, including supporting a coup, general strikes and opposition groups. Meanwhile, the Venezuelan opposition was in shambles following its referendum defeat, and the president who had been elected three times – two elections and one referendum – in six years was more popular than ever. By May 2005, as a result of his oil-funded 'revolution for the poor', Chávez's approval rating had surpassed 70 per cent.[37]

## The Bolivarian revolution

Chávez's popularity escalated following each failed attempt to remove him from power. Correspondingly, his legitimacy increased not only among a majority of Venezuelans, but also in the eyes of many throughout Latin America. His scathing critiques of the neo-liberal economic policies being imposed on nations of the South by the international financial institutions enhanced his popularity among marginalized peoples. At the United Nations in 2004, Chávez declared: 'Hunger and poverty are the most terrible of the effects of a world order based on neo-liberal globalization. ... A world without poor and hungry would be achievable only through an economic and social order radically different from that which now prevails.'[38] Chávez sought to achieve that radically different economic and social order through the implementation of his Bolivarian revolution.

With the launching of various oil-funded programmes known as 'missions', Chávez began implementing what he called 'social-ism for the twenty-first century'. The various missions provide healthcare, food, education, housing and job training to im-poverished Venezuelans. Chávez also sought to redistribute the country's wealth, including land, to benefit the 70 per cent of the population living in poverty. He exchanged oil for Cuban doctors in a barter agreement that sought to make free healthcare available to all Venezuelans. He also used the government's $30 billion in oil revenues to subsidize food and medicines, improve schools in poor areas, build housing and provide micro-credit to worker-owned cooperatives throughout the country.

The Venezuelan opposition and the Bush administration pointed to these policies as examples of Cuba's communist influence and claimed that Chávez was irresponsibly spending the country's oil wealth and ruining the economy. Venezuela's national petroleum wealth was no longer the personal money spigot of the country's elite and US oil companies; it was now being used to benefit the majority of citizens, particularly those on the lowest rungs of the socio-economic ladder. In February 2005, Foreign Minister Rodríguez Araque told a meeting of the OAS that the Venezuelan government viewed 'social justice as a fundamental component of democracy'. Rodríguez explained the government's priorities, declaring that 'democracy in a country like Venezuela, whose concrete reality is one of poverty, depends on giving the large majority of the country the opportunity to participate, that is, the overcoming of poverty becomes the government's first reason for being'.[39] Alleviating poverty was not the priority of all Venezuelans, however, particularly if it came at the expense of the 20 per cent of the population that constituted the middle and upper classes. Jairo González, a nineteen-year-old university student from a wealthy suburb of the oil-rich city of Maracaibo, clearly illustrated the class divide in Venezuela when he stated: 'We hate Chávez because he only helps the poor; those who support him. He doesn't help the middle and upper classes.'[40]

Unlike the Cuban revolution, where the country's economy was radically transformed from capitalism to socialism in a few years, Venezuela's Bolivarian revolution has been far less radical and implemented at a much slower pace. In many ways, despite the rhetoric emanating from the Bush administration and the opposition, Chávez's revolution has more closely resembled western European democratic socialism than Cuban communism. In the context of neo-liberalism, however, the Bolivarian revolution has appeared quite radical.

One of the early components of Chávez's 'revolution for the poor' included addressing the country's healthcare crisis. In 1999, Cuba deployed 450 doctors and medical technicians to help victims of the deadly floods in northern Venezuela. The following year, Venezuela began selling oil to Cuba and other Latin American and Caribbean nations under preferential financial terms. The deal with Cuba also included a barter agreement in which the Castro government would send doctors, medical technicians, physical fitness trainers and literacy experts to Venezuela in partial payment for 53,000 barrels of oil a day. The amount of Venezuelan oil shipped to Cuba would increase to 90,000 barrels a day by 2005.[41]

At the time of the signing of the Cuba deal, Venezuela's public health system was seriously under-funded and not readily accessible to poor Venezuelans living in urban shanty towns and rural areas. For the impoverished majority, visiting a doctor meant travelling long distances followed by hours spent waiting in line. According to Minister of Health and Social Development Francisco Armada, 'We practised neo-liberal politics during the last two decades of the last century, similar to what was happening in the rest of Latin America. This was setting us up legally for a private healthcare system a lot like the Chilean model, although not exactly.'[42] While privatization did not pose a problem for the country's middle and upper classes, who were already paying for quality private healthcare, it threatened to make access to healthcare for the poor even more difficult. To address the inequitable access to healthcare and reverse the privatization process, Article 83 of the Bolivarian constitution enshrined the right to free universal and equitable healthcare for all Venezuelans. Armada explained that 'as a country, we decided that health was a fundamental and prioritized human and social right, including being above other rights. For example, being above commercial rights.'[43]

The number of Cuban doctors working in poor Venezuelan neighbourhoods increased dramatically after the launching of Misión Barrio Adentro (Into the Neighbourhood Mission) in April 2003. Barrio Adentro was initiated in the impoverished municipality of Libertador, located on the steep hillsides surrounding Caracas. Armada described the project:

We had difficulty getting Venezuelan doctors to participate in this process, so we began working with Cuban doctors. The community itself established the places where the doctors would be located; many families contributed parts of their own homes. The community assumed the responsibility for the security of the doctors, sharing their food and many other aspects of the process. And it is this process, this combination of forces that we want to highlight, because in it we see the recipe for success with an organized community that not only makes demands, but also participates in its right to health.[44]

The goal of Barrio Adentro was to make quality healthcare available to all Venezuelans, particularly the marginalized poor. The objective was not only to cure the sick, but also to practise preventive medicine. One of the Cuban doctors' initial priorities was to increase the low numbers of poor Venezuelan children vaccinated against preventable diseases. The government set about building thousands of distinctive, small, two-storey, red-brick, hexagon-shaped primary care clinics called 'modules'. Doctors also worked in new primary care clinics that had been established in pre-existing buildings throughout poor urban barrios. At the end of 2004, there were more than twenty thousand Cuban medical personnel and physical trainers working in close to nine thousand primary care clinics throughout Venezuela.[45]

By 2005, in Barrio 23 de Enero (23rd of January), one of the largest poor neighbourhoods in Caracas, the government had used oil revenues to fund more than ninety primary care clinics, with over thirty of them situated in the newly constructed modules. The clinics served the community's 300,000 residents, many of whom lived in small brick houses stacked precariously on top of each other on steep hillsides overlooking the city centre. The Cuban doctors held office hours from eight in the morning until noon and performed house calls during the afternoons. They lived in the sector of the neighbourhood in which they worked and were on call twenty-four hours a day. According to a female patient waiting to see a Cuban doctor in one of the modules, 'The programme has been good for the community. There were no doctors in 23 de Enero before Barrio Adentro.'[46] Meanwhile, the physical fitness trainers were responsible for educating citizens about general health issues and how to care for their bodies. The trainers routinely held exercise classes and, along with the doctors, met regularly with health committees made up of local residents to discuss community health needs. Tibisay Miranda, a resident of the La Cañada section of Barrio 23 de Enero, claimed that 'people in the community who barely knew their neighbours before are now organizing themselves'.[47]

The Chávez administration's healthcare programme has gone beyond staffing modules with Cuban doctors and physical trainers. The government has used oil revenues to fund a three-tiered public health system. The modules constitute the first level, providing primary healthcare in communities. For more extensive treatment, patients are referred to 'popular clinics', which constitute the second level of the system. Significantly larger than the modules, the popular clinics have the capacity to perform X-rays, ultrasounds, podiatry, gynaecology, dentistry, minor surgery and diagnostic tests. By 2005, the Chávez administration had constructed more than 850 popular clinics throughout the country.[48] The third level in the system consists of hospitals for major surgery and serious diseases. The Chávez administration has also invested heavily in training thousands of new Venezuelan doctors both in domestic universities and in Cuba in order to eventually diminish the country's dependence on Cuban medical personnel.

While medical care is provided free of charge, it constitutes only one component of the government's overall health programme. The Chávez administration has also used the country's oil revenues to establish 'popular pharmacies' in poor communities. The state-subsidized pharmacies allow poor Venezuelans to purchase medicines at an 85 per cent discount. Before Chávez, even if poor Venezuelans could visit a doctor, the high cost of drugs posed a formidable barrier to addressing their medical needs.

Another component of the government's preventive medicine programme consists of ensuring that all Venezuelans, particularly children in poor areas, have access to basic foodstuffs that provide adequate nutrition. In addition to establishing 'popular kitchens', or soup kitchens, in poor neighbourhoods, the Chávez administration initiated the Mercal Mission in 2003 in response to the economic collapse brought about by the management-led oil strike. The government built Mercals, or food markets, that sell state-subsidized goods in poor barrios. Basic foodstuffs such as rice, beans, chicken, milk and bread are available at prices 30 to 40 per cent lower – free to those living in extreme poverty – than in the private supermarkets, which are often located far from the poor barrios. In addition to providing affordable basic foodstuffs, the Mercals have also generated employment. By the end of 2004, according to the government, the more than 13,000 state-subsidized Mercals had generated more than 41,000 jobs for local community members.[49]

The government has also sought to reform the country's education system, including making primary and secondary education free. The Chávez administration is transforming the country's primary and secondary schools from traditional institutions to Bolivarian schools. By 2005, more than eighty-five schools in Greater Caracas had completed the transformation.[50] The Bolivarian schools contain kitchens staffed with parents from the community who have completed an intensive state-funded nutrition course. The school kitchens provide children with breakfast, lunch and an afternoon snack in an attempt to lower the levels of malnutrition among poor Venezuelan children. The Bolivarian schools also contain computer labs so that all Venezuelan children, not only those from wealthy families, have the opportunity to become computer literate in the twenty-first century. In Barrio 23 de Enero, twelve of the neighbourhood's twenty-two schools had been transformed to the Bolivarian model by early 2005.

**Venezuela**

According to Arnaldo Sotillo, director of one of the Bolivarian schools in the barrio, the overall objective of the new schools is to emphasize 'social values and create a different citizen for the future, a better society overall. The only way to change society is through education.'[51]

At the same time, the government launched Misión Robinson (Robinson Mission), an adult literacy and education campaign that made the school computer labs available to adult community members in the evenings. The literacy programme also provides free computer classes and Internet access at public libraries and Infocentres that have been established throughout the country. By 2005, the Robinson Mission had made almost 1.5 million Venezuelans literate – about 90 per cent of the country's illiterate population.[52]

The Bolivarian revolution, according to its proponents, seeks to create a new society in which all citizens are politically empowered. One strategy utilized by the government to achieve this goal is educating people about their political, social and economic rights under the new constitution. In Venezuela, the constitution is everywhere. It is a best-selling book. There are cartoon depictions of it in schools. In the state-subsidized Mercals, many food packages are adorned with an article of the constitution and a cartoon illustrating the significance of that particular article. A package of sugar, for example, quotes Article 103, which states that all people have the right to a quality education for free. Above the writing is a cartoon illustration of independence hero Simón Bolívar taking his two children to school. Other food packages contain articles of the constitution addressing the right to food as well as the right to be free from police brutality and government corruption.

In Barrio 23 de Enero, the government's local representative, Lisandro Pérez, known as the Jefe Civil (Civil Authority), claims that the Bolivarian revolution seeks to empower citizens so that they become passionate about social change. This change, says Pérez, cannot come from above; it must be rooted in local communities. The objective is to create a new socialism that is different from the rigid centralized socialism of the twentieth century: 'When the Berlin Wall fell, we thought it was the fall of socialism, but that wasn't true. What was the significance of the fall of the Berlin Wall? In reality, it was the fall of the old models, the old orthodoxy, and something new was rising. ... It had to fall so that a new political project could rise, like President Chávez's, which is now under way.'[53] In other words, the new socialist project cannot be strictly dictated and controlled by the central government, as so often occurred during the twentieth century. Instead, the role of the national government is to facilitate and provide logistical support for community-based initiatives.

As part of its attempts to establish the foundation for a 'socialism for the twenty-first century', the Chávez administration has worked to restructure the country's unequal distribution of agricultural land. When Chávez came to power, 2 per cent of landowners in Venezuela owned more than 60 per cent of the country's farmland, much of it idle ranches.[54] In November 2001, Chávez enacted the Law on Land and Agricultural Development in an attempt to address Venezuela's grossly inequitable distribution of land and to work towards food sovereignty in order to reduce the country's dependence on imported foodstuffs. The government's plan to increase agricultural production is also intended to help diversify the country's economy and diminish the effect of Dutch Disease, which results from a hyper-dependence on a single export commodity. Despite being compared to Cuban agrarian reforms by the opposition, Venezuela's agrarian law clearly differs from the Cuban model in that it recognizes the right to private property. The law limits the size of privately owned property, however, to a maximum of 5,000 hectares, and if more than 20 per cent of the land lies fallow then the excess non-productive land is subject to higher taxes.[55]

By 2005, the government had redistributed 2.2 million hectares of state-owned land to 130,000 peasant families that had formed cooperatives.[56] PDVSA provided funding for technical training and assistance to help ensure that the peasant cooperatives became viable and productive. The Chávez administration also established an Intervention Commission to evaluate private landholdings in order to determine the size of the property, the degree of productivity and legality of ownership before making decisions on possible redistribution. By continuing to recognize private property while implementing agrarian reform, Chávez had attempted to perform a difficult balancing act between not discouraging private investment and addressing the needs of the country's landless majority.

Not all the cooperatives funded by PDVSA are in rural areas; some are manufacturing cooperatives located in the cities. In 2003, the state oil company turned an unused storage facility in Caracas into a community complex called Fabricio Ojeda, which contains three cooperatives producing textiles, footwear and agriculture. The Fabricio Ojeda complex also houses a popular clinic, a popular pharmacy, a Mercal, agricultural plots, various exercise facilities and an office that sells discounted urban transportation tickets to students. PDVSA provided loans to the textile cooperative established by 280 women from the local community. The women used the PDVSA funding to construct a building using local labour and to purchase the necessary machinery and materials to begin producing military and school uniforms, clothing, bags and other textile products. The cooperative is providing inexpensive uniforms to schools and the military, and selling its other products to stores and vendors around Caracas. By participating in the cooperative, previously marginalized women have achieved a sense of empowerment. As cooperative member Luisa

Ruiz stated: 'We are no longer staying in the house; we are business women now.'[57]

In conjunction with using oil revenues to establish agricultural and manufacturing cooperatives, Chávez launched a 'Made in Venezuela' campaign to urge people to purchase domestically produced goods. The campaign's objective is to help diversify the nation's economy away from its hyper-dependence on the oil sector by creating a domestic market for the new cooperative-produced goods. Additionally, in order to protect nascent domestic industries, the government increased tariffs on many imports. The campaign and protectionist policies are part of the Chávez administration's attempts to achieve an elusive goal sought by most oil-rich nations of the South: the 'sowing' of oil revenues to diversify the country's economy.

The Bolivarian revolution has not been a strictly nationalist project; Chávez has also placed great emphasis on regional integration as a means to more effectively confront Washington's global neo-liberal project. Venezuela proposed the Bolivarian Alternative for Latin America and the Caribbean (ALBA) as an alternative to the US-pushed Free Trade Area of the Americas (FTAA). The FTAA would require that all Latin American nations regardless of their level of development compete economically with the United States in a 'free' market. The ALBA, on the other hand, calls for solidarity with those countries with the weakest economies through the creation of a 'Compensatory Fund for Structural Convergence'. This fund would facilitate a transfer of resources from the better-performing economies to the weaker ones, similar to the transfer system utilized by member nations of the European Union. Chávez has shown that his desire to help the region reduce its dependency on the Washington-based international financial institutions is more than mere rhetoric. In July 2005, Venezuela loaned $300 million to Ecuador so that the country could avoid defaulting on its foreign debt. The loan was issued when the World Bank would not disburse a previously agreed $100 million loan because the IMF was not satisfied with Ecuador's efforts to implement neo-liberal reforms.[58]

The Bolivarian regional alternative also advocates agricultural policies that contribute to food self-sufficiency among member nations rather than neo-liberalism's export-oriented agricultural model. It also opposes the intellectual property rights called for under the FTAA.[59] In June 2005, as part of his ALBA initiative, Chávez announced the launching of Petrocaribe, which aimed to ensure the delivery of affordable oil to thirteen Caribbean nations in an effort to stave off the social unrest that often results from high fuel costs. Venezuela was already supplying subsidized oil to several Caribbean nations, but under Petrocaribe, Caracas agreed to absorb 40 per cent of the cost whenever the price of oil surpassed $50 a barrel – the price was above $60 a barrel for much of 2005.[60] One month after initiating Petrocaribe, a new twenty-four-hour South American cable news network funded by Venezuela, Argentina, Uruguay and Cuba began broadcasting throughout the continent. The Caracas-based network, called Telesur, was designed to provide Latin Americans with an alternative perspective to the US-owned Spanish-language CNN.

Venezuela has also sought to develop political and economic ties beyond the western hemisphere in order to develop strategic alliances and reduce Venezuela's dependence on the US oil market. In December 2004, Chávez signed a bilateral trade deal with Beijing under which Venezuela supplies China with 120,000 barrels of oil a month. The deal also allows the China National Petroleum Corporation (CNPC) to operate fifteen fields in eastern Venezuela, which could produce up to 1 billion barrels of oil, and to build refineries in the South American country to process the heavy crude.[61] The deal was a strategic move by Chávez that not only diminishes Venezuelan reliance on the US market, but also attempts to ensure that any US intervention in

Venezuela would pose a threat to Beijing because of the CNPC's vested oil interests in the South American country. For China, the agreement gives the world's second-highest oil-consuming country much-needed access to a new supply of the vital resource. Following the announcement of the agreement, Chávez declared: 'We've been producing and exporting petroleum for more than 100 years, but they were 100 years of domination by the United States. ... The streets of New York are paved with our oil. We'll keep selling to them, but not only to them.'[62] From Washington's perspective, Chávez's global and domestic oil policies, Bolivarian revolution, harsh critiques of neo-liberalism and calls for Latin American integration pose a serious challenge to US hegemony in the region.

## The US response

The Bush administration has not limited its response to Chávez's oil policies and his Bolivarian revolution to the afore-mentioned support for the coup, general strikes and the opposition's recall referendum drive. It has also worked to undermine the Venezuelan government by trying to create the impression both in Venezuela and internationally that Chávez, while being democratically elected, does not govern in a democratic manner. In 2003, Secretary of State Colin Powell declared: 'President Chávez has taken some actions during the course of his presidency that we have not approved of. He sometimes has some ideas with respect to democratic systems that don't quite comport with ours, or, we believe, with the views of the Venezuelan people.'[63] The theme was continued by Powell's successor Condoleezza Rice in June 2005 when, referring to the Venezuelan leader, she suggested that 'if you are democratically elected, that you govern democratically as well'.[64]

Both the Bush administration and the Venezuelan opposition have pointed to Chávez's use of executive decrees to introduce the hydrocarbon and agrarian reform laws as an example of his authoritarian behaviour. Missing from their rhetoric was the fact that past presidents also enacted laws by decree under the country's old constitution. In recent years, many democratically elected Latin American leaders have routinely and constitutionally enacted laws by decree to implement neo-liberal reforms. In Argentina, for example, President Carlos Menem, who was largely responsible for turning Argentina into a neo-liberal poster child, issued 336 decrees between 1989 and 1994.[65] US officials also neglected to point out that President Bush had issued an executive decree in 2001 to implement aspects of the national energy plan developed by Vice-President Cheney's energy task force.[66]

Chávez also came under fire for his proposal to increase the size of the Supreme Court from twenty to thirty-two justices, with critics claiming it was an undemocratic ploy to stack the court with judges loyal to the government. The Venezuelan president did not, however, implement the changes to the court through decree; a majority in the National Assembly approved the court's expansion in December 2004. Opposition members, however, argued that only a newly formed Constituent Assembly should have the authority to make such changes.

There was a similar response to the government's new media bill, entitled the Law of Social Responsibility in Radio and Television, which was passed by the National Assembly in November 2004. The law mandates that private media must broadcast government education and information programming for sixty minutes a week. It also stipulates that media companies can be fined or even shut down for broadcasting content that promotes public disorder. Human Rights Watch criticized the new law for its lack of clarity: 'Its vaguely worded restrictions and heavy penalties are a recipe for self-censorship by the press and arbitrariness by government authorities.'[67] The National Assembly passed the law in response to the private media's repeated attacks on the government, including promoting anti-government demonstrations, and the media's role in the April 2002 coup and support for the short-lived coup regime. In its criticism of the new media law, Human Rights Watch acknowledged the private media's anti-government position: 'Private television companies have often adopted a blatantly partisan position, and their news and debate programs have been extremely hostile to the Chávez government.'[68] Many critics also failed to note that during Chávez's time in office not a single journalist had been jailed and no television and radio stations or newspapers had been shut down, all of which commonly occurred under previous governments.[69]

At the same time that critics of the new media regulations were accusing the government of censorship, the Chávez administration was working to democratize media in Venezuela. Chávez sought to help facilitate the development of community media organizations as an alternative source of information to the corporate media outlets that were all opposed to the government. Under government regulations, to qualify as a community media outlet the television or radio station must be non-profit-making and community members must produce at least 70 per cent of its broadcast content. As journalist Gregory Wilpert notes: 'The primary role of Venezuela's community media has been to provide news coverage that reflects the community. ... In contrast, the opposition media, insofar as they represent the interests of large private companies, are completely removed from poor communities and stand for a diametrically opposite set of interests.'[70]

The Bush administration has backed dictatorial regimes in oil-rich countries that support US political and economic interests, such as Saudi Arabia, Kuwait, Kazakhstan, Azerbaijan, Equatorial Guinea and Gabon. Ironically, it has repeatedly challenged the democratic credentials of a president who has been popularly elected in two free and fair elections and one national referendum over a six-year span. Washington has chosen to ignore the more democratic and transparent aspects of Chávez's presidency, such as the mobile cabinet meetings that are held throughout the country. Chávez and his ministers travel to various parts of Venezuela to hold public cabinet meetings during which they answer questions raised by residents of that particular region. Like his weekly *Aló Presidente* television and radio show, these meetings often last for five or more hours and are broadcast live to the nation on the state-run television channel. As Chávez biographer Richard Gott notes, the Venezuelan president works hard to address the concerns of Venezuelans throughout the country:

> He never stops talking and he never stops working. He has time for everyone and never forgets a face. For several years he travelled incessantly around the country, to keep an eye on what was going on. This was not mere electioneering, for he would talk for hours to those who had hardly a vote among them. He exhausts his cadres, his secretaries and his ministers. I have travelled with him and them into the deepest corners of the country, and then, after a 16-hour day, he would call the grey-faced cabinet together for an impromptu meeting to analyse what they had discovered and what measures they should take.[71]

The Bush administration's claims that Chávez's views don't comport 'with the views of the Venezuelan people' stand in stark contrast to the Venezuelan president's public approval ratings of over 70 per cent. In actuality, many Venezuelans, particularly the poor, identify closely with Chávez's style of communicating and view him as one of their own. As Caracas taxi driver Otamendi Widmark pointed out: 'Chávez speaks clearly; he doesn't use the technical terms that most people can't understand.'[72]

The Bush administration has also accused Chávez of 'interfering' in the internal political affairs of Venezuela's neighbours.

In particular, the White House has made unsubstantiated claims that Chávez has supported Bolivia's non-violent peasant coca growers' movement led by Evo Morales and Colombia's leftist guerrilla group, the Revolutionary Armed Forces of Colombia (FARC). In reference to Venezuela during her confirmation hearing in January 2005, secretary of state nominee Condoleezza Rice noted that 'we do have to be vigilant and to demonstrate that we know the difficulties that that government is causing for its neighbors'.[73] In March, Roger Pardo-Maurer, deputy assistant secretary for western hemisphere affairs at the US Department of Defense, echoed Rice's concerns: 'Chávez is a problem because he is clearly using his oil money and influence to introduce his conflictive style into the politics of other countries. He's picking on the countries whose social fabric is the weakest. In some cases it's downright subversion.'[74] The same month, Assistant Secretary of State Roger Noriega told the US Senate Foreign Relations Committee: 'We are concerned that President Hugo Chávez's very personal agenda may undermine democratic institutions at home and among his neighbors.'[75]

Secretary of State Rice and Secretary of Defense Rumsfeld toured South America separately in early 2005 in attempts to rally the support of regional governments against the man Rumsfeld claimed was 'promoting radicalism and attempting to subvert the democratic governments in the region'.[76] The problem faced by the Bush administration was the fact that most South American governments, including in Brazil, Argentina, Uruguay, Ecuador and Chile, not only maintained good relations with Chávez, but were also sympathetic to his Bolivarian revolution.

In June 2005, despite a clear lack of regional support, Rice tabled a US proposal calling for the creation of a new body at the OAS to monitor democracy in the western hemisphere. The new body's mission would be to ensure that democratically elected leaders govern in a democratic manner or face OAS intervention.

Chávez immediately responded to the proposal, stating: 'If there is any government that should be monitored by the OAS, then it should be the US government, a government which backs terrorists, invades nations, tramples over its own people, seeks to install a global dictatorship.'[77] Perceiving the US proposal as a thinly veiled attempt at establishing the framework for a regional intervention in Venezuela, most Latin American nations, including Brazil, Argentina and Mexico, firmly rejected it. Fully conscious of Washington's history of intervention in the region, Latin American leaders instead pledged to uphold the OAS policy of non-intervention unless requested by the host government.

Also in June 2005, anti-neo-liberal protests by Bolivian miners, farmers and indigenous groups led to the resignation of Bolivian president Carlos Mesa. The Bush administration suggested that Chávez was behind the crisis when Assistant Secretary of State Noriega declared: 'Chávez's profile in Bolivia has been very apparent from the beginning.'[78] Certainly, protest leader Evo Morales is an admitted admirer of Chávez, and the Bolivian miners demanded that the government emulate Venezuela by nationalizing the country's oil and gas resources. There is a big difference, however, between 'interference' and 'influence'.[79] Following his ousting, former Bolivian president Mesa stated that he had seen no evidence of Venezuelan interference in the crisis.[80] For his part, Chávez blamed Bolivia's troubles on IMF-imposed neo-liberal policies that had brought economic hardship to the majority of Bolivians.

Given the history of US intervention in Latin America, the Bush administration's finger-pointing at Chávez has come across as a case of the pot calling the kettle black. Several months before the Bolivian crisis, Venezuelan Foreign Minister Rodríguez Araque warned the OAS about the possibility of future US intervention in Venezuela based on the Bush administration's repeated criticisms of Chávez:

The absurdity of the accusations levied against our government would not bother us in the least if a multitude of facts did not exist that prove that when such statements are made, it's because, sooner or later, an attack will follow. This is what occurred to stimulate the coup against the government in April 2002, and also with the attack on the oil industry and the Venezuelan economy in December of the same year. This is what happened with Allende. This is what happened in the Dominican Republic. It is what happened in Guatemala and countless other cases. For the same reason, we cannot dismiss information from our intelligence services concerning the physical liquidation of our president, the same man who has been legitimated every time he has been subjected to the scrutiny of the Venezuelan people.[81]

The Bush administration's policy towards Venezuela has been eerily reminiscent of the US-backed overthrows of the democratically elected Jacobo Arbenz in Guatemala in 1954 and Salvador Allende in Chile in 1973 to which Rodríguez Araque referred. Both Arbenz and Allende implemented social and economic policies that benefited the poor. These policies included placing stricter regulations on foreign companies, which interfered with US economic interests. In both cases, the United States responded by launching propaganda campaigns to demonize the democratically elected leaders. In Chile, the CIA funded a management-led strike to paralyse the country's economy. The US government then supported the coups that finally overthrew Arbenz and Allende. The ensuing US-backed military dictatorships immediately rescinded the social and economic reforms. Finally, in Chile, the brutal US-backed dictatorship of General Augusto Pinochet introduced neo-liberalism to Latin America under the stewardship of the 'Chicago Boys', a group of disciples of US economist Milton Friedman.

In August 2005, Christian evangelist Pat Robertson, a former

Republican presidential candidate and founder of the Christian Coalition of America, validated Venezuelan Foreign Minister Rodríguez Araque's concerns about the possible 'physical liquidation of our president'. During a broadcast of his religious television show, *The 700 Club*, Robertson illustrated the attitude of US conservatives towards Chávez's Bolivarian revolution when he called for the assassination of the Venezuelan leader. The evangelist told more than a million viewers that 'if [Chávez] thinks we're trying to assassinate him, I think that we really ought to go ahead and do it. It's a whole lot cheaper than starting a war.' Robertson went on to link US energy interests to his call for eliminating Chávez: 'And without question, this is a dangerous enemy to our south, controlling a huge pool of oil, that could hurt us very badly. We have the ability to take him out, and I think the time has come that we exercise that ability.'[82] While US State Department spokesman Sean McCormack called Robertson's remarks 'inappropriate', he did not condemn the preacher's call to assassinate Chávez.[83]

The Bush administration has repeatedly claimed that it is primarily concerned with the 'authoritarian' nature of Chávez and his 'meddling' in the region. In truth, it has been the Venezuelan leader's oil policies, his criticism of neo-liberalism and US foreign policy, and the 'bad example' he is setting for other Latin American nations which have made him Washington's nemesis. In April 2005, Secretary of State Rice alluded to the true nature of the Bush administration's problem with the Chávez government. To support her claim that there is 'no reason that the United States should not have good relations with democratically elected governments from across the political spectrum', Rice pointed to Washington's good relations with the 'leftist' regimes in Brazil and Chile. The secretary of state also noted: 'I think that in cases like Brazil or Chile, which is a leftist government, you have very successful economic programs, stable and sound economic policies.'[84] The 'stable and sound economic policies' that Rice was referring to were the neo-liberal economic policies pushed by the IMF and the World Bank that have been implemented by these two 'leftist' governments. In other words, there is no reason that the United States cannot have good relations with democratically elected governments from across the political spectrum as long as they implement the neo-liberal policies that Washington advocates. Venezuela's crime is not so much that its government is leftist, but that it is anti-neo-liberal, thereby acting contrary to the political and economic interests of the United States.

Rice also failed to mention that Venezuela's economy was outperforming the 'very successful economic programs' of both Brazil and Chile, even according to the macroeconomic indicators so highly valued by Washington and the international financial institutions. After enduring an economic decline brought on by the opposition-led general strikes in 2002 and 2003, the Venezuelan economy rebounded in 2004 with a record growth rate of 17.3 per cent, the highest in Latin America. What was even more impressive for an oil-exporting nation of the South was that Venezuela's non-oil economy grew by 17.8 per cent compared with a growth rate of 8.7 per cent for its oil sector.[85]

The Chávez government had achieved economic growth not by implementing neo-liberal policies that reduced government spending and opened the country up to multinational corporations, but by doing the exact opposite. Even more important than the macroeconomic indicators was the fact that the quality of life for many poor Venezuelans was improving. According to World Bank statistics from 2002 – the most recent non-governmental data available – even the early stages of Chávez's 'revolution for the poor' were making a difference as the country registered increases in the percentage of children enrolled in primary schools and in the number of people with access to potable water.[86] An important factor that the statistics failed to illustrate was the palpable sense of empowerment and hope that many poor Venezuelans were beginning to feel.

*Conclusion*

A 2004 United Nations Development Programme (UNDP) report on democracy in Latin America showed that increasing numbers of people in the region were becoming disenchanted with democratically elected leaders who were not addressing their social and economic concerns.[87] Rather than being accountable to their constituents, elected leaders who inherited huge foreign debts and economies devastated by corrupt dictatorships and civil wars were instead beholden to the dictates of the IMF and the World Bank. Consequently, for almost two decades elected officials in Latin America have been implementing the neo-liberal policies demanded by the international financial institutions. The result has been increased inequality, job insecurity due to an expansion of the informal economy, a shrinking social safety net and widespread disillusionment with democracy in many Latin American countries. In Venezuela, the Chávez administration abandoned the neo-liberal model and made the welfare of poor Venezuelans rather than macroeconomic performance the priority of government policy-making. As a result, Chávez has been vindicated repeatedly at the polls and maintains higher approval ratings than any other leader in the western hemisphere, including President Bush.

The Bush administration has found it far more difficult to vilify Chávez in the eyes of the international community than it was to demonize Saddam Hussein. The fact that Chávez was democratically elected, has huge popular support, poses no military threat to the United States and has not committed any crimes against humanity has proved problematic for the Bush White House in its attempts to isolate the Venezuelan leader. It is the Chávez government's social and economic policies that have been the real threat to the interests of both the United States and Venezuela's traditional privileged sectors. And it is the desire to protect these interests that has driven the Bush administration and Venezuela's elites to react so strongly to the Bolivarian revolution. As political scientist Terry Gibbs notes:

> They are bound to find the process of wealth redistribution somewhat painful and to view the policies associated with redistribution as 'authoritarian'. Interestingly, it is not said that this is the bitter medicine that the rich must swallow to see a more just and humane society. Whereas the poor, on the other hand, have been asked to swallow the bitter medicine of neo-liberal austerity for over two decades in the vain hope that some of the wealth would eventually trickle down.[88]

It has become increasingly apparent throughout Latin America that the wealth generated by neo-liberalism is not trickling down to the region's impoverished majority. The Chávez government has responded to this reality by implementing its 'revolution for the poor'. At the time of writing, the Bolivarian revolution was still in its formative stages, although it was clearly at the forefront of the growing challenge to neo-liberalism in Latin America. While poverty in Venezuela in 2004 remained at the same level as when Chávez assumed office five years earlier, the quality of life for impoverished Venezuelans had improved dramatically. The Barrio Adentro Mission had made healthcare and medicines available to the nation's poor population. Additionally, the Mercal Mission's provision of subsidized goods ensured that impoverished Venezuelans could afford basic foodstuffs. Because poverty is often determined by income, subsidized essentials such as food and healthcare can dramatically improve the standard of living for poor people who, technically, still remain in poverty. In its own way, Venezuela has partly achieved what Jordan's Prince Hassan, in his role as president of the Club of Rome, called for when he asked: 'Might we not redefine poverty in terms of human well-being rather than in terms of dollars and cents? Humanise economics and politics, putting human well-being at the centre of national, as well as global, policy-making.'[89]

Proponents of the Bolivarian revolution claim that by ensuring that all Venezuelans have access to essentials such as food, healthcare and education, and by making them stakeholders in the nation's economy through the establishment of agricultural and manufacturing cooperatives, the economic growth experienced in 2004 will not only continue, it will also dramatically improve the quality of life for most citizens and diminish the gross inequalities that marked the neo-liberal era. It is too early to determine if the Bolivarian model will develop into a truly viable economic alternative to neo-liberalism. What is already evident, though, is that Chávez has challenged the traditional doctrine under which oil-rich governments of the South manage their valuable natural resources. Venezuela has shown that oil does not have to be a curse cast upon the majority of a producing country's population; that it does not exist solely to serve the interests of national elites, foreign companies and the economies of the rich industrialized nations of the North.

# Conclusion

For much of the past two decades, the United States has been relatively successful at imposing neo-liberal reforms on oil-rich nations of the South in order to open up their economies, and resources, to multinational energy companies. In countries where neo-liberal reforms were not possible, or proved insufficient, such as in Iraq and Colombia, US military intervention occurred in conjunction with economic intervention. Under President George W. Bush, the historic links between US energy policy and US foreign policy became even more pronounced. The Bush administration's unilateralist and militaristic foreign policy has made evident the cracks in the new world order. In fact, in the face of a growing global resistance to the US-driven neo-liberal project, the Bush administration's military and economic policies have contributed to a new world disorder. US military interventions have further destabilized already embattled nations, while the Bush White House's support for authoritarian regimes and its insistence on promoting 'free market' reforms have spurred civil unrest among peoples of the South adamantly opposed to such policies.

In Iraq, the Bush administration clearly underestimated the degree of resistance that would result from its invasion and occupation of that nation. It has not only had to contend with a major indigenous armed insurgency, supplemented by foreign terrorist activity, but also with the election of a Shiite-led government naturally inclined towards strong relations with a US adversary, Iran, and deeply suspicious of long-term US designs in the country and the region. Ironically, Washington's war on terror in Iraq turned the country into a hotbed for terrorism. In

Central Asia, the United States mostly succeeded in incorporating much of that region into the global capitalist system during the 1990s, albeit at great cost to local populations that have endured dramatic increases in poverty. The Bush administration then used its global war on terror to establish a military presence in several Central Asian nations, although its support for authoritarian regimes has fuelled popular discontent, and in some cases revolt.

In West Africa, the Bush administration has backed corrupt regimes and brutal military apparatuses whose activities, in conjunction with the operations of foreign oil companies, have had devastating human rights and environmental consequences for peoples in oil-producing regions. Similarly, in Colombia, foreign oil companies have benefited from US policies conducted under the flexible banner of the wars on drugs and terror which have contributed to the worst human rights catastrophe in the western hemisphere.

While opposition to US policies is evident in many nations, it is most pronounced in Venezuela, where the people rejected their country's US-backed political and economic elites by electing Hugo Chávez to the presidency in 1998. Chávez has been an outspoken critic of US foreign policy, particularly Washington's neo-liberal project. He has also begun to radically revise the manner in which oil-rich nations of the South manage their natural resources. As a result, Chávez has become a symbol of hope for the region's impoverished majority, who have suffered from two decades of neo-liberalism. Not surprisingly, Chávez has incurred the wrath of the Bush administration, which has employed a variety of tactics in its attempts to achieve regime change in Venezuela – and quash this unwelcome experiment in economic and social justice before the contagion spreads.

Since the end of the cold war, the United States has succeeded in using IMF-imposed neo-liberal reforms to pressure many resource-rich nations of the South into offering oil concession contracts that favour multinational corporations. In Kazakhstan, oil companies pay between 2 and 6 per cent a barrel in royalties. In Colombia, they pay 8 per cent in all but two of the country's oilfields. In sharp contrast, Venezuela's anti-neo-liberal government collects between 20 and 30 per cent a barrel in royalties which, it should be noted, is comparable to the 25 per cent that oil companies operating in Alaska have to pay to the US government.[1] As a result, Venezuela's higher state revenues have allowed the Chávez administration to fund social and economic programmes that address the needs of the country's impoverished majority. Of course, economic sovereignty that allows a national government to increase its revenues does not automatically translate into those revenues being distributed equitably. Many past nationalist governments in the global South did little to help the majority of their populations, which subsisted in poverty. Instead, they served the interests of national elites. Economic sovereignty must exist in conjunction with a democratic system that reflects the aspirations of a majority of a country's citizens.[2] From Washington's perspective, despite official US rhetoric promoting democracy and development, economic sovereignty and participatory democracy in oil-rich nations of the South usually conflict with US political and economic interests, as the case studies in this book make evident. The US dependence on non-renewable fossil fuels to satiate its ever-growing thirst for energy has also set the United States on a collision course with China, whose emergence as a global economic power may well lead to a bipolar world in the coming decades.

The Bush administration has pursued a national energy policy that is neither economically nor environmentally sustainable. As global reserves of non-renewable fossil fuels are depleted, the prices of oil, gas and coal will inevitably increase. Consequently, the US reliance on fossil fuels will drive up the cost of gasoline, electricity and home heating fuel to the point that they are no longer economically sustainable. Some studies claim that global oil production will peak in 2012 or shortly thereafter, and that supplies will begin running low by 2050. Such a scenario makes it clear that alternative sources of energy will inevitably have to be developed at some point in the not too distant future. Adding another dimension to the crisis, as a substantial body of literature and evidence attests, the continued burning of fossil fuels is proving increasingly devastating to the environment. If the United States, China, India and others maintain their present rate of increase with regard to fossil fuel use, there is no telling what irreparable environmental damage will occur by the time the world's oil and coal reserves have been exhausted.

Tragically, a fundamental re-evaluation of US energy policy sooner rather than later appears unlikely as long as US administrations maintain close ties to US energy companies. If it were to occur, such a re-evaluation would likely lead the United States to intensify its efforts to develop alternative energy forms. The technology to develop safe, clean and renewable sources of energy already exists; the only resource lacking is political will. Between 2000 and 2004, the European Union increased its wind-generated electricity production by some 24,500 megawatts compared with an increase of only 4,500 megawatts in the United States during the same period.[3] By 2003, wind was providing 20 per cent of the electricity used in Denmark. In sharp contrast, wind accounted for less than one half of 1 per cent of US electricity usage, despite the fact that 24 per cent of the United States is suitable for utilizing wind to generate electricity. Furthermore, experts claim that wind could satisfy more than 30 per cent of US electricity needs at a per-kilowatt-hour cost that is on a par with oil, coal and natural gas.[4] While the use of wind-generated electricity would not cover all US energy needs, it could be effectively deployed in conjunction with other renewable energy forms such as solar and biomass in much the same way that a combination of oil, gas and coal is currently utilized.

A transition to renewable energy forms is unlikely to occur without direct government intervention of the sort that has occurred in the European Union. Such a transition cannot be left to market forces or it could be too late, both for the global environment and for millions of desperately poor and oppressed people in the South who are the primary victims of Washington's energy-driven foreign policy. As physicist Martin Hoffert has pointed out: 'Most of the modern technology that has been driving the US economy did not come spontaneously from market forces. The Internet was supported for 20 years by the military and for 10 more years by the National Science Foundation before Wall Street found it.'[5] Hoffert has warned that a failure by the US government to develop alternative energy forms will likely lead to an increased use of even dirtier fossil fuels after the world's oil reserves have been depleted: 'If we don't have a proactive energy policy, we'll just wind up using coal, then shale, then tar sands, and it will be a continually diminishing return, and eventually our civilization will collapse. But it doesn't have to end that way. We have a choice.'[6]

The failure of the United States to choose to reduce its reliance on fossil fuels has led it to implement a foreign policy that often undermines both democracy and the economies of oil-rich nations of the South. By diminishing its dependence on fossil fuels, the United States would no longer require a foreign policy partly based on resource exploitation. For oil-rich nations of the South to fully benefit, this change would have to occur in conjunction with a shift away from policies that seek to forcibly incorporate countries into a global capitalist system that mostly benefits the industrial nations of the North. Instead, Washington could initiate a foreign policy that supports democracies that prioritize the needs of their citizens rather than US economic interests, which would go a long way towards achieving sustainable peace and stability. Additionally, because the global market for oil would not disappear overnight, such a shift in US policy would provide an opportunity for resource-rich nations of the South to use their oil wealth to benefit their impoverished populations rather than national elites, multinational companies and the energy needs of Northern nations.

Unfortunately, the Bush administration's insistence on using fossil fuels to meet US energy needs – a stance unlikely to be challenged in its fundamentals by any successor administration, Republican or Democrat – means that US military and economic interventions in oil-rich nations of the South will likely continue. Undoubtedly, such interventions will meet with growing resistance from emerging nationalist movements rooted in ethnicity, culture, religion and ideology. These movements are challenging the neo-liberal belief that the political and economic structures of their nations should be determined in large part by US economic and energy needs. As the Venezuelan example has made clear, nations of the South are seeking increased sovereignty, not only over their resources, but also over their entire political and economic systems. How Washington decides to respond to these demands for independence will play a huge role in determining the sort of world we will live in during the twenty-first century. For its part, the Bush administration has responded with interventionist policies, particularly with regard to securing access to oil, that have only highlighted and exacerbated the global disorder that so often occurs when a hegemonic power begins its decline.

# Notes

## Introduction

1 'US Daily average supply and disposition of crude oil and petroleum products, 2004', US Department of Energy, 2004.

2 'President George W. Bush: top industries', Center for Responsive Politics, 21 July 2005.

## 1 Iraq

1 Dana Milbank, 'Upbeat tone ended with war: officials' forecasts are questioned', *Washington Post*, 29 March 2003.

2 Cesar G. Soriano and Steven Komarow, 'Poll: Iraqis out of patience', *USA Today*, 30 April 2004.

3 'US death toll in Iraq passes 1,000', CNN, 8 September 2004.

4 Les Roberts, Riyadh Lafta, Richard Garfield, Jamal Khudhairi and Gilbert Burnham, 'Mortality before and after the 2003 invasion of Iraq: cluster sample survey', *Lancet*, 29 September 2004.

5 James Akins, 'Interview with James Akins', PBS, *Frontline: The Survival of Saddam*, January 2000.

6 Dr Sami Abdul-Rahman, 'Interview with Dr. Sami Abdul-Rahman', PBS, *Frontline: The Survival of Saddam*, January 2000.

7 Efraim Karsh, 'Making Iraq safe for democracy', *Commentary*, April 2003.

8 'Whatever happened to the Iraqi Kurds?', Human Rights Watch, 11 March 1991.

9 'Petroleum imports by country of origin, 1960–2004', *Annual Energy Review 2004*, US Department of Energy.

10 Akins, 'Interview with James Akins'.

11 'Declaration of Howard Teicher', United States District Court, Southern District of Florida, 31 January 1995.

12 'Background on Iraqi use of chemical weapons', US State Department, 21 November 1983.

13 'Information memorandum: Iraq use of chemical weapons', US State Department, 1 November 1983.

14 Ibid.

15 'Rumsfeld mission: December 20 meeting with Iraqi [secret]', US State Department, 21 December 1983.

16 'Department press briefing: March 30, 1984', US State Department, 30 March 1984.

17 'US dual-use exports to Iraq: specific actions', US State Department, 9 May 1984.

18 Senator Donald W. Reigle, 'The Reigle Report: US chemical and biological warfare-related dual use exports to Iraq and their possible impact on the health consequences of the Gulf War', US Senate, 25 May 1994.

19  Rep. Henry B. Gonzalez, 'Details on Iraq's procurement network', Congressional Record, 10 August 1992.

20  Reigle, 'The Reigle Report'.

21  Akins, 'Interview with James Akins'.

22  Tarik Kafala, 'Flashback: Desert Storm', BBC News, 15 January 2001.

23  Frank Anderson, 'Interview with Frank Anderson', PBS, *Frontline: The Survival of Saddam*, January 2000.

24  Sarah Zaidi and Mary C. Smith Fawzi, 'Health of Baghdad's children', *Lancet*, 2 December 1995.

25  'Autopsy of a disaster: The US sanctions policy on Iraq', Institute for Public Accuracy, 13 November 1998.

26  'Iraq surveys show "humanitarian emergency"', UNICEF, 12 August 1999.

27  Akins, 'Interview with James Akins'.

28  'Oil for food – food basket adequacy assessment survey', WFP Iraq–North Coordination Office, November 2000.

29  'Iraqi oil sales fund humanitarian action', Office of the Iraqi Programme Oil-for-Food, United Nations, 21 November 2003.

30  'Petroleum imports by country of origin, 1963–2003', *Annual Energy Review 2003*, US Department of Energy.

31  Gellman Barton, 'Annan suspicious of UNSCOM role', *Washington Post*, 6 January 1999.

32  Scott Ritter, 'Interview with Scott Ritter', PBS, *Frontline: Spying on Saddam*, April 1999.

33  'Authorization for use of military force against Iraq, Resolution 2002', US Congress, 16 October 2002.

34  'Resolution 1441 (2002)', United Nations Security Council, 8 November 2002.

35  Ambassador John D. Negroponte, 'Explanation of vote by Ambassador John D. Negroponte, United States Permanent Representative to the United Nations, following the vote on the Iraq resolution, Security Council, November 8, 2002', United States Mission to the United Nations, 8 November 2002.

36  Ibid.

37  President George W. Bush, 'President Bush outlines Iraqi threat', Office of the Press Secretary, White House, 7 October 2002.

38  Anton LaGuardia and Toby Harnden, 'Saddam is "Months Away from a Nuclear Bomb"', *Daily Telegraph*, 9 September 2002.

39  Vice-President Dick Cheney, 'Vice President speaks at VFW 103rd National Convention', Office of the Press Secretary, White House, 26 August 2002.

40  Secretary Donald H. Rumsfeld, 'Testimony of US Secretary of Defense Donald H. Rumsfeld before the Senate Armed Forces Committee regarding Iraq', US Department of Defense, 19 September 2002.

41  President George W. Bush, 'Radio address by the President to the nation', Office of the Press Secretary, White House, 28 September 2002.

42  Bush, 'President Bush outlines Iraqi threat'.

43  Secretary Donald H. Rumsfeld, 'Secretary Rumsfeld contrasts Iraq and North Korea', US Department of Defense, 20 January 2003.

44  President George W. Bush, 'President delivers "State of the Union"', Office of the Press Secretary, White House, 28 January 2003.

45 Secretary Colin L. Powell, 'Remarks to the United Nations Security Council', US Department of State, 5 February 2003.

46 President George W. Bush and President Alvaro Uribe, 'President Bush, Colombia President Uribe discuss terrorism', Office of the Press Secretary, White House, 25 September 2002.

47 Greg Miller, 'Cheney is adamant on Iraq "evidence"', *Los Angeles Times*, 23 January 2003.

48 'Americans on Iraq and the UN inspections II', PIPA/Knowledge Networks Poll, 21 February 2003.

49 President George W. Bush, 'Presidential letter', Office of the Press Secretary, White House, 18 March 2003.

50 'Tripartite declaration on Iraq by France, Russia and Germany', Permanent Mission of Germany to the United Nations, 5 March 2003.

51 'Security Council bypassed, inspections swept aside by *Operation Iraqi Freedom*', *Disarmament Diplomacy*, April/May 2003.

52 Secretary-General Kofi Annan, 'The Hague, Netherlands – Secretary General's press conference', UN News Centre, 10 March 2003.

53 Cesar G. Soriano and Steven Komarow, 'Poll: Iraqis out of patience', *USA Today*, 30 April 2004.

54 Jason P. Howe, e-mail letter to author from Baghdad, 20 March 2004.

55 Darrell Anderson, interview with author, Sydney, Nova Scotia, Canada, 12 March 2005.

56 Soriano and Komarow, 'Poll: Iraqis out of patience'.

57 Roberts et al., 'Mortality before and after the 2003 invasion of Iraq'.

58 Celina R. De Leon, 'A soldier speaks: Kelly Dougherty', Altertnet, 24 August 2005.

59 President George W. Bush, 'Remarks by the President after meeting with members of the Congressional Conference Committee on Energy Legislation', Office of the Press Secretary, White House, 17 September 2003.

60 President George W. Bush, 'President Bush addresses United Nations General Assembly', Office of the Press Secretary, White House, 23 September 2003.

61 'The 9-11 Commission Report', National Commission on Terrorist Attacks upon the United States, 22 July 2004.

62 Ibid.

63 Hans Blix, 'Notes for the briefing of the Security Council on the thirteenth quarterly report of UNMOVIC', United Nations, 5 June 2003.

64 David Kay, 'Statement by David Kay on the interim progress report on the activities of the Iraq Survey Group (ISG)', House Permanent Select Committee on Intelligence, House Committee on Appropriations, Subcommittee on Defense, and the Senate Select Committee on Intelligence, 2 October 2003.

65 Ibid.

66 'The 9-11 Commission Report'.

67 Seymour M. Hersh, 'Torture at Abu Ghraib', *New Yorker*, 30 April 2004.

68 Ibid.

69 Robert Burns/Associated Press, 'Few foreigners are among insurgents captured in Fallujah', *Boston Globe*, 15 November 2004.

70 Howe, e-mail letter to author.

**One**

71 Paul Richter, 'US airs critical views of Arab TV', *Los Angeles Times*, 28 April 2004.

72 Harvey McGavin, 'The civilian death toll', *Independent*, 15 November 2004.

73 Anderson, interview with author.

74 Secretary-General Kofi Annan, 'Excerpts: Annan interview', BBC News, 16 September 2004.

75 President George W. Bush, 'Middle East Free Trade Initiative', Office of the United States Trade Representative, 27 February 2003.

76 William I. Robinson, 'What to expect from US "democracy promotion" in Iraq', *Focus on the Global South*, 1 July 2004.

77 Akins, 'Interview with James Akins'.

78 'National survey of Iraq June 2004', Oxford Research Council, June 2004.

79 Michael Isikoff and Mark Hosenball, 'Rethinking the Chalabi connection', *Newsweek,* 20 May 2004.

80 Richard Sale/UPI, 'The NSA's tangle with Chalabi', *Washington Times*, 29 July 2004.

81 Ariana Eunjung Cha, '$1.9 billion of Iraq's money goes to US contractors', *Washington Post*, 4 August 2004.

82 Ibid.

83 Greg Palast, 'Secret US plans for Iraq's oil', BBC News, 17 March 2005.

84 James A. Paul, 'The Iraqi oil bonanza: estimating future profits', Global Policy Forum, 28 January 2004.

85 David R. Francis, 'Exploring new oil fields in Iraq: a risky business', *Christian Science Monitor*, 3 January 2005.

86 Laurence Frost, 'Oil companies hopeful on Iraqi politics', Associated Press, 14 March 2005.

87 Tom Burgis, 'Iraq: the carve-up begins', *London Line*, 23 June 2005.

88 Ibid.

89 Francis, 'Exploring new oil fields in Iraq'.

90 Adel Abdul Mahdi, 'A conversation with Adel Abdul Mahdi, the Iraqi Minister of Finance', American Enterprise Institute, 6 October 2004.

91 'Iraq official vows tough action', CBS News, 18 June 2004.

92 'Children "starving" in new Iraq', BBC News, 30 March 2005.

93 David Enders and Daniel Howdon, 'Iraqi vote gives Shia parties a mandate for Islamic law', *Independent*, 14 February 2005.

94 Robin Wright, 'Iraq winners allied with Iran are the opposite of US vision', *Washington Post*, 14 February 2005.

95 Ibid.

96 Robinson, 'What to expect from US "democracy promotion".

## 2 *Central Asia*

1 'Oil: the world over a barrel', CBC *Newsworld*, 28 July 2004.

2 Deputy Secretary Strobe Talbott, 'A farewell to Flashman: American policy in the Caucasus and Central Asia', US Department of State dispatch, July 1997.

3 George Monbiot, 'Oil, Afghanistan and America's pipedream', *Dawn* magazine, 25 October 2001.

4 'The Silk Road Strategy Act of 1998', US Senate Committee on Foreign Relations, 9 October 1998.

5 'Silk Road Strategy Act of 1999', US Congress, 10 March 1999.

6 'Uzbekistan: country reports on human rights practices – 2000', US Department of State, 23 February 2001.

7 Shahram Akbarzadeh, 'Keeping Central Asia stable', *Third World Quarterly*, 25(4), 2004.

8 Talbott, 'A farewell to Flashman'.

9 Akbarzadeh, 'Keeping Central Asia Stable'.

10 'IMF approves stand-by credit for Kazakhstan', International Monetary Fund, 5 June 1995.

11 'IMF Concludes Article IV consultation with the Republic of Kazakhstan', International Monetary Fund, 1 July 1998.

12 Ibid.

13 'Legislative alert: changes to subsurface use taxation discussed in the Senate', Ernst and Young, 27 November 2003.

14 'Country analysis briefs: Venezuela', US Department of Energy, June 2004.

15 'OPIC welcomes Kazakh trade minister, urges US investment', Overseas Private Investment Fund, 21 December 2001.

16 '22 USC Sec. 2191', Office of the Law Revision Counsel, US House of Representatives, 6 January 2003.

17 'OPIC welcomes Kazakh trade minister'.

18 'IMF concludes Article IV consultation with the Republic of Kazakhstan'.

19 'Tengizchevroil celebrates two-year anniversary operating the giant Tengiz oil field in Kazakhstan', ChevronTexaco, 6 April 1995.

20 'ChevronTexaco in Eurasia', ChevronTexaco, 2004.

21 Heather Timmons, 'Kazakhstan: oil majors agree to develop field', *New York Times*, 26 February 2004.

22 'Kazakhstan country brief 2004', World Bank Group, September 2004.

23 Burt Herman, 'The losing side of the Kazakhstan oil boom', Associated Press, 21 July 2004.

24 'ChevronTexaco in Eurasia'.

25 'Poverty in Kazakhstan: causes and cures', United Nations Development Programme (UNDP), 11 May 2004.

26 'ChevronTexaco reports net income of $1.7 billion in fourth quarter and $7.2 billion for year', ChevronTexaco, 30 January 2004.

27 'Kazakhstan: living standards during the transition', World Bank Group, 1998.

28 'Poverty in Kazakhstan: causes and cures'.

29 'Measurement of poverty in Kazakhstan', United Nations Economic and Social Commission for Asia and the Pacific (UNESCAP), 13 February 2004.

30 'Poverty in Kazakhstan: causes and cures'.

31 Dr Alexandr Nemets and Dr Thomas Torda, 'The battle for Kazakhstan continues', NewsMax, 27 June 2002.

32 Office for Democratic Institutions and Human Rights, 'The Republic of Kazakhstan presidential elections 10 January 1999, Assessment Mission', Organization for Security and Cooperation in Europe, 5 February 1999.

33 Christopher H. Smith, 'Kazakhstan's presidential election', Congressional Record, 23 February 1999.

34 'Corruption Perceptions Index 2004', Transparency International, October 2004.

35 Associated Press, 'Tax rap for bribed oil exec', CBS News, 13 June 2003.

36 'Fuelling poverty: oil, war and corruption', Christian Aid, 12 May 2003.

37 'Kazakhstan: major oil and gas projects', US Department of Energy, July 2002.

38 'Company news: oil and gas', *Kazakhstan News*, 21 September 2004.

39 President Nursultan Nazarbayev, 'Democracy, with traditional values', *Kazakhstan's Echo*, 12 February 2004.

40 'Kazakhstan country analysis brief', US Department of Energy, November 2004.

41 Carol Migdalovitz, 'Armenia–Azerbaijan conflict', Congressional Research Division, 8 August 2003.

42 'World Report 2003: Azerbaijan', Human Rights Watch, 14 January 2003.

43 Dan Morgan and David B. Ottaway, 'Azerbaijan's riches alter the chess-board', *Washington Post*, 4 October 1998.

44 'IMF approves stand-by credit and second STF drawing for Azerbaijan Republic', International Monetary Fund, 17 November 1995.

45 'IMF approves combined ESAF/EFF financing for Azerbaijan', International Monetary Fund, 20 December 1996.

46 Ibid.

47 'IMF concludes Article IV consultation with Azerbaijan Republic', International Monetary Fund, 9 August 1999.

48 'Azerbaijan Human Development Report 2000', United Nations Development Programme (UNDP), March 2001.

49 Ibid.

50 Ibid.

51 'IMF approves US$18 million PRGF disbursement to the Azerbaijan Republic and requests for waivers of performance criteria and extension of arrangement', International Monetary Fund, 15 May 2003.

52 'USOCAR: a fitting partner for the world's great oil firms', *International Reports*, 2001.

53 'Turkmenistan Country Brief 2004', World Bank Group, September 2004.

54 Ibid.

55 Ibid.

56 'World Report 2003: Turkmenistan', Human Rights Watch, 14 January 2003.

57 John J. Maresca, 'Testimony before the House Committee on International Relations, Sub Committee on Asia and the Pacific', House Committee on International Relations, Sub Committee on Asia and the Pacific, 12 February 1998.

58 'Afghanistan country report on human rights practices for 1997', US Department of State, 30 January 1998.

59 'Country analysis briefs: Afghanistan', US Department of Energy, September 2001.

60 Deputy Secretary Strobe Talbott, 'A farewell to Flashman'.

61 'Oil: the world over a barrel'.

62 'World Report 2003: Uzbekistan', Human Rights Watch, 14 January 2003.

63 'World Report 2000: Uzbekistan', Human Rights Watch, January 2000.

64 'World Report 2003: Uzbekistan'.

65 'US assistance to Uzbekistan – fiscal year 2002', US Department of State, 9 December 2002.

66 Richard Boucher, 'Secretary of State decision not to certify Uzbekistan', US Department of State, 13 July 2004.

67 'Top US general tours Central Asian capitals, dispenses aid to Uzbekistan', *Eurasia Insight*, 13 August 2004.

68 R. Jeffrey Smith and Glenn Kessler, 'US opposed calls at NATO for probe of Uzbek killings', *Washington Post,* 14 June 2005.

69 'Uzbekistan: interview with Craig Murray, former UK ambassador', IRIN News, 18 February 2004.

70 Secretary Donald Rumsfeld, 'Secretary Rumsfeld and Ambassador Jon Purnell press conference in Uzbekistan', Department of Defense, 24 February 2004.

71 '"Hundreds killed" in Uzbekistan violence', *Guardian*, 14 May 2005.

72 'World Report 2003: Kyrgyzstan', Human Rights Watch, 14 January 2003.

73 Michael Mainville, 'US bases overseas show new strategy', *Pittsburgh Post-Gazette*, 26 July 2004.

74 'World Report 2003: Kyrgyzstan'.

75 Antoine Blua, 'Central Asia: Rumsfeld wraps up visit to Uzbekistan, Kazakhstan', Radio Free Europe/Radio Liberty, 20 February 2004.

## *3 West Africa*

1 Jim Landers, 'African oil fields: rewards and risks', *Dallas Morning News*, 6 October 2004.

2 'Corruptions Perceptions Index 2004', Transparency International, 20 October 2004.

3 'World proved reserves of oil and natural gas', US Department of Energy, 9 November 2004.

4 'Nigeria: country brief', World Bank Group, September 2004.

5 'The world factbook: Nigeria', US Central Intelligence Agency, 27 January 2005.

6 'Nigeria brief: harnessing gas', Shell Petroleum Development Company, August 1996.

7 'Human Rights Watch world report 1992', Human Rights Watch, 1992.

8 'Nigeria's drilling fields', *Multinational Monitor*, January/February 1995.

9 'Human Rights Watch World Report 1994: Nigeria', Human Rights Watch, 1994.

10 'Nigeria's drilling fields'.

11 Ibid.

12 'Diary: A letter from Ken Saro-Wiwa in prison', *Drillbits & Tailings*, 9 November 1999.

13 'Vital statistics: a sampling of Shell's activities in Nigeria over the last four years', *Drillbits & Tailings*, 9 November 1999.

14 Cameron Duodu, 'Shell admits importing guns for Nigerian police', *Observer*, 28 January 1996.

15 *Wiwa v. Royal Dutch Shell*, United States District Court for the Southern District of New York, 28 February 2002.

## Three

16 'US/Indonesia: Bush backtracks on corporate responsibility', Human Rights Watch, 7 August 2002. See also, William H. Taft IV, 'Letter to Honorable Louis F. Oberdorfer', Human Rights Watch, 29 July 2002.

17 Jim Lobe, 'Villagers vs oil giant: Ashcroft to the rescue', Inter Press Service, 19 May 2003.

18 'Warning to the boardroom: don't buddy up to corrupt, brutal regimes', Globalvision News Network, September 2001.

19 Haider Rizvi, 'Shell ordered to stop wasteful, poisonous "gas flaring" in Nigeria', *One World*, 15 November 2005.

20 'Behind the Shine: the other Shell report 2003', Friends of the Earth, 2004.

21 Michael Fleshman, 'Nigeria transition watch number 9: report from Nigeria 2', Africa Fund, 17 June 1999.

22 'Behind the Shine: the other Shell report 2003'.

23 Emeka Duruigbo, 'Oil development in Nigeria: a critical investigation of Chevron Corporation's performance in the Niger river delta', California Global Corporate Accountability Project, 2001.

24 Emeka Duruigbo, phone interview with author, 14 April 2005.

25 Michael Peel, 'Energy special: oil in troubled waters', *Financial Times*, 25 March 2005.

26 'Bowoto v. ChevronTexaco', EarthRights International, 29 November 2004.

27 Emeka Duruigbo, 'Oil development in Nigeria'.

28 'Country reports on human rights practices for 1999: Nigeria', US Department of State, February 2000.

29 'Rivers and blood: guns, oil and power in Nigeria's Rivers State', Human Rights Watch, February 2005.

30 Ibid.

31 'Warlord targets Nigerian oil', Associated Press, 1 July 2004.

32 'Rivers and blood'.

33 Ibid.

34 Duruigbo, 'Oil development in Nigeria'.

35 'A crude awakening: the role of the oil and banking industries in Angola's civil war and the plunder of state assets', Global Witness, December 1999.

36 'Country analysis briefs: Angola', US Department of Energy, January 2005.

37 Ibid.

38 'Time for transparency: coming clean on oil, mining and gas revenues', Global Witness, March 2004.

39 'Is the Angolan war really over?', *Alexander's Gas and Oil Connections*, 27 November 2002.

40 'World Report 2005: Angola', Human Rights Watch, January 2005.

41 'Angolan enclave of Cabinda blames oil for humanitarian misery', *Alexander's Gas and Oil Connections*, 22 April 2004.

42 'Angola: account for missing oil revenues', Human Rights Watch, 13 January 2004.

43 Fabrice Lhomme, 'Un témoignage éclaire les dessous des ventes d'armes à l'Angola', *Le Monde*, 22 April 2003.

44 'All the presidents' men: the devastating story of oil and banking in Angola's privatised war', Global Witness, March 2002.

45 Ibid.

46 Ibid.

47 Ibid.

48 'Time for transparency'.

49 'Angola: selected issues and statistical appendix', International Monetary Fund, April 2005.

50 Nick Tattersall, 'West African oil gives US new security challenge', Reuters, 17 December 2004.

51 'World Report 2003: Nigeria', Human Rights Watch, January 2003.

52 Gilbert Da Costa, 'US general proposes help in "monitoring" unstable West Africa oil gulf', Associated Press, 12 July 2004.

53 Nico Colombant, 'US helps West African navies', Voice of America, 1 February 2005.

54 'A crude awakening'.

55 'Africa: supporting human rights and democracy – the US record 2002–2003', US Department of State, 24 June 2003.

56 'Equatorial Guinea: country reports on human rights practices – 2004', US Department of State, 28 February 2005.

57 Ken Silverstein, 'US oil politics in the "Kuwait of Africa"', *The Nation*, 4 April 2002.

58 Ibid.

59 'Equatorial Guinea: Country Reports on Human Rights Practices – 2004'.

60 Alex Belida, 'US re-opening of embassy in oil-rich Equatorial Guinea not without controversy', Voice of America, 31 October 2003.

61 Ibid.

62 'Gabon: country reports on human rights practices – 2004', US Department of State, 28 February 2005.

63 'Background note: Gabon', US Department of State, April 2005.

64 Andy Denwood, 'Gabon's oil boom hangover', BBC News, 11 October 2004.

65 'Country analysis briefs: Gabon', US Department of Energy, November 2004.

66 'VAALCO Energy announces $30 million revolving credit facility with the International Finance Corporation', VAALCO Energy, 13 June 2005.

67 'VAALCO Energy announces 223% increase in first quarter 2005 results', VAALCO Energy, 2 May 2005.

68 'Background note: Gabon'.

69 'Gabon: oil pact with China aims to boost falling reserves', *IRIN News*, 5 February 2004.

70 'Country analysis briefs: Nigeria', US Department of Energy, April 2005.

71 Don Lee, 'China barrels ahead in oil market', *Los Angeles Times*, 14 November 2004.

## 4 Colombia

1 'Country analysis briefs: Colombia', US Department of Energy, June 2005.

2 Steven Dudley, 'Colombia's hopes for great oil field likely dashed', Knight Ridder Newspapers, 26 August 2004.

3 'Colombia: country reports on human rights practices – 2004', US Department of State, 28 February 2005.

4 Ana Carrigan, 'Colombia's best chance', *The Nation*, 21 January 1999.

5 Scott Wilson, 'Colombia's rebel zone: world apart', *Washington Post*, 18 October 2003.

6 'UN envoy triggers a debate in Colombia', Associated Press, 22 May 2003.

7 Liam Craig-Best, 'An interview with ELN commander Antonio García', *Colombia Journal,* 27 August 2000.

8 Scott Dalton, 'Kidnapped in Arauca', *NACLA Report on the Americas*, January/February 2003.

9 'Colombia: country reports on human rights practices – 2001', US Department of State, 4 March 2002.

10 President George H. W. Bush, 'Statement on trade initiatives for the Andean region', George Bush Presidential Library and Museum, 1 November 1989.

11 'Colombia at a glance: 1999', World Bank Group, 29 May 2000.

12 'Colombia poverty report', World Bank Group, March 2002.

13 'Colombia, UN discussing anti-coca mycoherbicide cooperation', US Department of State, 17 July 2000.

14 Dr Edgar Perea, interview with author, 10 February 2001, La Hormiga, Putumayo, Colombia. Author witnessed food crops destroyed by aerial fumigations in Putumayo.

15 Jair Giovani Ruiz, interview with author, 20 August 2002, Puerto Asís, Putumayo, Colombia.

16 Mario Cabal, interview with author, 20 August 2002, Puerto Asís, Putumayo, Colombia.

17 Catalina Diaz, interview with author, 22 August 2002, Bogotá, Colombia. All requests by this writer to obtain an interview with US embassy officials to discuss Plan Colombia were refused.

18 Incident witnessed by author, 17 August 2002, Putumayo, Colombia.

19 Bodies of the victims witnessed by author. Two local residents told author that paramilitaries were responsible for the massacre, 18 August 2002, Puerto Asís, Putumayo, Colombia.

20 'Clinton leaves Colombia after defending aid package', CNN, 30 August 2000.

21 'Plan Colombia: US anti drug aid fueling civil war', Washington Office on Latin America, 2001.

22 Ingrid Vaicius and Adam Isacson, 'The "war on drugs" meets the "war on terror"', Center for International Policy, February 2003.

23 Ibid.

24 'Testimony of Francis X. Taylor, Coordinator of Counterterrorism', House Committee on International Relations, US House of Representatives, 10 October 2001.

25 Secretary Colin L. Powell, 'Testimony on the international campaign against terrorism', Senate Foreign Relations Committee, US Senate, 25 October 2001.

26 Sen. Bob Graham, 'Excerpt from press conference with Sen. Bob Graham (D-Florida)', Center for International Policy, 25 October 2001.

27 'Supplemental aid for 2002', Center for International Policy, 1 August 2003.

28  General James Hill, 'Regarding US narcotics policy in Colombia', Senate Caucus on International Narcotics Control, US Senate, 3 June 2003.

29  'Statement of Lawrence P. Meriage, Vice President, Executive Services and Public Affairs, Occidental Oil and Gas Corporation', House Government Reform Subcommittee on Criminal Justice, Drug Policy and Human Resources, US House of Representatives, 15 February 2000.

30  'The 2003 aid request', Center for International Policy, 24 February 2003.

31  'Colombia: human rights concerns raised by the security arrangements of transnational oil companies', Human Rights Watch, April 1998.

32  Steven Dudley, 'In Colombia, a dispute fueled by oil', *Washington Post*, 21 February 2000.

33  T. Christian Miller, 'Cutoff of aid a sign to Bogotá', *Los Angeles Times*, 14 January 2003.

34  Daniel Kovalik, 'US State Department intervenes to protect Occidental against lawsuit for human rights crimes', ZNet, 13 January 2005.

35  Marta Lucía Ramírez, 'Democratic security, transnational threats and the rule of law', Colombian Ministry of Defence, 8 October 2002.

36  Frances Robles, 'Colombian court nullifies tough security measures', *Miami Herald,* 28 November 2002.

37  'A laboratory of war: repression and violence in Arauca', Amnesty International, 20 April 2004.

38  Secretary Colin Powell, 'Press conference from Bogotá', US Department of State, 4 December 2002.

39  'Alerta frente a las cifras gobernamentales sobre derechos humanos en Colombia', Comisión Colombiana de Juristas, 4 July 2003. See also 'The effectiveness of the Colombian democratic security and defence policy', Colombian Ministry of Defense, August 2003.

40  'The effectiveness of the Colombian democratic security and defence policy'.

41  Amaranta Wright, 'In Colombia's jungles, echoes of Argentina's "disappeared"', *San Francisco Chronicle*, 12 January 2004.

42  'UN urges Colombia rights action', BBC News, 14 July 2005.

43  Wright, 'In Colombia's jungles'. See also Alfredo Castro, 'Colombia's disappeared: 25 people a week go missing', *Counterpunch*, 29 July 2002.

44  'Desplazamiento en cifras', Human Rights and Displacement Consultancy (CODHES), 31 March 2005.

45  'Internal displacement in the Americas', Global IDP Project of the Norwegian Refugee Council, March 2005.

46  Chip Mitchell, 'Government reduces aid to the displaced', *Colombia Week*, 5 April 2004.

47  Harvey Suarez Morales, interview with author, 13 June 2003, Bogotá, Colombia.

48  'Amnesty International report 2004: Colombia', Amnesty International, 26 May 2004.

49  'Colombia: country reports on human rights practices – 2002', US Department of State, 31 March 2003.

50  'Colombia: rights defenders under attack', Inter Press Service, 1 September 2003.

**Four**

51 'Colombia: en contravía de las recomendaciones internacionales sobre derechos humanos, balance de la política de seguridad democrática y la situación de derechos humanos y derecho humanitario, agosto 2002 a agosto 2004', Colombian Commission for Jurists (CCJ), 15 October 2004.

52 'Colombia: rights defenders under attack'.

53 'El embrujo autoritario: primer año de gobierno de Álvaro Uribe Vélez', Plataforma Colombiana de Derechos Humanos, Democracia y Desarollo, September 2003.

54 President Alvaro Uribe, 'Palabras del Presidente Uribe en posesión de nuevo comandante de la FAC', Presidency of the Republic, 8 September 2003.

55 'Democratic security and defence policy', Colombian Ministry of Defence, 16 June 2003.

56 President Alvaro Uribe, 'Discurso del Presidente Uribe en la Asamblea de Naciones Unidas', Presidency of the Republic, 30 September 2003. See also US Secretary Colin L. Powell, 'Remarks after meeting with Colombian President Alvaro Uribe', US Department of State, 30 September 2003.

57 Commander Enrique, interview with author, 7 February 2001, La Hormiga, Putumayo, Colombia.

58 'Statement of Lawrence P. Meriage'.

59 Adam Isacson, 'Firm hand, large heart', *Human Rights Dialogue*, Fall 2002.

60 'The massacre at Mulatos in Colombia: an investigative report', Colombia Support Network, 26 June 2005.

61 James J. Brittain, 'The reactionary restriction of justice in Colombia', *Colombia Journal*, 2 May 2005.

62 'Listado de victimas de violencia sociopolítica en Colombia', Colombian Commission of Jurists, August 2004.

63 Juan Forero and Monica Trujillo, 'New Colombia law grants concessions to paramilitaries', *New York Times*, 23 June 2005.

64 'Colombia: new report reveals paramilitary demobilisation strategy is a deadly illusion', Amnesty International, 2 September 2005.

65 'IMF approves a US$2.1 billion stand-by credit for Colombia', International Monetary Fund, 15 January 2003.

66 John Price, 'Colombia: balancing war with growth', Infoamericas Tendencias: Latin American Market Report, 5 July 2002.

67 'Economist Intelligence Unit – executive briefing: Colombia', *Economist*, 1 December 2004.

68 'Colombia breaks up state agencies in deficit-cutting plan', Bloomberg News, 27 June 2003.

69 Phil Stewart, 'Oil declining, Colombia offers new deal in Houston', Reuters, 9 March 2004.

70 Ecopetrol official, interview with author, 5 March 2004, Bogotá, Colombia.

71 'Harken energy subsidiary acquires new 85,000 acre exploration and production contract for the Los Hatos area in Colombia', Harken Energy, 4 November 2004.

72 José Armando Zamora, 'El contrato de asociación no da más', *Carta Petrolera*, August–October 2003.

73 Spokesperson for Occidental Petroleum, interview with author, 10 February 2003, Bogotá, Colombia.

74 'The real costs of pipeline protection in Arauca: corporate welfare with deadly consequences', Witness for Peace, July 2002. Witness for Peace's $3.70 per barrel figure was based on the $98 million in aid requested by the Bush administration. Congress approved only $93 million, which brought the cost of subsidization down to $3.55 per barrel.

75 'Protecting the pipeline: the US military mission expands', Washington Office on Latin America, May 2003.

76 Spokesperson for Occidental Petroleum interview.

77 Major Joaquín Enrique Aldana, interview with author, 4 February 2003, Saravena, Arauca, Colombia.

78 Ibid.

79 Mayor José Trinidad Sierra, interview with author, 6 February 2003, Saravena, Arauca, Colombia.

80 Brigadier General Carlos Lemus, interview with author, 9 August 2002, Arauca City, Arauca, Colombia.

81 Gary Marx, 'Imperiled pipeline gets US troops in Colombia', *Chicago Tribune*, 12 November 2002.

82 'Fear for safety/possible disappearance: Colombia indigenous and peasant farmer communities in Tame municipality, department of Arauca', Amnesty International, 3 June 2003.

83 'Amnesty International Report 2004', Amnesty International, 26 May 2004.

84 US Army special forces soldier, interview with author, 5 February 2003, Saravena, Arauca, Colombia.

85 Author witnessed activities on 6 February 2003, Saravena, Arauca, Colombia.

86 Paola Alzate Acosta, interview with author, 6 February 2003, Saravena, Arauca, Colombia.

87 Ibid.

88 Interview conducted by Colombian human rights group with a local resident on 5 February 2003 in Saravena, Arauca, Colombia.

89 US Army special forces soldier, interview with author.

90 'Colombia: trade unionists and human rights defenders under attack', Amnesty International, 27 August 2003.

91 Ibid.

92 Mayor Jorge Bernal and deputy mayor, interview with author, 9 June 2003, Tame, Arauca, Colombia.

93 'Colombia: mass arrests of politicians', Associated Press, 22 October 2003.

94 '25 Colombians suspected of rebel ties', Associated Press, 21 October 2003.

95 'Colombia cracks down', Washington Office on Latin America, July 2002.

96 Juan Forero, 'Bogotá says army killed union chiefs', *New York Times*, 8 September 2004.

97 Fernando Londoño Hoyos, 'Quién defiende a los defensores?', *El Tiempo*, 21 July 2005.

98 T. Christian Miller, 'US troops answered oil firm's pleas', *Los Angeles Times*, 30 December 2004.

99 Lieutenant Colonel Francisco Javier Cruz, interview with author, 2 March 2004, Orito, Putumayo, Colombia.

**Four**

100 Edgar Dyes, phone interview with author, 15 March 2004.

101 Cruz interview.

102 Steven Benedetti, interview with author, 5 March 2004, Bogotá, Colombia.

103 Cruz interview.

104 Anonymous, interview with author, 2 March 2004, Orito, Putumayo, Colombia.

105 Javier, interview with author, 2 March 2004, Orito, Putumayo, Colombia.

106 Ibid.

107 Jason Webb, 'Colombian rebels free soldier in gesture on hostages', Reuters, 22 July 2005.

108 Anonymous, interview with author, 4 March 2004, Puerto Asís, Putumayo, Colombia.

109 'Colombia: en contravía de las recomendaciones internacionales sobre derechos humanos'.

110 'Colombia: UN Human Rights office calls for end to arbitrary detentions', UN News Centre, 18 August 2005.

## 5 Venezuela

1 Douglas McKinnon, 'Is Venezuela going nuclear? Conversations with Iran give cause for concern', *Houston Chronicle*, 22 May 2005.

2 'Country analysis briefs: Venezuela', US Department of Energy, June 2004.

3 'OPEC revenues: country details', US Department of Energy, June 2005.

4 César Baena, 'The internationalization strategy of PDVSA: a policy-making analysis', Centre d'Etudes et de Recherches Internationales, November 1999.

5 Bernard Mommer, 'Venezuelan oil politics at the crossroads', Oxford Institute for Energy Studies, March 2001.

6 Paul Krugman, 'Venezuela's debt a monument to domestic mismanagement', Unofficial Paul Krugman archive, 27 March 1989.

7 'Venezuela: financial position in the Fund as of April 30, 2005', International Monetary Fund, 30 April 2005.

8 'Venezuela: financial position in the fund as of April 30, 2005'.

9 'Venezuela: statistical appendix', IMF Staff Country Report no. 99/111, International Monetary Fund, September 1999.

10 'Human Development Report Venezuela, 2000: Ways to overcome poverty', United Nations Development Programme, 2000.

11 'Venezuela: country report on human rights practices for 1998', US Department of State, 26 February 1999.

12 Nikolas Kozloff, 'Venezuela's Chávez: "oil is a geopolitical weapon"', Council on Hemispheric Affairs, 28 March 2005.

13 'Cuba, Venezuela sign oil deal', Associated Press, 30 October 2000.

14 'Ley Orgánico de Hidrocarburos', Gaceta Oficial de la República Bolivariana de Venezuela, 13 November 2001.

15 Brian Ellsworth, 'Harvest accepts oil deal', *Houston Chronicle*, 6 August 2005.

16 Kim Bartley and Donnacha O'Briain, *The Revolution Will Not be Televised*, The Irish Film Board, 2003.

17 Gregory Wilpert, 'Coup in Venezuela: an eyewitness account', ZNet, 12 April 2002.

18 *The Revolution Will Not be Televised.*

19 Ibid.

20 Ed Vulliamy, 'Venezuela coup linked to Bush team', *Observer*, 21 April 2002.

21 'Senior executive intelligence brief', Central Intelligence Agency, 11 March 2002.

22 'Senior executive intelligence brief', Central Intelligence Agency, 6 April 2002.

23 'A review of US policy toward Venezuela: November 2001–April 2002', US Department of State, July 2002.

24 Statement by George Folsom, 'IRI President Folsom praises Venezuelan civil society's defence of democracy', International Republican Institute (IRI), 12 April 2002.

25 'Hugo Chávez departs', *New York Times*, 13 April 2002.

26 'US papers hail Venezuelan coup as pro-democracy move', Fairness and Accuracy in Reporting (FAIR), 18 April 2002.

27 'Senior executive intelligence brief', 6 April 2002.

28 George Tenet, 'Current and projected national security threats to the United States', Hearing before the Select Committee on Intelligence of the United States Senate, 6 February 2002.

29 'Venezuela leader vows to break strike', BBC News, 13 December 2002.

30 Jonah Gindin, 'Made in Venezuela: the struggle to reinvent Venezuelan labor', *Monthly Review*, June 2005, p. 76.

31 'Artículo 72', *Constitución de la República Bolivariana de Venezuela* (Caracas: Gaceta Oficial de la República Bolivariana de Venezuela, 2000), p. 23.

32 'Last phase of the Venezuelan recall referendum: Carter Center Report', Carter Center, 21 August 2004.

33 Jimmy Carter, 'President Jimmy Carter: Venezuela election trip report, Aug 13–18, 2004', Carter Center, 19 August 2004.

34 'Grant agreement no. 2003-548.0 between National Endowment for Democracy and Súmate', National Endowment for Democracy, 29 September 2003.

35 Ibid.

36 'Venezuela: Iniciativa para la construción de confianza', Democratic Alternatives Incorporated, 20 August 2003.

37 Peter Millard, 'Venezuela Chávez's approval rating at 70.5%', Dow Jones Newswires, 2 May 2005.

38 President Hugo Chávez, 'Do we want to end poverty? Let us empower the poor (the Venezuelan experience)', United Nations, September 2004.

39 Minister Ali Rodríguez Araque, 'Canciller de la República Bolivariana de Venezuela, Dr Ali Rodríguez Araque en sesión extraordinaria del Consejo Permanente', Organization of American States, 23 February 2005.

40 Jairo González, interview with author, 2 May 2005, Maracaibo, Venezuela.

41 'Cuba, Venezuela sign oil deal', Associated Press, 30 October 2000.

42 Minister Francisco Armada, interview with author, 18 May 2005, Caracas, Venezuela.

**Five**

43 Ibid.

44 Ibid.

45 Ibid.

46 Anonymous, interview with author, 29 April 2005, Caracas, Venezuela.

47 Tibisay Miranda, interview with author, 17 May 2005, Caracas, Venezuela.

48 Armada interview.

49 'Misión Mercal: garantía de seguridad alimentaria', Ministerio de Comunicación e Información, January 2005.

50 Arnaldo Sotillo, director, Escuela Basica Integral Bolivariana Estado Vargas, interview with author, 17 May 2005, Caracas, Venezuela.

51 Ibid.

52 Armada, interview with author.

53 Lisandro Pérez, interview with author, 29 April 2005, Caracas, Venezuela.

54 Seth R. DeLong, 'Chávez's agrarian land reform: more like Lincoln than Lenin', Council on Hemispheric Affairs, 25 February 2005.

55 'Decreta con fuerza de Ley de Tierras y Desarrollo Agrario', *Gaceta Oficial de la República Bolivariana de Venezuela*, 9 November 2001.

56 Seth R. DeLong, 'Chávez's agrarian land reform'.

57 Luisa Ruiz, interview with author, 19 May 2005, Caracas, Venezuela.

58 Sophia Hoffman, 'Venezuela loans money to Ecuador', *Emerging Markets*, 2 August 2005.

59 Teresa Arreaza, 'ALBA: Bolivarian alternative for Latin America and the Caribbean', Venezuela Analysis, 30 January 2004.

60 'Caribbean oil initiative launched', BBC News, 30 June 2005.

61 'Venezuela and China sign oil deal', BBC News, 24 December 2004.

62 'Chávez seals strategic alliance with Beijing', MercoPress, 28 December 2004.

63 Secretary Colin Powell, 'Powell says terrorist arrests illustrate US, Russian cooperation', US Department of State, 13 April 2003.

64 Glenn Kessler, 'Rice urges OAS to back democracy', *Washington Post*, 6 June 2005.

65 Monica Barczak, 'Representation by consultation? The rise of direct democracy in Latin America', *Latin American Politics and Society*, 43(3): 46.

66 'Executive Order 13211 of May 18, 2001: Actions concerning regulations that significantly affect energy supply, distribution, or use', *Federal Register*, 22 May 2001.

67 'Venezuela: media law undercuts freedom of expression', Human Rights Watch, 24 November 2004.

68 Ibid.

69 Edgard Hernandez, 'The Inter-American Dialogue Institute's report on Venezuela: another unjustified attack on Chávez', *Venezuela Analysis*, 22 July 2005.

70 Gregory Wilpert, 'Community airwaves in Venezuela', *NACLA Report on the Americas*, January/February 2004.

71 Richard Gott, 'Two fingers to America', *Guardian*, 25 August 2005.

72 Otamendi Widmark, interview with author, 28 April 2005, Caracas, Venezuela.

73 'Transcript: confirmation hearing of Condoleezza Rice', *New York Times*, 18 January 2005.

74 Andy Webb-Vidal, 'Bush orders policy to "contain" Chávez', *Financial Times*, 14 March 2005.

75 Roger F. Noriega, 'Assistant Secretary Noriega's statement before the Senate Foreign Relations Committee', US Department of State, 2 March 2005.

76 Secretary Donald Rumsfeld, 'Hemisphere's security tied to CAFTA's passage', *Duluth News Tribune*, 11 June 2005.

77 Kessler, 'Rice urges OAS to back democracy', *Washington Post*, 6 June 2005.

78 Jane Bussey, 'Washington and Venezuela trade barbs over Bolivia at OAS conference in Fort Lauderdale', *Miami Herald*, 7 June 2005.

79 Teo Ballvé, 'Is Venezuela the new Cuba?', *NACLA Report on the Americas*, July/August 2005.

80 'US behind Bolivia crisis – Chávez', BBC News, 13 June 2005.

81 Rodríguez Araque, 'Canciller de la República Bolivariana de Venezuela ... '.

82 'Robertson is pilloried for assassination call', *New York Times*, 23 August 2005.

83 Sean McCormack, 'Daily press briefing', US Department of State, 23 August 2005.

84 'Rice outlines US vision for western hemisphere', US Department of State, 28 April 2005.

85 'Venezuela's oil revenue fuels record growth', Dow Jones Newswires, 17 February 2005.

86 'Millennium Development Goals', World Bank, April 2004. The 2002 figures were the most recent available non-governmental statistics for Venezuela.

87 'Informe sobre la democracia en América Latina: hacia una democracia de ciudadanas y ciudadanos', United Nations Development Programme, April 2004.

88 Terry Gibbs, 'Business as unusual: what the Chávez era tells us about democracy under globalization', *Third World Quarterly*, 25(4): 2006, August 2005.

89 Prince El Hassan bin Talal, 'A new world order without ideologies', Club of Rome, 4 February 2003.

## Conclusion

1 'Alaska Petroleum Taxes', Tax Division, State of Alaska, 20 November 2005. In Alaska, oil companies pay a royalty rate of 12.5 per cent on a well for the first five years and 15 per cent thereafter In addition, they pay a 12.25 per cent production tax, which is another form of royalty.

2 Terry Gibbs, 'Business as unusual: what the Chávez era tells us about the theory and practice of democracy under globalization', Unpublished paper, August 2005.

3 Michael Parfit, 'Future power: where will the world get its next energy fix?', *National Geographic*, August 2005.

4 Dawn Levy, 'Harnessing the wind: one quarter of the United States is suited for wind power production, researchers find', *Stanford Report*, 21 May 2003.

5 Parfit, 'Future power'.

6 Ibid.

# Bibliography

Akiner, S. (1995) *Formation of Kazakh Identity: From Tribe to Nation-state*, London: Royal Institute for International Affairs

Aranguren Molina, M. (2001) *Mi confesión: Carlos Castaño revela sus secretos*, Bogotá: Editorial La Oveja Negra

Bagarov, S., I. Akhmedov and S. Tsalik (2003) 'State oil fund of the Azerbaijan Republic', in R. Ebel (ed.), *Caspian Oil Windfalls: Who Will Benefit?*, New York: Open Society Institute

Buxton, J. (2003) 'Economic policy and the rise of Hugo Chávez', in S. Ellner and D. Hellinger (eds), *Venezuelan Politics in the Chávez Era: Class, Polarization and Conflict*, Boulder, CO: Lynne Rienner Publishers

Ewell, J. (1996) *Venezuela and the United States: From Monroe's Hemisphere to Petroleum's Empire*, Athens: University of Georgia Press

Human Rights Watch (1999) *The Price of Oil: Corporate Responsibility and Human Rights Violations in Nigeria's Oil Producing Communities*, New York: Human Rights Watch

Kleveman, L. (2003) *The New Great Game: Blood and Oil in Central Asia*, New York: Grove Press

Maier, K. (2002) *This House Has Fallen: Nigeria in Crisis*, Oxford: Westview Press

Mommer, B. (2003) 'Subversive oil', in S. Ellner and D. Hellinger (eds), *Venezuelan Politics in the Chávez Era: Class, Polarization and Conflict*, Boulder, CO: Lynne Rienner Publishers

Nakash, Y. (2003) *The Shi'is of Iraq*, Princeton, NJ: Princeton University Press

Tripp, C. (2000) *A History of Iraq*, Cambridge: Cambridge University Press

Turner, T. E. and L. S. Brownhill (2003) *Why Women are at War with Chevron: Nigerian Subsistence Struggles against the International Oil Industry*, New York: International Oil Working Group

UNDP (United Nations Development Programme) (1993) *Human Development Report 1993*, Oxford: Oxford University Press

— (2004) *Human Development Report 2004: Cultural Liberty in Today's Diverse World*, New York: United Nations Development Programme

UNSC (United Nations Security Council) (1987) *Resolutions and Decisions of the Security Council 1986*, New York: United Nations

# Index